P9-DFQ-675

# UML and the
# Unified
# Process

# The Addison-Wesley Object Technology Series

Grady Booch, Ivar Jacobson, and James Rumbaugh, Series Editors

For more information check out the series web site [http://www.aw.com/cseng/otseries/].

# Component Software Series

Clements Szyperski, Series Editor

JIM ARLOW AND ILA NEUSTADT

# UML and the Unified Process

## Practical object-oriented analysis and design

Addison-Wesley

*An imprint of* **Pearson Education**

Boston · San Francisco · New York · Toronto · Montreal
London · Munich · Paris · Madrid · Cape Town
Sydney · Tokyo · Singapore · Mexico City

PEARSON EDUCATION LIMITED

Head Office:
Edinburgh Gate
Harlow CM20 2JE
Tel: +44 (0)1279 623623
Fax: +44 (0)1279 431059

London Office:
128 Long Acre
London WC2E 9AN
Tel: +44 (0)20 7447 2000
Fax: +44 (0)20 7240 5771

Website: www.informit.com

First published in Great Britain in 2002

© Pearson Education Limited 2002

The rights of Jim Arlow and Ila Neustadt to be identified as the Authors of this Work have been asserted
by them in accordance with the Copyright, Designs and Patents Act 1988.

ISBN 0 201 77060 1

*British Library Cataloguing in Publication Data*
A CIP catalogue record for this book can be obtained from the British Library.

*Library of Congress Cataloging-in-Publication Data*
Arlow, Jim, 1960-
    UML and the unified process : practical object-oriented analysis and design/Jim
Arlow, Ila Neustadt.
        p. cm.
    Includes bibliographical references and index.
    ISBN 0-201-77060-1 (pbk.: alk. paper)
      1. Object-oriented methods (Computer science) 2. Computer software--Development.
    3. UML (Computer science) I. Neustadt, Ila. II. Title.

    QA76.9.O35 A75 2002
    005.1'17--dc21                                          2001055223

All rights reserved; no part of this publication may be reproduced, stored in a retrieval system,
or transmitted in any form or by any means, electronic, mechanical, photocopying, recording, or
otherwise without either the prior written permission of the Publishers or a licence permitting
restricted copying in the United Kingdom issued by the Copyright Licensing Agency Ltd,
90 Tottenham Court Road, London W1P 0LP. This book may not be lent, resold, hired out or
otherwise disposed of by way of trade in any form of binding or cover other than that in which it is
published, without the prior consent of the Publishers.

Many of the designations used by manufacturers and sellers to distinguish their products are claimed as trademarks.
Pearson Education Limited has made every attempt to supply trademark information about manufacturers and their
products mentioned in this book.

10 9 8 7 6 5 4 3 2 1

Typeset by Pantek Arts Ltd, Maidstone, Kent.
Printed and bound in Great Britain by Biddles Ltd of Guildford and King's Lynn.

*The Publishers' policy is to use paper manufactured from sutainable forests.*

**To our parents**

# Acknowledgments

We would like to thank Fabrizio Ferrandina, Wolfgang Emmerich and our friends at Zühlke Engineering for encouraging us to create the UML training course that led to this book. Thanks to Sue and David Epstein for essential support throughout the course of the project. Thanks to Andy Pols for sharing his thoughts on use cases and software engineering with us. Thanks to Alison Birtwell and her colleagues at Addison-Wesley for their great work on the text. Thanks to the Neustadt family for their patience. Thanks to Al Toms for light relief. And thanks to our cats, Homer and Isis, for the many hours they spent sleeping on the various drafts of the manuscript.

Finally, we must acknowledge the "Three Amigos" – Grady Booch, Jim Rumbaugh and Ivar Jacobson – for their fine work on UML and UP that this book is all about.

# Contents

# Preface

## About this book

The aim of this book is to take you through the process of object-oriented (OO) analysis and design using the Unified Modeling Language (UML) and the Unified Process (UP).

UML provides the visual modeling syntax for OO modeling, and UP provides the software engineering process framework that tells us how we perform OO analysis and design.

We have tried to make our presentation of UML and UP as straightforward and accessible as possible.

## Conventions

To help you navigate through the book we have provided each chapter with an outline in the form of a UML activity diagram. These diagrams indicate reading activities and the order in which sections should be read. An example is shown in Figure 0.1.

Most of the diagrams in this book are UML diagrams. The annotations, in gray, are not part of UML syntax.

Notes indicate
important information.

We have provided notes in the margin to highlight important information. We have used the UML note icon for this. An example is shown in the margin.

We have used different fonts throughout the book:

This font is for UML modeling elements.

This font is for code.

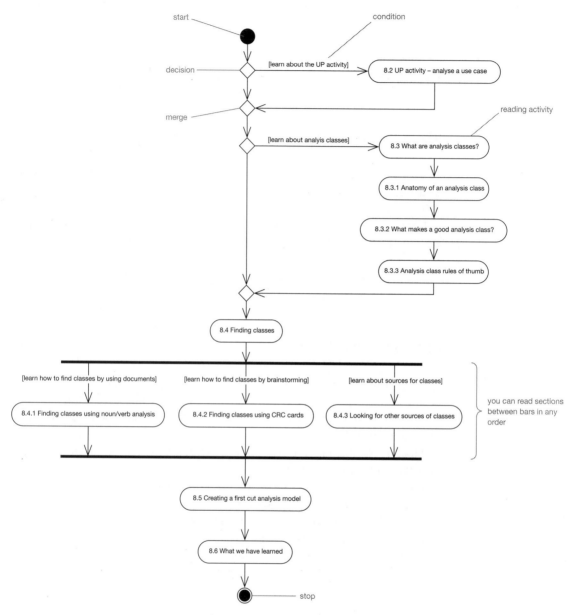

**Figure 0.1**

## How to read this book

So many books, so little time to read them all! With this in mind we have designed this book so that you can read it in several different ways (as well as cover to cover) according to your needs.

## Fast Track

Choose Fast Track if you just want an overview of the whole book or a particular chapter. This is also the "management summary".

- Choose a chapter.
- Read the chapter roadmap so that you know where you're going.
- Go through the chapter looking at the figures and reading the margin notes.
- Read the "What we have learned" section.
- Go back to any section that takes your interest and read it.

Fast Track is a quick and efficient way to read this book. You may be pleasantly surprised at how much you can pick up! Note that Fast Track works best if you can first formulate a clear idea of the information you want to obtain. For example "I want to understand how to do use case modeling."

## Reference

If you need to know a particular part of UML or learn a particular technique, we have provided a detailed index and table of contents that should help you to locate the information you need quickly and efficiently.

## Revision

If you need to refresh your knowledge of UML as quickly and efficiently as possible, read the outline summaries of each chapter in the "What we have learned" section. When you don't understand something, go back and read the appropriate section.

## Dipping

If you have a few minutes to spare, you might pick up the book and open it at random. We have tried to ensure that there is something interesting on every page. Even if you already know UML quite well, you may still discover some new things to learn.

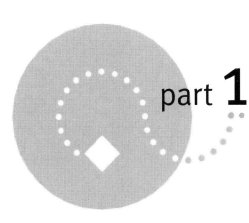

part **1**

# Introducing
# UML and UP

# chapter **1**
# What is UML?

## 1.1   Chapter roadmap

This chapter provides a brief overview of the history and high-level structure of the UML. We mention many topics that will be expanded in later chapters.

    Beginners should start by learning about UML history and principles. If you have experience in UML, or are satisfied that you already know enough about UML history, then you can skip straight to Section 1.6 and the discussion of UML structure. There are three main strands to this discussion, which may be read in any order. You can find out about UML building blocks (1.7), UML common mechanisms (1.8), and architecture and UML (1.9).

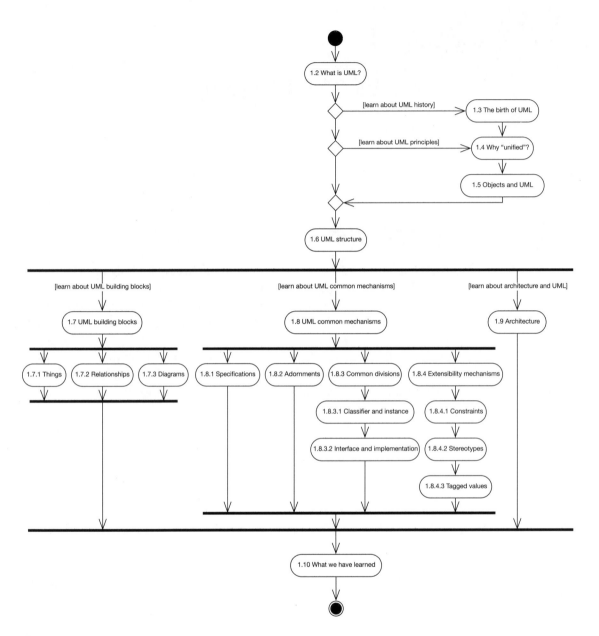

**Figure 1.1**

## 1.2    What is UML?

The Unified Modeling Language (UML) is a general purpose visual modeling language for systems. Although UML is most often associated with modeling OO software systems, it has a much wider application than this due to its in-built extensibility mechanisms.

UML was designed to incorporate current best practice in modeling techniques and software engineering. As such, it is explicitly designed to be implemented by computer-assisted software engineering (CASE) tools. This is in recognition of the fact that large, modern software systems generally require CASE support. UML diagrams are human-readable and yet are easily rendered by CASE programs.

It is important to realize that UML does *not* give us any kind of modeling methodology. Naturally, some aspects of methodology are implied by the elements that comprise a UML model, but UML itself just provides a visual syntax that we can use to construct models.

> UML is not a methodology – it is a universal visual modeling language. UP is a methodology.

The Unified Process (UP) *is* a methodology – it tells us the workers, activities and artefacts that we need to utilize, perform or create in order to model a software system.

UML is *not* tied to any specific methodology or lifecycle, and indeed it is capable of being used with all existing methodologies. UP uses UML as its underlying visual modeling syntax and you can therefore think of UP as being the *preferred* method for UML, as it is the best adapted to it, but UML itself can (and does) provide the visual modeling support for other methods.[1]

The goal of UML and UP has always been to support and encapsulate best practice in software engineering based on the experience of the last decade. To do this UML and UP *unify* previous attempts at visual modeling languages and software engineering processes into a best-of-breed solution.

## 1.3    The birth of UML

Prior to 1994, the OO methods world was a bit of a mess. There were several competing visual modeling languages and methodologies all with their strengths and weaknesses and all with their supporters and detractors. In terms of visual modeling languages (summarized in Figure 1.2), the clear leaders were Booch (the Booch Method) and Rumbaugh (Object Modeling Technique or OMT) who between them had over half the market. On the

---

[1] For a specific example of a mature methodology that also uses UML as its visual syntax, see the OPEN (Object-oriented Process, Environment and Notation) method at www.open.org.au

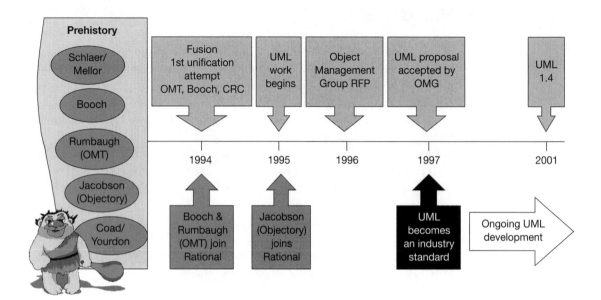

**Figure 1.2**

methodologies side, Jacobson had by far the strongest case as although many authors claimed to have a "method", all that many of them actually had was a visual modeling syntax and a collection of more or less useful aphorisms and guidelines.

There was a very early attempt at unification in 1994 with Coleman's Fusion method. However, although laudable, this attempt did not involve the original authors of the constituent methods (Booch, Jacobson, and Rumbaugh) and was also quite late to market with a book explaining the approach. Fusion was rapidly overtaken by the course of events when, in 1994, Booch and Rumbaugh joined Rational Corporation to work on UML. This worried a lot of us at the time, as it gave Rational over half the methods market. However, these fears have proved to be entirely unfounded and UML has since become an open industry standard.

In 1996, the Object Management Group (OMG) produced a request-for-proposal (RFP) for an OO visual modeling language, and UML was submitted. In 1997, OMG accepted the UML and the first open, industry standard OO visual modeling language was born. Since then, all of the competing methods have faded away and UML stands unchallenged as the industry standard OO modeling language. As we write this book, UML 1.4 has just been released and we are well on the way to UML 2.0.

UML is the open, industry standard visual modeling language approved by the OMG.

In one of his books, Grady Booch says "If you have a good idea then it's mine!" In a way this summarizes the UML philosophy – it takes the best of that which has gone before and integrates and builds on it. This is reuse in its broadest sense, and the UML incorporates many of the best ideas from the "prehistoric" methods while rejecting some of their more idiosyncratic extremes.

## 1.4 Why "unified"?

UML unification is not just historical in scope, UML attempts (and largely succeeds) in being unified across several different domains.

- Development lifecycle – UML provides visual syntax for modeling right through the software development lifecycle from requirements engineering to implementation.

- Application domains – UML has been used to model everything from hard real-time embedded systems to management decision support systems.

- Implementation languages and platforms – UML is language and platform neutral. Naturally, it has excellent support for pure OO languages (Smalltalk, Java, C#, etc.) but it is also effective for hybrid OO languages such as C++ and object-based languages such as Visual Basic. It has even been used to model for non-OO languages such as C.

- Development processes – although UP and its variants are probably the preferred development processes for OO systems, UML can (and does) support many other software engineering processes.

- Its own internal concepts – UML valiantly tries to be consistent and uniform in its application of a small set of internal concepts. It doesn't (as yet) always succeed, but it is still a big improvement on prior attempts.

## 1.5 Objects and UML

UML models the world as systems of interacting objects. An object is a cohesive cluster of data and function.

The basic premise of UML is that we can model software and other systems as *collections of collaborating objects*. This is clearly a great fit with OO software systems and languages, but it also works very well for business processes and other applications.

There are two aspects to a UML model.

- Static structure – this describes what types of objects are important for modeling the system and how they are related.

- Dynamic behavior – this describes the lifecycles of these objects and how they collaborate together to deliver the required system functionality.

These two aspects of the UML model go hand-in-glove, and one is not truly complete without the other.

We look at objects (and classes) in full detail in Chapter 7. Until we get there, just think of an object as being a cohesive cluster of data and behavior. In other words, objects contain information and can perform functions.

## 1.6   UML structure

You can begin to understand how UML works as a visual language by looking at its structure. This is illustrated in Figure 1.3 (as you will see later, this is a valid UML diagram). This structure consists of:

● building blocks – these are the basic UML modeling elements, relationships and diagrams;

● common mechanisms – common UML ways of achieving specific goals;

● architecture – the UML view of system architecture.

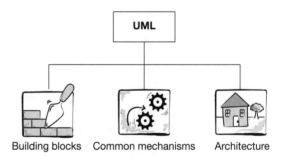

Building blocks    Common mechanisms    Architecture

**Figure 1.3**

Understanding the structure of UML gives us a useful organizing principle for the rest of the information presented in this book. It also highlights that UML is, itself, a designed and architected system. In fact, UML has been modeled and designed using UML! This design is the UML *metamodel*.

## 1.7   UML building blocks

According to *The Unified Modeling Language User Guide* [Booch 2], UML is composed of just three building blocks:

- things – these are the modeling elements themselves;

- relationships – these tie things together – relationships specify how two or more things are semantically related;

- diagrams – these are *views* into UML models – they show collections of things that "tell a story" about the software system and are our way of visualizing *what* the system will do (analysis-level diagrams) or *how* it will do it (design-level diagrams).

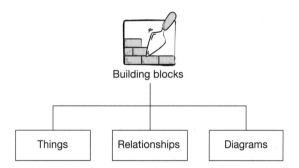

Building blocks

Things     Relationships     Diagrams

**Figure 1.4**

We'll look at things, relationships and diagrams in a little more detail in the next three sections.

 ### 1.7.1 Things

UML things may be partitioned into:

> In UML, modeling elements are called "things".

- structural things – the nouns of a UML model such as class, interface, collaboration, use case, active class, component, node;

- behavioral things – the verbs of a UML model such as interactions, state machines;

- grouping things – the package, which is used to group semantically related modeling elements into cohesive units;

- annotational things – the note, which may be appended to the model to capture ad hoc information, very much like a yellow sticky note.

We'll look at all of these things, and how they are usefully applied in UML modeling, in Part 2 onwards.

## 1.7.2   Relationships

Relationships allow you to show on a model how two or more things relate to each other. Thinking of families, and the relationships between all of the people in a family, gives you a pretty good idea of the role relationships play in UML models – they allow you to capture meaningful (semantic) connections between things. Relationships apply to the structural and grouping things in a model and are depicted in Figure 1.5.

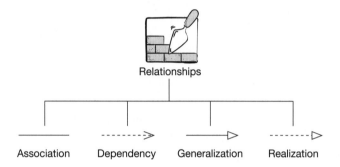

Relationships

Association        Dependency        Generalization        Realization

**Figure 1.5**

Understanding the exact semantics of the different types of relationship is a very important part of UML modeling, but we will defer a detailed exploration of these semantics until later sections of the book. For now, Table 1.1 gives a brief summary to give you some idea.

**Table 1.1**

| Type of relationship | Brief semantics | Section |
| --- | --- | --- |
| Association | The description of a set of links between objects | 9.4 |
| Dependency | A change to a thing affects the semantics of a dependent thing | 9.5 |
| Generalization | One element is a specialization of another and may be substituted for the more general element | 10.2 |
| Realization | A relationship between classifiers where one classifier specifies a contract that the other classifier guarantees to carry out | 12.3 |

## 1.7.3   Diagrams

In all UML CASE tools, when you create a new thing or new relationship, it is added to the model. The model is the repository of all of the things and relationships that you have created to help describe the required behavior of the software system you are trying to design.

Diagrams are only
views into the model.

Diagrams are *windows* or *views* into the model. The diagram is *not* the model itself! This is actually a very important distinction, as a thing or relationship may be deleted from a diagram, or even from all diagrams, but may still exist in the model. In fact, it will stay in the model until explicitly deleted from it. A common error of novice UML modelers is to delete things from diagrams, but leave them in the model.

There are a total of nine different types of UML diagram and these are listed in Figure 1.6. We can usefully divide this set of diagrams into those that model the static structure of the system (the so-called static model) and those that model the dynamic structure of the system (the dynamic model). The static model captures the things and the structural relationships between things; the dynamic model captures how things interact to generate the required behavior of the software system. We'll look at both the static and dynamic models from Part 2 onwards.

There is no specific order in which UML diagrams are created, although you typically start with a use case diagram to define the system scope. In fact, you often work on several diagrams in parallel, refining each one as you uncover more and more information and detail about the software system you are designing. Thus, the diagrams are both a view of the model and the primary mechanism for entering information into the model.

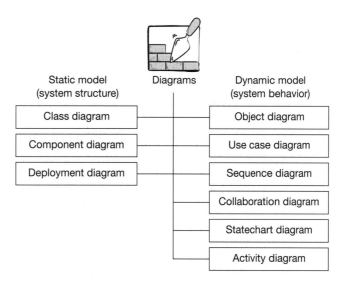

**Figure 1.6**

## 1.8   UML common mechanisms

UML has four common mechanisms that apply consistently throughout the language. They describe four strategies for approaching object modeling which are applied again and again in different contexts throughout UML. Once again, we see that UML has a simple and elegant structure (Figure 1.7).

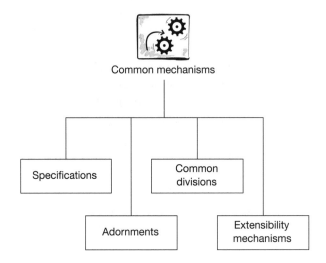

**Figure 1.7**

### 1.8.1   Specifications

UML models have at least two dimensions – a graphical dimension that allows you to visualize the model using diagrams and icons, and a textual dimension that consists of the specifications of the various modeling elements. Specifications are textual descriptions of the semantics of an element.

For example, we may visually represent a class, such as a BankAccount class, as a box with various compartments (Figure 1.8), but this representation doesn't really tell us anything about the business semantics of that class. The semantics behind modeling elements are captured in their specifications, and without these specifications you can only guess what a modeling element actually represents.

The set of specifications is the real "meat" of the model, and forms the *semantic backplane* that holds the model together and gives it meaning. The various diagrams are just views or visual projections of that backplane.

Diagrams present views into the backplane.

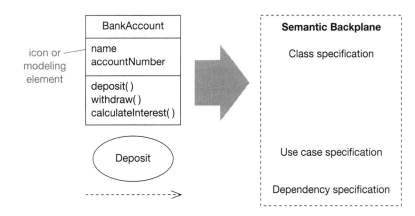

**Figure 1.8**

This semantic backplane is typically maintained using a CASE tool that provides ways to enter, view and modify specifications for each modeling element.

UML allows a great deal of flexibility in constructing models. In particular, models may be:

● elided – some elements are present in the backplane, but hidden in any particular diagram in order to simplify the view;

● incomplete – some elements of the model may be missing entirely;

● inconsistent – the model may contain contradictions.

The fact that the completeness and consistency constraints are relaxed is important, as you will see that models evolve over time and undergo many changes. However, the drive is always toward *consistent models* that are *sufficiently complete* to allow construction of a software system.

It is common practice in UML modeling to start with a largely graphical model, which allows you to visualize the system, and then to add more and more semantics to the backplane as the model evolves. However, for a model to be considered in any way useful or complete, the model semantics *must* be present in the backplane. If not, you don't have a model, just a meaningless collection of boxes and blobs connected by lines! In fact, a common modeling error made by novices might be called "death by diagrams" – the model is over-diagramed but under-specified.

 ## 1.8.2 Adornments

A very nice feature of UML is that every modeling element has a very simple symbol, to which may be added a number of adornments when more information is to be shown on a diagram.

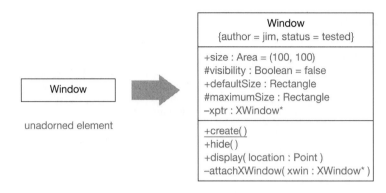

unadorned element

element with adornments

**Figure 1.9**

We adorn model
elements on UML
diagrams to highlight
important details.

This means that you can start by constructing a very high-level model by using just the basic symbols with perhaps one or two adornments, and then you can refine the model over time by adding more and more adornments until the modeling element is sufficiently detailed for your purposes.

It is important to remember that any UML diagram is only a view of the model, and so you should only show adornments when they increase the overall clarity and readability of the diagram, or if they highlight some important feature of the model. There is generally no need to show everything on a diagram – it is more important that the diagram is clear, illustrates exactly the points you want it to make, and is easy to read.

Figure 1.9 shows that the minimal icon for a class is a box with the class name in it. However, you can expose various features of the underlying model as adornments to extend this minimal view. The text in gray indicates optional possible adornments.

## 1.8.3  Common divisions

Common divisions describe particular ways of thinking about the world. There are two common divisions in UML – classifier and instance, and interface and implementation.

### 1.8.3.1  Classifier and instance

UML considers that we might have the abstract notion of a type of thing (such as a bank account) and then specific, concrete instances of that abstraction such as "my bank account" or "your bank account". The abstract notion of a type of thing is a classifier, and the specific, concrete things themselves are instances. This is a very important concept that is

> Classifier – an abstract notion, e.g. a type of bank account. Instance – a concrete thing, e.g. your bank account or my bank account.

actually quite easy to grasp. Classifiers and instances surround us. Just think of this UML book – we might say that the abstract idea of the book is "UML and the Unified Process" and that there are many instances of this book, such as the one you are reading right now. We will see that this notion of classifier/instance is a key concept that permeates UML.

In UML an instance usually has the same icon as the corresponding classifier, but for instances the name on the icon is underlined. At first, this can be quite a subtle visual distinction to grasp.

UML provides the classifiers listed in Table 1.2 – we will look at all of these in detail in later sections.

**Table 1.2**

| Classifier | Semantics | Section |
|---|---|---|
| Actor | A role played by an outside user of the system to whom the system delivers some value | 4.3.2 |
| Class | A description of a set of objects that share the same features | 7.4 |
| Classifier role | A classifier restricted to a particular role in a collaboration | 12.5 |
| Component | A physical and replaceable part of a system that conforms to and realizes one or more interfaces – good examples of components would be ActiveX controls or JavaBeans | 22.2 |
| Datatype | A type whose values have no identity such as the primitive types, int, float and char found in languages like C++ and Java – for example, all instances of int that have the value 4 are precisely the same and can't be distinguished from each other Pure OO languages such as Smalltalk don't have datatypes | |
| Interface | A collection of operations that are used to specify a service offered by a class or component | 17.2 |
| Node | A physical, run-time element that represents a computational resource – an example might be a PC | 23.2 |
| Signal | An asynchronous message passed between objects | 13.10 |
| Subsystem | A grouping of elements – some of these may specify the behavior offered by contained elements | 17.6 |
| Use case | A description of a sequence of actions that a system performs to yield value to a user | 4.3.3 |

### 1.8.3.2  *Interface and implementation*

> Interface, e.g. the buttons on the front of your VCR. Implementation, e.g. the mechanism inside your VCR.

The principle here is to separate what something does (its interface) from how it does it (its implementation). For example, when you drive a car you are interacting with a very simple and well-defined interface. This interface is implemented in different ways by many different physical cars.

An interface defines a contract (which has much in common with a legal contract) that specific implementations guarantee to adhere to. This separation of what something promises to do from the actual implementation of that promise is an important UML concept. We discuss this in detail in Chapter 17.

Concrete examples of interfaces and implementations are everywhere. For example, the buttons on the front of a video recorder provide a (relatively) simple interface to what is actually a very complex mechanism. The interface shields us from this complexity by hiding it from us.

 ## 1.8.4 Extensibility mechanisms

UML is an extensible modeling language.

The designers of UML realized that it was simply not possible to design a completely universal modeling language that would satisfy everyone's needs present and future, so UML incorporates three simple extensibility mechanisms that we summarize in Table 1.3.

We'll look at these three extensibility mechanisms in more detail in the next three sections.

**Table 1.3**

| UML extensibility mechanisms | |
|---|---|
| Constraints | These extend the semantics of an element by allowing us to add new rules |
| Stereotypes | A stereotype allows us to define a new UML modeling element based on an existing one – we define the semantics of the stereotype ourselves |
| | Stereotypes add new elements to the UML metamodel |
| Tagged values | These provide a way of extending an element's specification by allowing us to add new, ad hoc information to it |

### 1.8.4.1 Constraints

Constraints allow us to add new rules to modeling elements.

A constraint is simply a text string in braces ({ }) that specifies some condition or rule about the modeling element that *must* be maintained as true. In other words, it constrains some feature of the element in some way. You'll come across examples of constraints throughout the book.

### 1.8.4.2 Stereotypes

Stereotypes allow us to define new modeling elements based on existing ones.

*The UML Reference Manual* [Rumbaugh 1] states, "A stereotype represents a variation of an existing model element with the same form (such as attributes and relationships) but with a different intent."

Stereotypes allow you to introduce new modeling elements based on *existing* elements. You can do this by appending the stereotype name in guillemots («...») to the new element. Each model element can have at most one stereotype.

Each stereotype may define a set of tagged values and constraints that apply to the stereotyped element. You can also associate an icon, color or texture with the stereotype. Typically, use of color and texture should be avoided in UML models as some readers (the color blind for example) may have trouble interpreting the diagrams, and diagrams often have to be printed in black and white anyway. However, it is common practice to associate a new icon with a stereotype. This allows you to extend the UML graphical notation in a controled manner.

Because stereotypes introduce *new* modeling elements with different intent, you have to define the semantics of these new elements somewhere. How do you do this? Well, if the CASE tool doesn't provide in-built support for documenting stereotypes, most modelers just put a note in the model, or insert a reference to an external document in which the stereotypes are defined. At present, CASE tool support for stereotypes is rather patchy – most tools support stereotypes to some degree, but not all tools provide facilities for capturing stereotype semantics.

You can model stereotypes themselves by using the class element (Chapter 7) with the special predefined UML stereotype «stereotype». This creates a metamodel of your system of stereotypes. It is a metamodel because it is a model of a modeling element and is on a completely different level of abstraction to the usual UML system or business models. Because this is a metamodel, you must *never* merge it with your normal models – you must always keep it as a separate model. Creating a new model just for the stereotypes is only really worth doing when there are a lot of stereotypes. This is very rare, so most modelers tend to document stereotypes with a note or an external document.

There is a lot of flexibility in how stereotypes can be displayed. However, most modelers just use the stereotype name in « » or the icon. The other variants don't tend to be used that much and the CASE tool often limits what you can do. Some examples are shown in Figure 1.10. (N.B. The stars are *not* part of UML syntax – they just highlight the most useful display options.)

Notice that you can stereotype relationships as well as classes. You'll see many uses for this throughout the book.

### 1.8.4.3 Tagged values

> Tagged values allow you to add your own properties to model elements.

In UML, a property is any value attached to a model element. Most elements have large numbers of predefined properties. Some of these are displayable on diagrams, and others are just part of the semantic backplane of the model.

UML allows you to add your own properties to modeling elements by using tagged values. A tagged value is a very simple idea – it is just a keyword

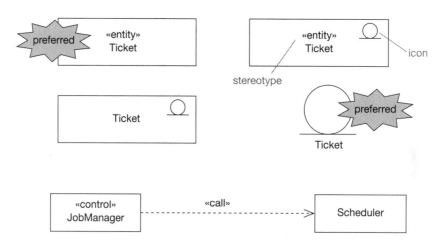

**Figure 1.10**

which can have a value attached. The syntax for tagged values is shown here: { tag1 = value1, tag2 = value2, ..., tagN = valueN }. This is a comma-delimited list of tag/value pairs separated by an equals sign. The list of tags is enclosed in curly brackets.

Some tags are just extra information applied to a model element, such as {author = Jim Arlow}. However, other tags indicate properties of new modeling elements defined by a stereotype. You should not apply these tags directly to model elements, rather you should associate them with the stereotype itself. Then, when the stereotype is applied to a model element, it also gets the tags associated with that stereotype.

## 1.9   Architecture

*The UML Reference Manual* [Rumbaugh 1] defines system architecture as, "The organizational structure of a system, including its decomposition into parts, their connectivity, interaction, mechanisms and the guiding principles that inform the design of a system." The IEEE defines system architecture as, "The highest-level concept of a system in its environment."

Architecture is all about capturing the strategic aspects of the high-level structure of a system. In order to be able to capture all the essential aspects of system architecture, UML defines four different views of the system – the logical view, the process view, the implementation view, and the deployment view. These are all integrated by a fifth view, the use case view, as shown in Figure 1.11.

UML captures the strategic aspects of a system in a "4+1 view" of architecture – logical view, process view, implementation view, deployment view, and use case view.

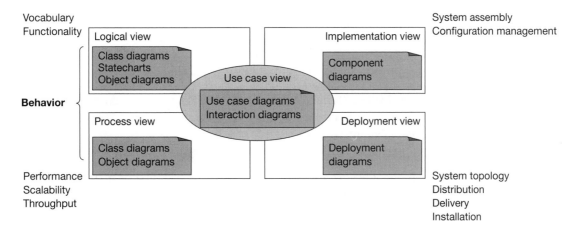

**Figure 1.11**   Adapted from Figure 5.1 [Kruchten 1] with permission from Addison-Wesley

Let's look at each of these views in turn.

- Logical view – captures the vocabulary of the problem domain as a set of classes and objects. The emphasis is on showing how the objects and classes that compose the system, implement the required system behavior.

- Process view – models the executable threads and processes in our system as active classes. It is really a process-oriented variation on the logical view, and contains all the same artefacts.

- Implementation view – models the files and components that make up the physical code base of the system. It is also about illustrating dependencies between components, and about configuration management of sets of components to define a version of the system.

- Deployment view – models the physical deployment of components onto a set of physical, computational nodes such as computers and peripherals. It allows you to model the distribution of components across the nodes of a distributed system.

- Use case view – all of the other views derive from the use case view. This view captures the basic requirements for the system as a set of use cases (see Chapter 4) and provides the basis for the construction of the other views.

Once we have created this 4+1 architecture, we have explored all of the key aspects of the system with UML models. If we follow the UP lifecycle, this 4+1 architecture is not created in one go, rather it evolves over time. The process of UML modeling within the framework of the UP is therefore a process of stepwise refinement towards a 4+1 architecture that captures *just enough* information about the system to allow it to be built.

## 1.10   What we have learned

This chapter has provided an introduction to UML history, structure, concepts and key features. You have learned the following.

- The Unified Modeling Language (UML) is an open, extensible industry standard visual modeling language approved by the Object Management Group.

- UML is not a methodology.

- The Unified Process (UP), or a variant, is the type of methodology that best complements UML.

- Object modeling regards the world as systems of interacting objects. Objects contain information and may perform functions. UML models have:
  - static structure – what types of object are important and how they are related;
  - dynamic behavior – how objects collaborate together to perform the functions of the system.

- UML is composed of three building blocks:
  - things:
    - structural things are the nouns of a UML model;
    - behavioral things are the verbs of a UML model;
    - there is only one grouping thing, the package – this is used to group semantically related things;
    - there is only one annotational thing, the note – this is just like a yellow sticky note;
  - relationships link things together;
  - diagrams show interesting views of the model.

- UML has four common mechanisms:
  - specifications are textual descriptions of the features and semantics of model elements – the meat of the model;
  - adornments are items of information exposed on a modeling element in a diagram to illustrate a point;
  - common divisions:
    - classifier and instance: classifier – the abstract notion of a type of thing, e.g. a bank account; instance – a specific instance of a type of thing, e.g. my bank account;

- interface and implementation: interface – a contract that specifies the behavior of a thing; implementation – the specific details of how the thing works;

— extensibility mechanisms:

- constraints allow us to add new rules to modeling elements;

- stereotypes introduce new modeling elements based on old ones;

- tagged values allow us to add new properties to model elements – a tagged value is a keyword with an associated value.

- UML is based on a 4+1 view of system architecture:

— logical view – system functionality and vocabulary;

— process view – system performance, scalability and throughput;

— implementation view – system assembly and configuration management;

— deployment view – system topology, distribution, delivery and installation;

— these are united by the use case view, which describes stakeholder requirements.

# chapter 2
# What is the Unified Process?

## 2.1 Chapter roadmap

The purpose of this chapter is to give a very concise overview of the Unified Process (UP). Beginners should start by learning about UP history. If you already know this, then you may choose to skip ahead to Section 2.4, a discussion of UP and the Rational Unified Process (RUP), or to Section 2.5 which discusses how you may apply UP on your project.

Our interest in UP, as far as this book is concerned, is to provide a process framework within which the techniques of OO analysis and design may be presented. You will find a complete discussion of UP in [Jacobson 1] and excellent discussions of the related RUP in [Kruchten 1] and [Ambler 1], [Ambler 2], and [Ambler 3].

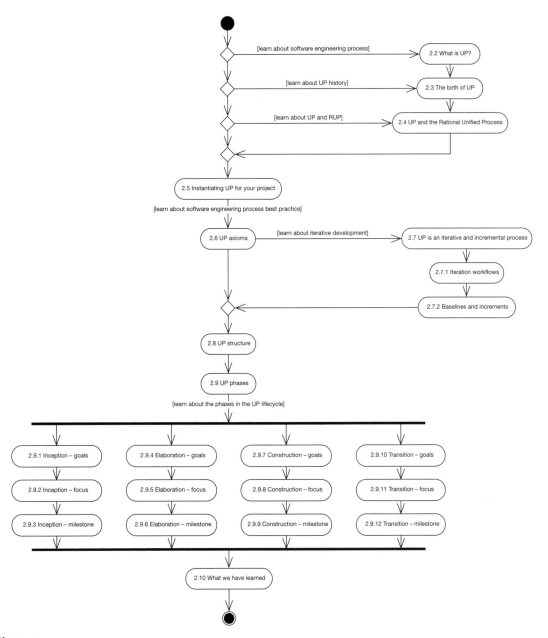

**Figure 2.1**

## 2.2 What is UP?

A software development process (SDP), also known as a software engineering process (SEP), defines the *who*, *what*, *when* and *how* of developing software. As illustrated in Figure 2.2, a SEP is the process in which we turn user requirements into software.

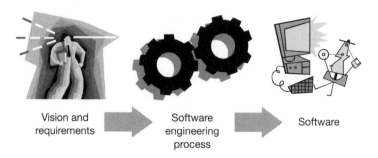

Figure 2.2

The Unified Software Development Process (USDP) is an industry standard SEP from the authors of the UML. It is commonly referred to as the Unified Process or UP [Jacobson 1]. We shall use the term UP throughout this book.

The UML project was meant to provide both a visual language *and* a software engineering process. What we know today as UML is the visual language part of the project – UP is the process part.

UP is based on process work conducted at Ericsson (the Ericsson approach, 1967), at Rational (the Rational Objectory Process, 1996 to 1997) and other sources of best practice. As such, it is a pragmatic and tested method for developing software that incorporates best practice from its predecessors.

> A software engineering process describes how requirements are turned into software.

## 2.3   The birth of UP

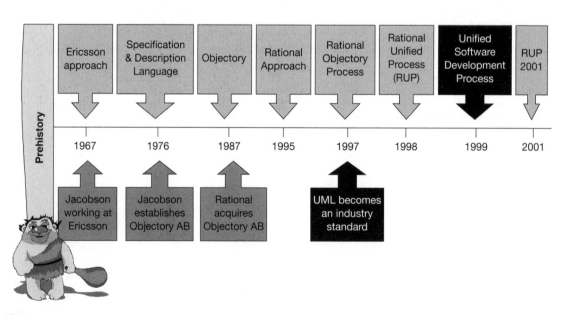

Figure 2.3

When we look at the history of UP, depicted in Figure 2.3, it is fair to say that its development is intimately tied to the career of one man, Ivar Jacobson. In fact, Jacobson is often thought of as being the father of UP. This is not to minimize the work of all of the other individuals (especially Booch) who have contributed to the development of UP, rather it is to emphasize Jacobson's pivotal contribution.

UP goes back to 1967 and the Ericsson approach, which took the radical step of modeling a complex system as a set of interconnected blocks. Small blocks were interconnected to form larger blocks building up to a complete system. The basis of this approach was "divide and conquer" and it is known today as component-based development.

> SEP work that was to develop into the UP began in 1967 at Ericsson.

Although a complete system might be incomprehensible to any individual who approaches it as a monolith, when broken down into smaller components it can be made sense of by understanding the services each component offers (the interface to the component) and how these components fit together. In the language of UML, large blocks are called subsystems, and each subsystem is implemented in terms of smaller blocks called components.

Another Ericsson innovation was a way of identifying these blocks by creating "traffic cases" that described how the system was to be used. These "traffic cases" have evolved over time and are now called use cases in UML. The result of this process was an architecture representation that described all the blocks and how they fitted together. This was the forerunner of the UML static model.

As well as the requirements view (the "traffic cases") and the static view (the architecture description), Ericsson also had a dynamic view that described how all the blocks communicated with each other over time. This consisted of sequence, collaboration, and statechart diagrams, all of which are still found in UML, albeit in a much refined form.

The next major development in OO software engineering was the release of the Specification and Description Language (SDL) from the international standards body CCITT. This language was designed to capture the behavior of telecommunications systems. Systems were modeled as a set of components that communicated by sending signals to each other. In fact, SDL was the first object modeling standard. It is still used today.

In 1987, Jacobson founded Objectory AB in Stockholm. This company developed and sold a software engineering process, based on the Ericsson Approach, called Objectory (*Object* Fac*tory*). The Objectory SEP consisted of a set of documentation, a rather idiosyncratic CASE tool, and some probably much needed consultancy from Objectory AB.

Perhaps the most important innovation during this time was that the Objectory SEP was viewed as a system in its own right. The workflows of the process (requirements, analysis, design, implementation, test) were expressed in a set of diagrams. In other words, the Objectory process was modeled and developed just like a software system. This paved the way for the future development of the process. Objectory, like UP, was also a process framework and needed vigorous customization before it could be applied to any specific project. The Objectory process product came with some templates for various types of software development project, but it almost invariably needed to be heavily customized further. Jacobson recognized that all software development projects are different, and so a "one size fits all" SEP was not really feasible or desirable.

When Rational acquired Objectory AB in 1995, Jacobson went to work unifying the Objectory process with the large amount of process-related work that had already been done at Rational. A 4+1 view of architecture based around four distinct views (logical, process, physical and development) plus a unifying use case view was developed. This still forms the basis of the UP and UML approaches to system architecture. In addition, iterative development was formalized into a sequence of phases (Inception, Elaboration, Construction, and Transition) that combined the discipline of the waterfall lifecycle with the dynamic responsiveness of iterative and incremental development. The main participants in this work were Walker Royce, Rich Reitmann, Grady Booch (inventor of the Booch method), and Philippe Kruchten. In particular, Booch's experience and strong ideas on architecture were incorporated into the Rational Approach (see [Booch 1] for an excellent discussion of his ideas).

The Rational Objectory Process (ROP) was the result of the unification of Objectory with Rational's process work. In particular, ROP improved areas where Objectory was weak – requirements other than use cases, implementation, test, project management, deployment, configuration management, and development environment. Risk was introduced as a driver for ROP, and architecture was defined and formalized as an "architecture description" deliverable. During this period Booch, Jacobson, and Rumbaugh were developing UML at Rational. This became the language in which ROP models, and ROP itself, were expressed.

From 1997 onward, Rational acquired many more companies bringing in expertise in requirements capture, configuration management, testing, etc. This led to the release of the Rational Unified Process (RUP)[1] in 1998. Since then, there have been many releases of RUP, each one consistently better than the previous.

In 1999, an important book was published, the *Unified Software Development Process* [Jacobson 1], which describes the Unified Process. Whereas RUP is a Rational process product, UP is an open SEP from the authors of UML. Not surprisingly, UP and RUP are very closely related. We have chosen to use UP rather than RUP in this book as it is an open SEP, accessible to all, and is not tied to any specific product or vendor.

UP is a mature, open SEP from the authors of UML.

---

[1]  See www.rational.com and [Kruchten 1].

## 2.4 UP and the Rational Unified Process

RUP is a commercial product that extends UP.

There are several commercial variants of UP available. If we think in UML terms, then UP defines a class of software development processes and these commercial variants are like subclasses of UP. What this means is that the commercial variants take all of the features of UP, override some, and add new ones.

The most widely used commercial variant is RUP. This product supplies all of the standards, tools, etc. that are not included in UP and that one would otherwise have to provide oneself. It also provides a rich web-based environment including process documentation and "tool mentors" for each of the Rational tools.

RUP must still be instantiated on a per project basis, but the amount of work that needs to be done is much less than starting from raw UP. In fact, it is unrealistic to view any of the current crop of UP subclasses as complete and ready to go "out of the box". Expect to invest a certain amount of time in customization, and budget for some consultancy from the SEP vendor.

UP and RUP are much more similar than they are different.

Back in 1999, it was reasonable to view RUP as just a commercial implementation of UP. However, RUP has moved on a lot since then and now extends UP in many important ways. Nowadays, we should view UP as the open, general case, and RUP as a specific commercial subclass that both extends and overrides UP features. But RUP and UP still remain much more similar than different. The main differences are those of completeness and detail rather than semantic or ideological matters. The basic workflows of OO analysis and design are sufficiently similar that a description from the UP perspective will be just as useful for RUP users. By choosing to use UP in this book, we make the text suitable for the majority of OO analysts and designers who are not using RUP, and also for the significant minority who are.

Both UP and RUP model the *who*, *when* and *what* of the software development process, but they do so very slightly differently. The latest version of RUP (RUP 2001) has some terminological and syntactic differences to UP although semantics of the process elements remain essentially the same. Figure 2.4 shows how the RUP 2001 process icons map on to the UP icons we use in this book. Notice that there is a «trace» relationship between the RUP 2001 icon and the original UP icon. In UML a «trace» relationship is a special type of dependency between model elements that indicates that the element at the beginning of the «trace» relationship is an historical development of the element on the end. This fits the UP and RUP model elements perfectly.

To model the "who" of the SEP, UP introduces the concept of the worker. This describes a role played by an individual or team within the project. In RUP workers are actually called roles but the semantics remain the same.

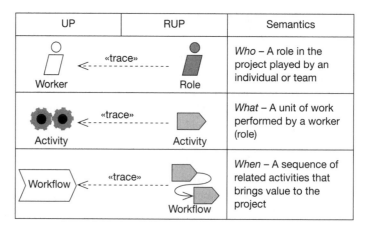

| UP | RUP | Semantics |
|---|---|---|
| Worker «trace» | Role | *Who* – A role in the project played by an individual or team |
| Activity «trace» | Activity | *What* – A unit of work performed by a worker (role) |
| Workflow «trace» | Workflow | *When* – A sequence of related activities that brings value to the project |

**Figure 2.4**

UP models the "when" as activities. These are tasks that will be performed by individuals or teams in the project. These individuals or teams will always *adopt specific roles* when they perform certain activities and so, for any activity, UP (and RUP) can tell us the workers (roles) that participate in that activity. Activities may be broken down into finer levels of detail as needed. A sequence of related activities is known as a workflow in both UP and RUP.

The "what" of the SEP is described in both RUP and UP as artefacts. These are things that are inputs and outputs to the project – they may be source code, executable programs, standards, documentation, etc. Artefacts may have many different icons.

## 2.5 Instantiating UP for your project

UP is a generic software development process that has to be instantiated for an organization and then for each particular project. This recognizes that all software projects tend to be different, and that a "one size fits all" approach to SEP just doesn't work. The instantiation process involves defining and incorporating:

UP and RUP must be instantiated for each project.

● in-house standards;

● document templates;

● tools – compilers, configuration management tools, etc;

● databases – bug tracking, project tracking, etc;

● lifecycle modifications – e.g. more sophisticated quality control measures for safety-critical systems.

Details of this customization process are outside the scope of this book, but are described in [Rumbaugh 1].

## 2.6 UP axioms

UP has three basic axioms. It is:

- use case and risk driven;
- architecture centric;
- iterative and incremental.

We'll look at use cases in great depth in Chapter 4, but for now let's just say that they are a way of capturing requirements – so we could accurately say that UP is requirements driven.

> UP is a modern SEP that is driven by user requirements and risk.

Risk is the other UP driver because if you don't actively attack risks they will actively attack you! Anyone who has worked in a software development project will no doubt agree with this sentiment, and UP addresses this by predicating software construction on the analysis of risk. However, this is really a job for the project manager and architect, and so we don't cover it in any detail in this book.

The UP approach to developing software systems is to develop and evolve a robust system architecture. Architecture describes the strategic aspects of how the system is broken down into components, and how those components interact and are deployed on hardware. Clearly, quality system architecture will lead to a quality system, rather than just an ad hoc collection of source code that has been hacked together with little forethought.

Finally, UP is iterative and incremental. The iterative aspect of UP means that we break the project into small subprojects (the iterations) that deliver system functionality in chunks, or increments, leading to a fully functional system. In other words, we build software by a process of stepwise refinement to our final goal. This is a very different approach to software construction compared to the old waterfall lifecycle of analysis, design, and build that occur in a more or less strict sequence. In fact, we return to key UP workflows, such as analysis, several times throughout the course of the project.

## 2.7 UP is an iterative and incremental process

> UP aims to build a robust system architecture incrementally.

To understand UP, we need to understand iterations. The idea is fundamentally very simple – history shows that, generally speaking, human beings find small problems easier to solve than large problems. We therefore break a large software development project down into a number of smaller "mini projects" which are easier to manage and to complete successfully. Each of these "mini projects" is an iteration. The key point is that each iteration contains *all* of the elements of a normal software development project:

- planning;
- analysis and design;
- construction;
- integration and test;
- an internal or external release.

Each iteration generates a baseline that comprises a *partially complete* version of the final system and any associated project documentation. Baselines build on each other over successive iterations until the final finished system is achieved.

The difference between two consecutive baselines is known as an increment – this is why UP is known as an iterative and incremental lifecycle.

As you will see in Section 2.8, iterations are grouped into phases. Phases provide the macrostructure of UP.

### 2.7.1    Iteration workflows

In each iteration, there are five core workflows that specify what needs to be done and the skills needed to do it. As well as the five core workflows there will be other workflows such as planning, assessment and anything else specific to that particular iteration. However, these are not covered in UP. The five core workflows are:

> UP has five core workflows.

- requirements – capturing what the system should do;
- analysis – refining and structuring the requirements;
- design – realizing the requirements in system architecture;
- implementation – building the software;
- test – verifying that the implementation works as desired.

Some possible workflows for an iteration are illustrated in Figure 2.5. We will look at the requirements, analysis, design and implementation workflows in more detail later in the book (the test workflow is out of scope).

Although each iteration may contain all of the five core workflows, the emphasis on a particular workflow depends on where the iteration occurs in the project lifecycle.

Breaking the project down into a series of iterations allows a flexible approach to project planning. The simplest approach is just a time-ordered sequence of iterations, where each leads on to the next. However, it is often possible to schedule iterations in parallel. This implies an understanding of the dependencies between the artefacts of each iteration, and requires an approach to software development predicated on architecture and modeling. The benefit of parallel iterations is better time-to-market and perhaps better utilization of the team, but careful planning is essential.

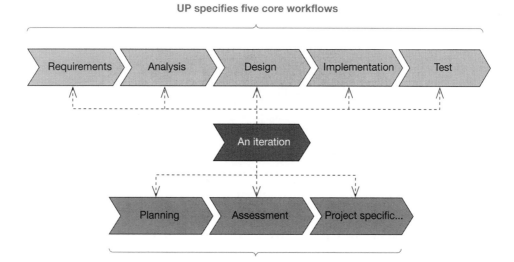

**Figure 2.5**

### 2.7.2   Baselines and increments

Every UP iteration generates a baseline. This is an internal (or external) release of the set of reviewed and approved artefacts generated by that iteration. Each baseline:

● provides an agreed basis for further review and development;

● can be changed *only* through formal procedures of configuration and change management.

Increments, however, are just the *difference* between one baseline and the next. They constitute a step toward the final, delivered system.

## 2.8   UP structure

UP has four phases, each of which ends with a major milestone.

Figure 2.6 shows the structure of UP. The project lifecycle is divided into four phases – Inception, Elaboration, Construction, and Transition – each of which ends with a major milestone. Within each phase we can have one or more iterations, and in each iteration we execute the five core workflows and any extra workflows. The exact number of iterations per phase depends on the size of the project, but each iteration should last no more than two to three months. The example is typical for a project that lasts about 18 months and is of medium size.

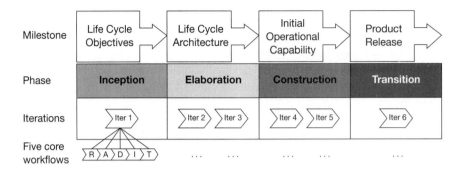

**Figure 2.6**

As can be seen from Figure 2.6, UP consists of a sequence of four phases, each of which terminates with a major milestone:

- Inception – Life Cycle Objectives;
- Elaboration – Life Cycle Architecture;
- Construction – Initial Operational Capability;
- Transition – Product Release.

As the project shifts through the phases of the UP, so the amount of work that is done in each of the five core workflows changes.

Figure 2.7 is really the key to understanding how UP works. Along the top, we have the phases. Down the left-hand side, we have the five core

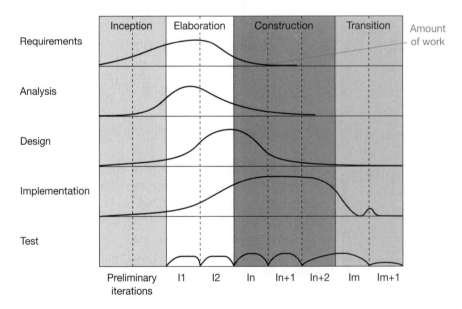

**Figure 2.7**    Adapted from Figure 1.5 [Jacobson 1] with permission from Addison-Wesley

workflows. Along the bottom, we have some iterations. The curves show the relative amount of work done in each of the five core workflows, as the project progresses through the phases.

As Figure 2.7 shows, in the Inception phase most of the work is done in requirements and analysis. In Elaboration the emphasis shifts to require-ments, analysis and some design. In Construction the emphasis is clearly on design and implementation. Finally, in Transition the emphasis is on implementation and test.

In the rest of this chapter, we will give a brief overview of each of the UP phases.

> The amount of work done in each core workflow varies according to the phase.

## 2.9   UP phases

Every phase has a goal, a focus of activity with one or more core workflows emphasized, and a milestone. This will be our framework for investigating the phases.

### 2.9.1   Inception – goals

The goal of Inception is to "get the project off the ground". Inception involves:

> Inception is about initiating the project.

- establishing feasibility – this may involve some technical prototyping to validate technology decisions or proof of concept prototyping to vali-date business requirements;
- creating a business case to demonstrate that the project will deliver quantifiable business benefit;
- capturing essential requirements to help scope the system;
- identifying critical risks.

The primary workers in this phase are the project manager and system architect.

### 2.9.2   Inception – focus

The primary emphasis in Inception is on requirements and analysis work-flows. However, some design and implementation might also be done if it is decided to build a technical, or proof of concept, prototype. The test work-flow is not generally applicable to this phase, as the only software artefacts are prototypes that will be thrown away.

### 2.9.3 Inception – milestone: Life Cycle Objectives

While many SEPs focus on the creation of key artefacts, UP adopts a different approach that is goal-oriented. Each milestone sets certain goals that *must* be achieved before the milestone can be considered to have been reached. Some of these goals might be the production of certain artefacts and some might not.

The milestone for Inception is the Life Cycle Objectives. The conditions that must be met for this milestone to be attained are given in Table 2.1.

**Table 2.1**

| Conditions of satisfaction | Deliverable |
| --- | --- |
| The stakeholders have agreed the project objectives | A vision document that states the project's main requirements, features and constraints |
| System scope has been defined and agreed with the stakeholders | An initial use case model (only about 10% to 20% complete) |
| Key requirements have been captured and agreed with the stakeholders | A Project Glossary |
| Cost and schedule estimates have been agreed with the stakeholders | An initial Project Plan |
| A business case has been raised by the project manager | Business Case |
| The project manager has performed a risk assessment | A Risk Assessment document or database |
| Confirmation of feasibility through technical studies and/or prototyping | One or more throwaway prototypes |
| An outline architecture | An initial architecture document |

### 2.9.4 Elaboration – goals

The goals of Elaboration may be summarized as follows:

- create an executable architectural baseline;
- refine the Risk Assessment;
- define quality attributes (defect discovery rates, acceptable defect densities, etc.);
- capture use cases to 80% of the functional requirements (you'll see exactly what this involves in Chapters 3 and 4);
- create a detailed plan for the construction phase;
- formulate a bid that includes resources, time, equipment, staff and cost.

> Elaboration is about creating a partial but working version of the system – an executable architectural baseline.

The main goal of Elaboration is to create an executable architectural baseline. This is a real, executable system that is built according to the specified architecture. It is *not* a prototype (which is throwaway), but rather the "first cut" of the desired system. This initial executable architectural baseline will be added to as the project progresses, and will evolve into the final delivered system during the Construction and Transition phases. Because future phases are predicated on the results of Elaboration, this is perhaps the most critical phase. In fact, the focus of this book will be very much on the Elaboration activities.

### 2.9.5 Elaboration – focus

In the Elaboration phase, the focus in each of the core workflows is as follows:

- requirements – refine system scope and requirements;
- analysis – establish what to build;
- design – create a stable architecture;
- implementation – build the architectural baseline;
- test – test the architectural baseline.

The focus in Elaboration is clearly on the requirements, analysis and design workflows, with implementation becoming very important at the end of the phase when the executable architectural baseline is being produced.

### 2.9.6 Elaboration – milestone: Life Cycle Architecture

The milestone is the Life Cycle Architecture. The conditions of satisfaction for this milestone are summarized in Table 2.2.

**Table 2.2**

| Conditions of satisfaction | Deliverable |
|---|---|
| A resilient, robust executable architectural baseline has been created | The executable architectural baseline |
| The executable architectural baseline demonstrates that important risks have been identified and resolved | UML Static Model |
| | UML Dynamic Model |
| | UML Use Case Model |
| The vision of the product has stabilized | Vision document |
| The risk assessment has been revised | Updated Risk Assessment |
| The business case has been revised and agreed with the stakeholders | Updated Business Case |
| A project plan has been created in sufficient detail to enable a realistic bid to be formulated for time, money and resources in the next phases | Updated Project Plan |
| The stakeholders agree to the project plan | |
| The business case has been verified against the project plan | Business Case and Project Plan |
| Agreement is reached with the stakeholders to continue the project | Sign-off document |

### 2.9.7 Construction – goals

Construction evolves the executable architectural baseline into a complete, working system.

The goal of Construction is to complete all requirements, analysis and design, and to evolve the architectural baseline generated in Elaboration into the final system. A key issue in Construction is *maintaining the integrity of the system architecture*. It is quite common once delivery pressure is on and coding begins in earnest, for corners to be cut leading to a corruption of the architectural vision and a final system with low quality and high maintenance costs. Clearly, this outcome should be avoided.

### 2.9.8 Construction – focus

The emphasis in this phase is on the implementation workflow. Just enough work is done in the other workflows to complete requirements capture, analysis and design. Testing also becomes more important – as each new increment builds on the last, both unit and integration tests are now needed. We can summarize the kind of work undertaken in each workflow as follows:

- requirements – uncover any requirements that had been missed;
- analysis – finish the analysis model;
- design – finish the design model;
- implementation – build the Initial Operational Capability;
- test – test the Initial Operational Capability.

### 2.9.9 Construction – milestone: Initial Operational Capability

In essence, this milestone is very simple – the software system is finished ready for beta testing at the user site. The conditions of satisfaction for this milestone are given in Table 2.3.

**Table 2.3**

| Conditions of satisfaction | Deliverable |
|---|---|
| The software product is sufficiently stable and of sufficient quality to be deployed in the user community | The software product |
| | The UML model |
| | Test suite |
| The stakeholders have agreed and are ready for the transition of the software to their environment | User manuals |
| | Description of this release |
| The actual expenditures vs. the planned expenditures are acceptable | Project Plan |

### 2.9.10 Transition – goals

The Transition phase starts when beta testing is completed and the system is finally deployed. This involves fixing any defects found in the beta test and preparing for rollout of the software to all the user sites. We can summarize the goals of this phase as follows:

- correct defects;
- prepare the user site for the new software;
- tailor the software to operate at the user site;
- modify the software if unforeseen problems arise;
- create user manuals and other documentation;
- provide user consultancy;
- conduct a post project review.

> Transition is about deploying the completed system into the user community.

### 2.9.11 Transition – focus

The emphasis is on the implementation and test workflows. Sufficient design is done to correct any design errors found in beta testing. Hopefully, by this point in the project lifecycle, there should be very little work being done in the requirements and analysis workflows. If this is not the case, then the project is in trouble.

- Requirements – not applicable.
- Analysis – not applicable.
- Design – modify the design if problems emerge in beta testing.
- Implementation – tailor the software for the user site and correct problems uncovered in beta testing.
- Test – beta testing and acceptance testing at the user site.

### 2.9.12 Transition – milestone: Product Release

This is the final milestone – beta testing, acceptance testing and defect repair are finished and the product is released and accepted into the user community. The conditions of satisfaction for this milestone are given in Table 2.4.

**Table 2.4**

| Conditions of satisfaction | Deliverable |
|---|---|
| Beta testing is completed, necessary changes have been made, and the users agree that the system has been successfully deployed | The software product |
| The user community is actively using the product | |
| Product support strategies have been agreed with the users and implemented | User support plan<br>User manuals |

## 2.10  What we have learned

- A software engineering process (SEP) turns user requirements into software by specifying *who* does *what, when.*

- The Unified Process (UP) has been in development since 1967. It is a mature, open SEP from the authors of UML.

- Rational Unified Process (RUP) is a commercial extension of UP. It is entirely compatible with UP but is more complete and detailed.

- UP (and RUP) must be instantiated for any specific project by adding in-house standards, etc.

- UP is a modern SEP that is:
  — risk and use case (requirements) driven;
  — architecture centric;
  — iterative and incremental.

- In UP software is built in iterations:
  — each iteration is like a "mini project" that delivers a part of the system;
  — iterations build on each other to create the final system.

- Every iteration has five core workflows:
  — requirements – capturing what the system should do;
  — analysis – refining and structuring the requirements;
  — design – realizing the requirements in system architecture (how the system does it);
  — implementation – building the software;
  — test – verifying that the implementation works as desired.

● UP has four phases, each of which ends with a major milestone:
   — inception – getting the project off the ground: Life Cycle Objectives;
   — elaboration – evolving the system architecture: Life Cycle Architecture;
   — construction – building the software: Initial Operational Capability;
   — transition – deploying the software into the user environment: Product Release.

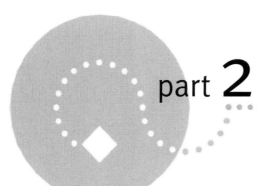

part 2

# Requirements

# chapter 3
# The requirements workflow

## 3.1  Chapter roadmap

This chapter is all about understanding system requirements. We'll discuss the details of the UP requirements workflow and introduce the notion of requirements. Also, we'll present a UP extension for dealing with requirements *without* using UML use cases.

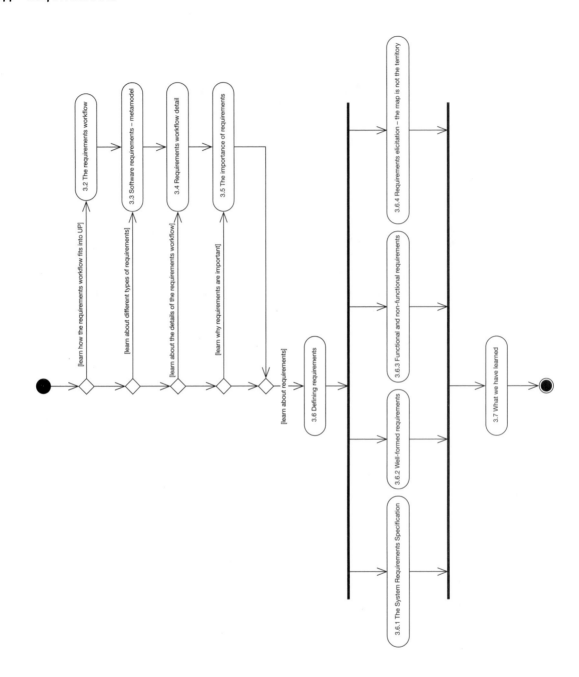

## 3.2   The requirements workflow

As shown in Figure 3.2, most of the work in the requirements workflow occurs throughout the Inception and Elaboration phases right at the beginning of the project lifecycle. This is hardly surprising, as you can't progress beyond Elaboration until you know roughly what you are going to build!

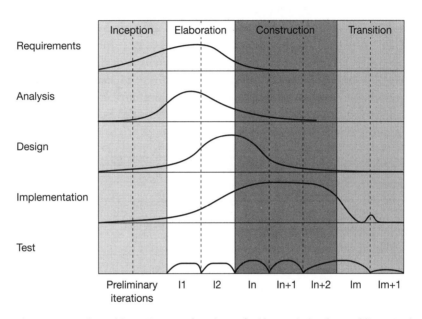

**Figure 3.2**   Adapted from Figure 1.5 [Jacobson 1] with permission from Addison-Wesley

Before you can even begin to work on OO analysis and design, you have to have some idea of what you are trying to achieve, and this is the purpose of the requirements workflow – to discover and reach agreement on what the system should do, expressed in the language of the users of the system. You create a very high-level specification for what the system should do – this is known as requirements engineering.

For any given system, there may be many different stakeholders – many types of user, maintenance engineers, support staff, salespeople, managers, etc. Requirements engineering is about eliciting and prioritizing the requirements that these stakeholders have for the system. It is a process of negotiation as there are often conflicting requirements which must be

> Most requirements work is done at the beginning of the project in the Inception and Elaboration phases.

balanced. For example, one group might want to add many users, which may result in unrealistic traffic on the existing database and communications infrastructure. This is a very common conflict at the moment as more and more companies are opening up parts of their system to a huge user base via the internet.

Many UML books (and indeed training courses) state that the UML notion of use cases is the only way to capture requirements, but this doesn't really stand up to close examination. Use cases can only really capture functional requirements, which are statements about *what the system will do*. However, there is another set of non-functional requirements that are statements about *constraints on the system* (performance, reliability, etc.), which are not really suitable for capture by use cases. We therefore present in this book a robust "requirements engineering" approach where we illustrate powerful and complementary ways to capture *both* sets of requirements.

## 3.3    Software requirements – metamodel

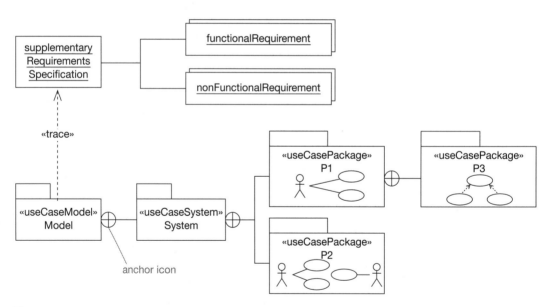

**Figure 3.3**

Figure 3.3 shows the metamodel for our approach to requirements engineering in this book. It contains quite a lot of UML syntax that we have not covered yet. Don't worry! We will cover these things in depth later on. For now, the following is all you need to know.

- The icons that look like folders are UML packages. They are the UML grouping mechanism and contain groups of UML modeling elements. In effect, they act very much like real folders in a filing system in that they are used to organize and group related things.

- The anchor icon indicates that the thing at the circle end contains the thing at the other end of the line.

- Our metamodel shows that the supplementaryRequirementsSpecification document (which we have modeled as an object) contains many functionalRequirements and many nonFunctionalRequirements. As we will see later, object names are always underlined.

- The dashed arrow labeled «trace» illustrates that we can form the use case model by a consideration of the supplementaryRequirementsSpecification and indicates an historical relationship between them.

- The use case model is composed of exactly one use case system. This system is made up of many use case packages (we only show three here) that contain use cases, actors and relationships.

So what are requirements, use cases and actors? We'll cover requirements in the rest of this chapter, and use cases and actors in the next.

## 3.4   Requirements workflow detail

Figure 3.4 shows the specific tasks for the UP requirements workflow. A diagram such as this is known as a workflow detail as it details the component tasks of a specific workflow.

UP workflow details are modeled as workers (the icons on the left-hand side) and tasks (the icons that look like cogs). UP variants such as RUP may use different icons but the semantics are the same (see Section 2.4 for a brief discussion of the relationship between UP and RUP). The arrows are relationships that show the normal flow of work from one task to the next. However, it is worth bearing in mind that this is only an approximation of the workflow in the "average" case and might not be a particularly exact representation of what happens in practice. In the real world, you can

A workflow detail shows us the workers and activities involved in a particular workflow.

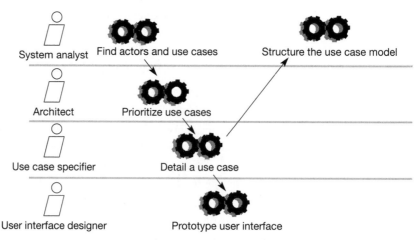

**Figure 3.4**  Reproduced from Figure 7.10 [Jacobson 1] with permission from
Addison-Wesley

expect some tasks to be done in a different order or in parallel according to
circumstances.

Because this is an analysis and design book, we will only be focusing on
the tasks important to OO analysts and designers. In this case, the tasks we
are interested in are:

- Find actors and use cases;
- Detail a use case;
- Structure the use case model.

The other tasks in the requirements workflow are not that relevant to us as
analyst/designers. "Prioritize use cases" is primarily an architecture and project
planning activity, and "Prototype user interface" is a programming activity. If
you need to, you can learn more about these activities in [Jacobson 1].

In Figure 3.4 you can see that the standard UP workflow focuses on use
cases to the exclusion of any other requirements elicitation techniques.
This is fine as far as it goes but, as we have said, it doesn't really address the
non-functional aspect of requirements particularly well. In order to deal
with requirements rigorously, we make a simple extension to the UP
requirements workflow to add the following new tasks:

> We extend the UP
> requirements
> workflow to deal with
> requirements
> expressed in
> structured English.

- Find functional requirements;
- Find non-functional requirements;
- Prioritize requirements;
- Trace requirements to use cases.

We have also introduced a new worker – the requirements engineer. The
new tasks and workers are shown in Figure 3.5.

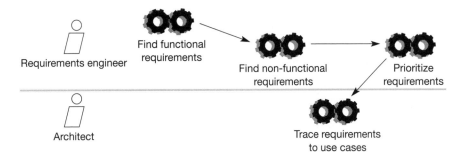

**Figure 3.5**

## 3.5  The importance of requirements

Requirements engineering is a term used to describe the activities involved in eliciting, documenting, and maintaining a set of requirements for a software system. It is about discovering what the stakeholders need the system to do for them.

Several studies have shown that failure in requirements engineering is the major cause of software project failure.

The next most important contributor to software project failure is lack of user involvement. Given that the users are our key source of requirements, this also amounts to a failure in requirements engineering!

As the final software system is predicated on a set of requirements, effective requirements engineering is a critical success factor in software development projects.

## 3.6  Defining requirements

We can define a requirement as "a specification of what should be implemented". There are basically two types of requirements:

- functional requirements – what behavior the system should offer;
- non-functional requirements – a specific property or constraint on the system.

Requirements tell us what we should build, not how we should build it.

Requirements are (or at least should be) the basis of all systems. They are essentially a statement of what the system should do. In principle, requirements should *only* be a statement of *what* the system should do, and not *how* it should do it. This is an important distinction. We can specify *what* a system should do and what behavior a system should exhibit without necessarily saying anything about *how* this functionality may be actually realized.

While it is certainly attractive in theory to separate the "what" from the "how", in practice a set of requirements (known as a System Requirements Specification, or just as a Requirements Specification) will tend to be a mix of "what" and "how". This is partly because it is often easier to write and understand an implementation description, rather than an abstract statement of the problem, and partly because there may be implementation constraints that predetermine the "how" of the system.

Despite the fact that system behavior and, ultimately, end user satisfaction is predicated on requirements engineering, many companies still don't recognize this as an important discipline. As we have seen, the primary reason that software projects fail is due to problems in requirements.

### 3.6.1   The System Requirements Specification

Many companies produce System Requirements Specifications (SRS) that specify what the software systems will do. This is typically written in natural language but special requirements engineering tools such as Requisite Pro (Rational Corporation) or DOORS[1] are sometimes used to great advantage.

The SRS is really the very beginning of the software construction process. It is often the initial input to OO analysis and design. Over the years we have seen many SRSs and they have varied widely from company to company and project to project. They come in all shapes and sizes and in varying degrees of usefulness. In fact, the essential questions to be asked of *any* SRS are "how useful is it to me?" and "Does it help me to understand what the system should do or not?" This is the bottom line.

### 3.6.2   Well-formed requirements

UML does not provide any recommendations on writing an SRS. In fact UML deals with requirements entirely by the mechanism of use cases, which we will examine later. However, many modelers (us included) believe that use cases are not enough, and that we still need SRSs and requirements management tools.

We recommend a very simple format for stating requirements (see Figure 3.6). Each requirement has a unique identifier (usually a number), a keyword (shall) and a statement of function. The advantage of adopting a uniform structure is that requirements management tools such as DOORS can parse an SRS more easily.

> Use simple "shall" statements to capture requirements.

---

[1] Details of the DOORS requirements management tool can be found at www.telelogic.com

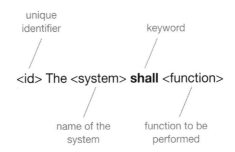

**Figure 3.6**

### 3.6.3   Functional and non-functional requirements

It is useful to divide requirements into functional and non-functional requirements. There are many other ways of categorizing requirements, but we will keep things as simple as possible and work initially with these two categories.

A functional requirement is a statement of what the system should do – it is a statement of system function. For example, if you were collecting requirements for an automated teller machine (ATM), some functional requirements might be:

> Functional requirement – what the system should do. Non-functional requirement – a constraint on the system.

1.   The ATM system shall check the validity of the inserted ATM card.

2.   The ATM system shall validate the PIN number entered by the customer.

3.   The ATM system shall dispense no more than $250 against any ATM card in any 24-hour period.

A non-functional requirement is a constraint placed on the system. For your ATM system, non-functional requirements might be:

1.   The ATM system shall be written in C++.

2.   The ATM system shall communicate with the bank using 256-bit encryption.

3.   The ATM system shall validate an ATM card in three seconds or less.

4.   The ATM system shall validate a PIN in three seconds or less.

You can see that non-functional requirements specify, or constrain, how the system will be implemented.

### 3.6.4   Requirements elicitation – the map is not the territory

Whenever you work with people to capture the requirements for a software system, you are trying to elicit from them an accurate picture, or map, of their model of the world. According to Noam Chomsky, in his 1975 book *Syntactic Structures* [Chomsky 1] on transformational grammar, this map is

The three filters of deletion, distortion and generalization shape natural language.

created by the three processes deletion, distortion and generalization. This is entirely necessary, as we just don't have the cognitive equipment to capture every nuance and detail of the world in an infinitely detailed mental map, so we have to be selective. We make our selection from the vast array of possible information by applying these three filters:

- deletion – information is filtered out;
- distortion – information is modified by the related mechanisms creation and hallucination;
- generalization – the creation of rules, beliefs and principles about truth and falsehood.

These filters shape natural language. It is important to know about them when you are doing detailed requirements capture and analysis, as you may need to actively identify and challenge them to recover information.

Below are some examples from a library management system. For each there is a challenge to the filter and a possible response to that challenge.

- Example: "They use the system to borrow books" – deletion.
  — Challenge: Who specifically uses the system to borrow books? All users of the system, or just some?
  — Response: Some users just use the system for stock control.

- Example: "Borrowers can't borrow another book until all overdue books have been returned" – distortion.
  — Challenge: Are there any circumstances under which someone could borrow a new book before all overdue books had been returned?
  — Response: Actually, there are two circumstances under which a borrower's right to borrow books may be restored. Firstly, all borrowed books are returned; secondly, any borrowed book that has not been returned has been paid for.

- Example: "Everyone must have a ticket to borrow books" – generalization.
  — Challenge: Is there any user of the system who might not need to have a ticket?
  — Response: Some users of the system, such as other libraries, may not need a ticket or may have a special type of ticket with different terms and conditions.

The last two cases are particularly interesting as they are examples of a very common language pattern – the universal quantifier. Universal quantifiers are words such as:

- all

- everyone

- always

- never

- nobody

- none.

Whenever you encounter a universal quantifier, you may have found a deletion, distortion, or a generalization. They often indicate that you have reached the limits, or bounds of someone's mental map. As such, when doing analysis it is often a good idea to challenge universal quantifiers. We almost wrote "it is *always* a good idea to challenge universal quantifiers", but then we challenged ourselves!

## 3.7 What we have learned

This chapter has presented the UP requirements workflow and a general discussion of software requirements. You have learned the following.

- Most of the work in the requirements workflow occurs in the Inception and Elaboration phases of the UP project lifecycle.

- Our requirements metamodel (Figure 3.3) shows that there are two ways of capturing requirements – as functional and non-functional requirements and as use cases and actors.

- The UP requirements workflow detail contains the following activities that are of interest to us as OO analysts and designers:
  — Find actors and use cases;
  — Detail a use case;
  — Structure the use case model.

- We extend the standard UP requirements workflow with:
  — actor: Requirements engineer;
  — activity: Find functional requirements;
  — activity: Find non-functional requirements;
  — activity: Prioritize requirements;
  — activity: Trace requirements to use cases.

- About 25% of projects fail due to problems with requirements engineering.

- There are two types of requirement:
  - –- functional requirements – what behavior the system should offer;
  - — non-functional requirements – a specific property or constraint on the system.

- Well-formed requirements should be expressed in simple structured English using shall statements, so that they can be easily parsed by requirements engineering tools.

- The System Requirements Specification contains the functional and non-functional requirements for a system. This may be:
  - — a document;
  - — a database in a requirements management tool.

- The map is not the territory. Natural language contains:
  - — deletions – information is filtered out;
  - — distortions – information is modified;
  - — generalizations – rules, beliefs and principles are created about truth and falsehood.

- Universal quantifiers ("all," "every," etc.) can indicate the boundary of someone's mental map of their world – we should challenge them.

# chapter 4

# Use case modeling

## 4.1 Chapter roadmap

In this chapter, we're going to discuss the basics of use case modeling, which is another form of requirements engineering. We will take you through the process of use case modeling as defined by UP. We will be concentrating on specific techniques and strategies that the OO analyst/designer can use to perform use case modeling effectively. To focus on these techniques, we'll keep the use cases in this section as simple as possible. There is a complete (and more complex) worked example on our website at www.umlandtheunifiedprocess.com.

UML does not specify any formal structure for the use case specification. This is problematic, as different modelers adopt different standards. To help with this, we have adopted a simple and effective standard in this chapter and in our worked example. In order to help you to apply our approach, our website provides open source XML (eXtensible Markup Language) Schema for use cases and actors that you are free to use in your projects. These templates are based on industry best practice and provide a simple, yet effective, standard for capturing use case specifications.

Our website also includes a very simple XSL (eXtensible Stylesheet Language) stylesheet that transforms XML use case documents into HTML for display in a browser. This stylesheet is a useful example that can be easily customized to incorporate branding or other document standards for different organizations. A detailed discussion of XML is beyond the scope of this book, and you may need to refer to XML texts such as [Pitts 1] and [Kay 1] to utilize these documents effectively.

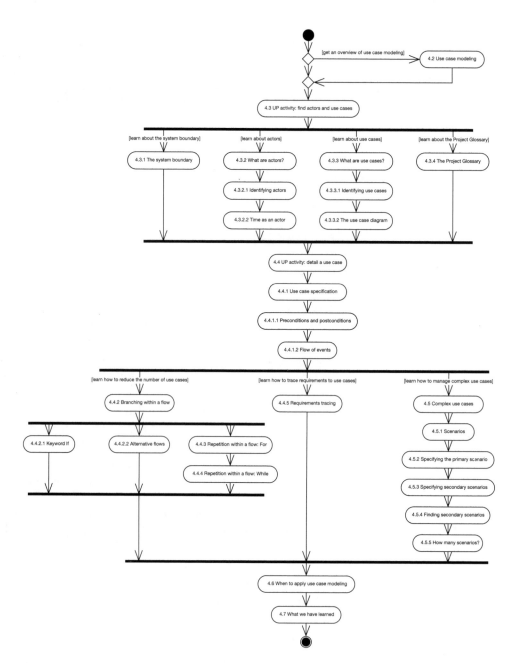

**Figure 4.1**

## 4.2 Use case modeling

Use case modeling is a form of requirements engineering. In Section 3.6, you saw how to create an SRS in what we might call the "traditional" way. Use case modeling is a different and complementary way of eliciting and documenting requirements. Use case modeling typically proceeds as follows.

- Find the system boundary.
- Find the actors.
- Find the use cases:
  a. specify the use case;
  b. create scenarios.

The output of these activities is the use case model. There are four components of this model:

Use cases are a way of capturing requirements.

- actors – roles played by people or things that use the system;
- use cases – things that the actors can do with the system;
- relationships – meaningful relationships between actors and use cases;
- system boundary – a box drawn around the use cases to denote the edge or boundary of the system being modeled.

In addition, the use case model provides a prime source for objects and classes. It is the primary input to class modeling.

## 4.3 UP activity: find actors and use cases

Use case modeling involves finding actors and use cases.

In this section, we will be focusing on the activity "Find actors and use cases" from the requirements workflow (see Section 3.4). This is shown in Figure 4.2. We will go on in Section 4.4 to look at the activity "Detail a use case".

### 4.3.1 The system boundary

The system boundary separates the system from the rest of the world.

The first thing you need to do when you are thinking about building a system is to decide where the boundaries of the system are. In other words, you need to define what is *part* of your system (inside the system boundary) and what is *external* to your system (outside the system boundary). This sounds obvious, but there have been many projects where severe problems arose from an uncertain system boundary. The positioning of

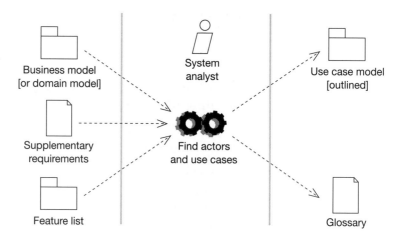

**Figure 4.2**   Reproduced from Figure 7.11 [Jacobson 1] with permission from Addison-Wesley

the system boundary typically has an enormous impact on the functional (and sometimes non-functional) requirements, and we have already seen that incomplete and ill-specified requirements can be the primary reason that projects fail.

The system boundary is defined by who or what uses the system (i.e. the actors), and what specific benefits the system offers to those actors (i.e. the use cases).

The system boundary is drawn as a box, labeled with the name of the system, with the actors drawn *outside* the boundary and the use cases *inside*. You will start use case modeling with only a tentative idea of where the system boundary actually lies. As you find the actors and use cases, the system boundary becomes more and more sharply defined.

### 4.3.2   What are actors?

Actors are roles adopted by things that interact *directly* with the system.

An actor specifies a role that some external entity adopts when interacting with your system directly. It may represent a user role, or a role played by another system, that touches the boundary of your system.

Actors are represented in UML as shown in Figure 4.3. The actor is just a stereotype of class with its own special icon. Both forms of the actor nota-

**Figure 4.3**

tion are valid, but many modelers prefer to use the "stick man" form to represent roles that are likely to be played by people, and the "box" form to represent roles likely to be played by other systems.

Actors are external to the system.

It is important to realize that actors are always *external* to the system. For example, if you are using an e-commerce system such as an online bookstore to buy a book, then you are external to that system. However, it is interesting to note that although actors themselves are always external to the system, systems often maintain some internal representation of one or more actors. In the case given above, the online bookstore e-commerce system maintains a customer details record for most customers. This contains name, address, etc. This is an internal system representation of the Customer actor. Now, it's important to be crystal clear about this difference – the Customer actor is *external* to the system, but the system might maintain a CustomerDetails class, which is an *internal* representation of individuals who play the role of Customer actor.

### 4.3.2.1   Identifying actors

In order to identify the actors, you need to consider who or what uses the system, and what roles they play in their interactions with the system. You can arrive at the roles that people and things play in relation to a system by a consideration of cases of specific people and things, and then generalizing. Asking the following questions will help you to identify actors.

To find actors ask: "Who or what uses or interacts with the system?"

- Who or what uses the system?
- What roles do they play in the interaction?
- Who installs the system?
- Who starts and shuts down the system?
- Who maintains the system?
- What other systems interact with this system?
- Who gets and provides information to the system?
- Does anything happen at a fixed time?

In terms of modeling actors, remember the following points.

- Actors are always external to the system – they are therefore outside your control.
- Actors interact directly with the system – this is how they help to define the system boundary.
- Actors represent roles that people and things play in relation to the system, not specific people or specific things.

- One person or thing may play many roles in relation to the system simultaneously or over time. For example, if you were both writing and delivering training courses, from the perspective of a course planning system you would play two roles – "Trainer" and "Course Author".

- Each actor needs a short name that makes sense from the business perspective.

- Each actor must have a short description (one or two lines) that describes what this actor is from a business perspective.

- Like classes, actors may have compartments that show attributes of the actor and events that the actor may receive. Typically these compartments are not used that much and are rarely shown on use case diagrams. We won't consider them any further.

### 4.3.2.2    *Time as an actor*

When you need to model things that happen to your system at a specific point in time but which *don't* seem to be triggered by any actor, you can introduce an actor called Time as illustrated in Figure 4.4. An example of this would be an automatic system backup that runs every evening.

Time

**Figure 4.4**

## 4.3.3    What are use cases?

*The UML Reference Manual* [Rumbaugh 1] defines a use case as "A specification of sequences of actions, including variant sequences and error sequences, that a system, subsystem or class can perform by interacting with outside actors."

A use case is something an actor wants the system to do. It is a "case of use" of the system by a specific actor:

A use case describes behavior that the system exhibits to benefit one or more actors.

- use cases are *always* started by an actor;

- use cases are *always* written from the point of view of an actor.

We usually think of use cases at the system level but, as the definition states, we may also apply use cases to describe "cases of use" of a subsystem (part of a system) or even an individual class. Use cases can also be very effective in business process modeling, although we don't address that aspect in this book.

The UML icon for use cases is shown in Figure 4.5.

**Figure 4.5**

The name of the use case may be written inside or underneath the oval.

### 4.3.3.1   *Identifying use cases*

> To find use cases ask "How does each actor use the system?" and "What does the system do for each actor?"

The best way of identifying use cases is to start with the list of actors, and then consider how each actor is going to use the system. Using this strategy you can obtain a list of candidate use cases. Each use case must be given a short, descriptive name that is a verb phrase – after all, the use case is *doing* something!

As you identify use cases, you may also find some new actors – this is OK. Sometimes you have to consider system functionality very carefully before you find all the actors, or all the *right* actors.

Use case modeling is iterative and proceeds via a process of stepwise refinement. You begin with just a name for a use case, and fill in the details later. These details consist of an initial short description that is refined into a complete specification. Here is a helpful list of questions that you can ask when trying to identify use cases.

● What functions will a specific actor want from the system?

● Does the system store and retrieve information? If so, which actors trigger this behavior?

● Are any actors notified when the system changes state?

● Are there any external events that affect the system? What notifies the system about those events?

### 4.3.3.2   *The use case diagram*

In the use case diagram we represent the system boundary by a box labeled with the name of the system. You show actors outside the system boundary (external to the system) and use cases, which constitute the system behavior, inside the system boundary (internal to the system). This is illustrated in Figure 4.6.

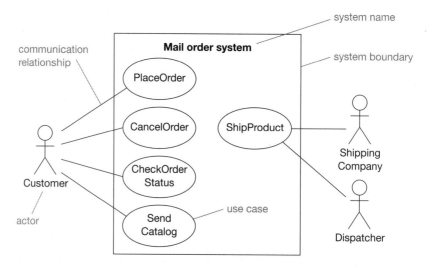

**Figure 4.6**

The relationship between an actor and a use case is shown using a solid line, which is actually the UML association symbol. You'll see much more of associations in Chapter 9. There is always assumed to be an implicit «communication» stereotype on this association to indicate that the actor and the use case communicate in some way. This stereotype is never shown explicitly on the use case diagram.

## 4.3.4 The Project Glossary

Capture business language and jargon in the Project Glossary.

The Project Glossary may well be one of the most important project artefacts. Every business domain has its own unique language, and the primary purpose of requirements engineering and analysis is to understand and capture that language. The glossary provides a dictionary of key business terms and definitions. It should be understandable by everyone in the project, including all the stakeholders.

As well as defining key terms, the Project Glossary must resolve synonyms and homonyms.

- Synonyms are different words that mean the same thing. As an OO analyst you must choose one of these words (the one that seems to be used most widely) and stick with it. The other variants must be completely excluded from your models. This is because if you allow the use of synonyms, you may well end up with two classes that do more or less the same thing, but have different names. Also, if you allow the use of all the synonyms on an ad hoc basis, then you can be sure that the actual semantics of the words will gradually diverge over time.

- Homonyms occur when the same word means different things to different people. This always gives rise to difficult communication problems as the various parties are quite literally speaking different languages when they all *believe* that they are speaking the same language. Again, the way to resolve this is to choose one meaning for the term, and perhaps introduce new terms for the other homonyms.

In the Project Glossary, you should record the preferred term and list any synonyms under the definition. This may involve encouraging some business stakeholders to become accustomed to different terminology. It is often a hard task to get stakeholders to change their use of language and yet, with persistence, it can be done.

UML does not set any standards for a Project Glossary. It is good practice to keep it as simple and concise as possible. Use a format like that of a dictionary with an alphabetically sorted list of words and definitions. A simple text-based document may suffice, but large projects may well require an online HTML- or XML-based glossary or even a simple database. Remember that the more accessible and the easier the glossary is to use, the more positive an impact it is likely to have on the project.

One issue with the Project Glossary is that terms and definitions in the glossary will also be used in the UML model. You have to ensure that the two documents are kept synchronized. Unfortunately, most UML CASE tools do not provide any support for this and so it is usually a manual activity.

## 4.4   UP activity: detail a use case

Having created a use case diagram and identified the actors and key use cases, you then need to begin to specify each use case in turn. This is the UP activity known as "Detail a use case" – it is summarized in Figure 4.7.

It is important at this point to note that, typically, you don't do things in an exact sequence, and you can choose to specify some, or all, of the use cases as you find them. It is always difficult to present parallel activities in a book that, by its very nature, is linear!

The output of this activity is a more detailed use case. This consists of at least the use case name and a use case specification. There may also (optionally) be a short description of the use case.

### 4.4.1   Use case specification

There is no UML standard for a use case specification. However, the template shown in Figure 4.8 is in common use. There are more complex templates in use but, on the whole, it is best to keep use case modeling as simple as possible. The use case in Figure 4.8 is about paying VAT – a form of sales tax levied in many European countries.

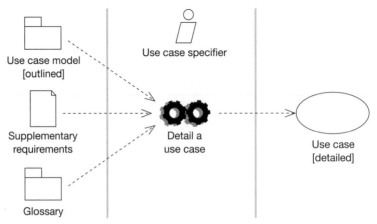

**Figure 4.7**    Reproduced from Figure 7.14 [Jacobson 1] with permission from
Addison-Wesley

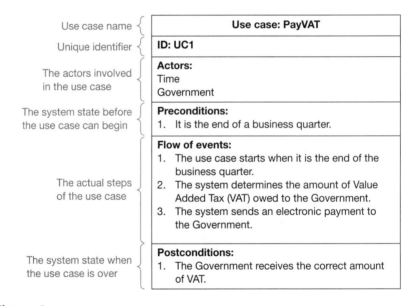

**Figure 4.8**

Each use case has a name and a specification. The specification consists of:

- Preconditions – these are things that must be true before the use case can execute – they are constraints on the state of the system;
- Flow of events – the steps in the use case;
- Postconditions – things that must be true at the end of the use case.

In the example above, the government always gets its tax one way or another, and so we state this as a postcondition of the use case.

### 4.4.1.1 *Preconditions and postconditions*

Preconditions and postconditions are constraints.

Preconditions
constrain the state of
the system before the
use case can start.
Postconditions
constrain the state of
the system after the
use case has executed.

- Preconditions constrain the state of the system before the use case can start. Think of them as gatekeepers that prevent an actor from triggering the use case until all their conditions are met.
- Postconditions constrain the state of the system after the use case has executed.

Another way of looking at this is that preconditions specify what must be true *before* the use case can be triggered, and postconditions specify what will be true *after* the use case has executed. Preconditions and postconditions help you to design systems that function correctly.

Preconditions and postconditions should always be simple statements about the state of the system that will evaluate to true or false – these are known as Boolean conditions.

### 4.4.1.2 *Flow of events*

The flow of events
describes steps in a
use case.

The flow of events lists the steps in a use case. It always begins by an actor doing something to trigger the use case. A good way to start a flow of events is:

1. The use case starts when an <actor> <function>.

Remember that time can be an actor, so the use case may also start with a time expression in place of the actor, as in Figure 4.8.

The flow of events consists of a sequence of short steps that are declarative, numbered, and time-ordered. Each step in the use case flow should be in the form:

<number> The <something> <some action>.

The use case flow of events can also be captured as prose. However, we don't recommend this, as it is generally far too imprecise.

We can show alternatives in a use case flow by branching or listing behavior fragments under an Alternative Flow heading in the use case. We'll look at both of these techniques in Section 4.4.2.

Here is an example of a couple of steps in a PlaceOrder use case:

1. The use case starts when the customer selects place order.
2. The customer enters his or her name and address into the form.

These are well-formed steps. In both cases we have a simple declarative statement of some thing performing some action. An example of an ill-formed use case step would be:

2. Customer details are entered.

This sentence actually contains three important deletions.

- Who is it that enters the customer details? Who triggers this use case?
- Into what are the details entered?
- What specifically are the "customer details"?

It is important to recognize and avoid deletions when writing use case flows. Even though you may be able to tell by context, or guess what is meant, this is not really the point. The point is that the use case should be a precise statement of a piece of system functionality!

When you encounter vagueness, deletions, or generalizations during the process of analysis, it is useful to ask the following questions.

- Who specifically...?
- What specifically...?
- When specifically...?
- Where specifically...?

## 4.4.2   Branching within a flow

> Branching within a flow can simplify by reducing the number of use cases, but use sparingly!

You often need to indicate that there are many possibilities within the flow of events of a use case. A very good way to do this is to use "structured English" (or German or whatever your native language is). We introduce a simple set of keywords that you can use to express branching, repetition, and even alternative flows.

It is worth knowing that some use case modelers may frown on branching within use cases. They argue that wherever there is a branch, a new use case should be written. Strictly speaking, this argument has merit – however, we take the more pragmatic stance that a small amount of simple branching is desirable as it reduces the total number of use cases and leads to a more compact representation of the requirements. You'll see specific techniques for dealing with really complicated use cases where branching may be entirely inappropriate, in Section 4.5.

### 4.4.2.1   *Keyword* If

You use the keyword If to indicate a branch in the flow of events. The example in Figure 4.9 shows a very nicely structured flow of events with three branches. Each branch is prefixed with the keyword If, and begins with a simple Boolean expression such as "If the user types in a new quantity", which is true or false. The indented text under the If statement is what will

| Use case: ManageBasket |
| --- |
| **ID: UC10** |
| **Actors:**<br>Customer |
| **Preconditions:**<br>1.   The shopping basket contents are visible. |
| **Flow of events:**<br>1.   The use case starts when the Customer selects<br>      an item in the basket.<br>2.   If the Customer selects "delete item"<br>      2.1  The system removes the item from<br>            the basket.<br>3.   If the Customer types in a new quantity<br>      3.1  The system updates the quantity of the<br>            item in the basket. |
| **Postconditions:**<br>1.   The basket contents have been updated. |

**Figure 4.9**

happen if the Boolean expression is true. You can clearly indicate the body of the If statement by careful use of indentation and numbering without needing to introduce an endif, or some other statement-closing syntax.

### 4.4.2.2   *Alternative flows*

Sometimes you can't easily express branching using If. This is particularly true for things that can happen at any point in time. Where in the main flow could the If statement be put for such an event? A typical case is shown in Figure 4.10.

It is best to express branching that can happen at any point in the flow of events as one or more alternative flows. You can do this as follows.

1.   Specify the preconditions for the use case – these must be true for all possible paths through the use case.

2.   Specify the normal flow of events.

3.   Specify the postconditions for the normal flow of events.

You can then append a new section to the end of the use case for each alternative flow. This section must contain the following.

1.   The flow of events for the alternative flow. Normally, this should be kept very simple (just a few steps at most) and must *always* begin with a Boolean condition that causes the flow to be executed.

2.   The postconditions for this flow of events.

| Use case: DisplayBasket |
| --- |
| **ID: UC11** |
| **Actors:**<br>Customer |
| **Preconditions:**<br>1.  The Customer is logged on the system. |
| **Flow of events:**<br>1.  The use case starts when the Customer selects "display basket".<br>2.  If there are no items in the basket<br> 2.1 The system informs the Customer that there are no items in the basket yet.<br> 2.2 The use case terminates.<br>3.  The system displays a list of all items in the Customer's shopping basket including product ID, name, quantity and item price. |
| **Postconditions:** |
| **Alternative flow 1:**<br>1.  At any time the Customer may leave the shopping basket screen. |
| **Postconditions:** |
| **Alternative flow 2:**<br>1.  At any time the Customer may leave the system. |
| **Postconditions:** |

**Figure 4.10**

You can't just add the postconditions for the alternative flows to the postconditions for the main flow, as the alternative flow may or may not be executed.

## 4.4.3  Repetition within a flow: **For**

Sometimes you have to repeat an action several times within a flow of events. To be frank, this doesn't occur very often in use case modeling, but when it does, it is useful to have a strategy to deal with it. You can model repetition by using the keyword For. The format is:

n. For (iteration expression)
    n.1. Do something
    n.2. Do something else
    n.3. ...
n+1.

The iteration expression is some expression that evaluates to a positive whole number of iterations. Each indented line after the For statement is repeated for the number of iterations specified in the iteration expression. An example is given in Figure 4.11.

| Use case: FindProduct |
|---|
| **ID: UC12** |
| **Actors:**<br>Customer |
| **Preconditions:** |
| **Flow of events:**<br>1.  The Customer selects "find product".<br>2.  The system asks the Customer for search criteria.<br>3.  The Customer enters the requested criteria.<br>4.  The system searches for products that match the Customer's criteria.<br>5.  If the system finds some matching products then<br>    5.1. For each product found<br>        5.1.1.  The system displays a thumbnail sketch of the product.<br>        5.1.2.  The system displays a summary of the product details.<br>        5.1.3.  The system displays the product price.<br>6.  Else<br>    6.1. The system tells the Customer that no matching products could<br>       be found. |
| **Postconditions:** |
| **Alternative flow:**<br>1.  At any point the Customer may move to different page. |
| **Postconditions:** |

**Figure 4.11**

## 4.4.4   Repetition within a flow: **While**

You use the While keyword to model a sequence of actions in the flow of events that is performed while some Boolean condition is true. The format is:

n. While (Boolean condition)
    n.1. Do something
    n.2. Do something else
    n.3. ...
n+1.

Like For it's not used very frequently. An example is shown in Figure 4.12. The sequence of indented lines after the While statement is repeated until the Boolean condition specified in the While clause becomes false.

| Use case: ShowCompanyDetails |
|---|
| **ID: UC13** |
| **Actors:**<br>Customer |
| **Preconditions:** |
| **Flow of events:**<br>1.  The use case starts when the Customer selects "show company details".<br>2.  The system displays a web page showing the company details.<br>3.  While the Customer is browsing the company details<br>  3.1. The system plays some background music.<br>  3.2. The system displays special offers in a banner ad. |
| **Postconditions:** |

**Figure 4.12**

## 4.4.5   Requirements tracing

> Requirements tracing links requirements in the System Requirements Specification to the use case model.

With an SRS and a set of use cases, we effectively have two "databases" of functional requirements. It is very important to relate the two to find out if there is anything in our SRS that is not covered by the use cases and vice versa. This is one aspect of requirements tracing.

Tracing functional requirements to use cases is complicated by the fact that there is a many-to-many relationship between individual functional requirements as recorded in the SRS and use cases. One use case will cover many individual functional requirements, and one functional requirement may be manifest in several different use cases.

Hopefully, you will have CASE support for requirements tracing, and indeed requirements engineering tools such as Rational Requisite Pro and DOORS allow you to link individual requirements in their requirements database to specific use cases and vice versa. In fact, UML provides pretty good support for requirements tracing. Using tagged values, you can associate a list of requirement ID numbers with each use case. In the requirements tool, you can link one or more use case names to specific requirements.

If you have no CASE support, then you must do the job manually. A good approach is to create a Requirements Traceability Matrix. This is simply a grid with the ID numbers of individual requirements down one axis, and use case names (and/or ID numbers) along the other. A cross is put in all cells where a use case and requirement intersect. Requirements Traceability Matrices are often created in spreadsheets. An example is given in Table 4.1.

**Table 4.1**

| | | Use case | | | |
|---|---|---|---|---|---|
| | | UC1 | UC2 | UC3 | UC4 |
| Requirement | R1 | ✗ | | | |
| | R2 | | ✗ | ✗ | |
| | R3 | | | ✗ | |
| | R4 | | | | ✗ |
| | R5 | ✗ | | | |

A Requirements Traceability Matrix is a very useful tool for checking consistency. If there is a requirement that doesn't map to any use case, then there is a use case missing. Conversely, if there is a use case that doesn't map to any requirement, then you know that your set of requirements is incomplete.

## 4.5 Complex use cases

As a rule of thumb, use cases should be kept as simple as possible. Occasionally, however, you will encounter irreducible complexity and will need to formulate complex use cases. Rather than trying to capture this complexity with lots of branching and alternative flows, it is easier, and less error prone, to model the main flows through this branching network as separate scenarios.

### 4.5.1 Scenarios

> A scenario is one specific path through a use case.

Scenarios are another way of looking at use cases. A scenario is one specific path through a use case.

When you document a use case, if you tease out specific paths that can be taken through the use case flow of events, then each of these paths is a scenario. The important feature of scenarios is that they *do not branch*. Therefore, each possible branch in the use case flow of events potentially generates a *separate* scenario.

Each use case has exactly one primary scenario. This is the "happy day", or "perfect world", path through the complex flow. For the primary scenario everything goes as expected and desired, and there are no errors, deviations, interrupts, or branches.

> Each use case has one primary scenario and may have many secondary scenarios.

Each use case also has many secondary scenarios – these are alternative paths to the primary scenario through the flow of events.

It is sometimes useful to think of a complex use case as being like a river delta with many branching channels. Every use case has one primary scenario that is the main channel through the delta. The other, smaller, channels in the river delta are the secondary scenarios. These secondary scenarios can capture errors (often known as exception scenarios), branches, and interrupts to the main flow.

## 4.5.2 Specifying the primary scenario

When you use the scenario approach for documenting use cases, the use case specification contains the primary scenario and a list of the names of the secondary scenarios under an appropriately titled section. The secondary scenarios are typically documented separately and in much the same way as use cases are documented. An example is given in Figure 4.13.

| Use case: Checkout |
|---|
| **ID: UC14** |
| **Actors:**<br>Customer |
| **Preconditions:** |
| **Primary scenario:**<br>1.  The use case begins when the Customer selects "go to checkout".<br>2.  The system displays the customer order.<br>3.  The system asks for the customer identifier.<br>4.  The Customer enters a valid customer identifier.<br>5.  The system retrieves and displays the Customer's details.<br>6.  The system asks for credit card information – name on card, card number and expiry date.<br>7.  The Customer enters the credit card information.<br>8.  The system asks for confirmation of the order.<br>9.  The Customer confirms the order.<br>10. The system debits the credit card.<br>11. The system displays an invoice. |
| **Secondary scenarios:**<br>InvalidCustomerIdentifier<br>InvalidCreditCardDetails<br>CreditCardLimitExceeded<br>CreditCardExpired |
| **Postconditions:** |

**Figure 4.13**

### 4.5.3 Specifying secondary scenarios

You should specify secondary scenarios in the same way that you specify use cases. You must always state clearly how the scenario begins and ensure that it is just one specific path through the use case flow of events with no branching.

Each secondary scenario must be traceable back to its use case. The simple naming convention shown in Figure 4.14 is a good way to do this. Notice that secondary scenarios can reference the primary scenario in their flow of events.

| **Use case: Checkout**<br>**Secondary scenario: InvalidCustomerIdentifier** |
|---|
| **ID: UC15** |
| **Actors:**<br>Customer |
| **Preconditions:** |
| **Secondary scenario:**<br>1. The use case begins in step 3 of the use case Checkout when the Customer enters an invalid customer identifier.<br>2. For three invalid entries<br>    2.1. The system asks the Customer to enter the customer identifier again.<br>3. The system informs the Customer that their customer identifier was not recognized. |
| **Postconditions:** |

**Figure 4.14**

### 4.5.4 Finding secondary scenarios

Secondary scenarios are identified by inspection of the primary scenarios. At each step in the primary scenario, look for:

- possible alternative flows;
- errors that might be raised;
- interrupts that might occur to the flow – things that might happen at any time.

Each of these is a possible source of a secondary scenario.

### 4.5.5 How many scenarios?

Only document the most important secondary scenarios.

As we've said, there is exactly one primary scenario per use case. However, there may be *many* secondary scenarios. The question is – how many? You should try to limit the number of secondary scenarios to the necessary minimum. There are two strategies for this.

- Pick the most important secondary scenarios and document those.
- Where there are groups of secondary scenarios that are all very similar, document one member of the group as an exemplar and (if necessary) add notes to this explaining how the others differ from it.

Going back to the river delta analogy – in addition to the main channel, there can be many branching and twisting alternative flows through the delta. You can't really afford to map them all, so you just choose the main ones. Also, many of these branches flow in pretty much the same direction with only minor differences. You can therefore map one exemplar channel in detail, and just provide notes explaining how the other, smaller channels deviate from this. This is a very efficient and effective way of modeling a complex use case.

The basic principle in use case modeling is to keep the amount of information captured to the *necessary minimum*. This means that many secondary scenarios may never be specified at all – the one-line description of them in the use case may be enough detail to allow understanding of the functioning of the system. This is an important point – it is very easy to get swamped in scenarios, and we have seen more than one use case modeling activity fail because of this. Remember that you are capturing use cases and scenarios to *understand the desired behavior* of the system, and not just for the sake of creating a complete use case model. You therefore stop use case modeling when you feel that you have achieved that understanding. Also, because the UP is an iterative lifecycle, you can always go back to a use case and do more work if there is some aspect of the system's behavior that you decide you don't really understand.

## 4.6 When to apply use case modeling

Use cases are good at capturing system functionality. They are poor at capturing system constraints.

Because use cases capture system function from the point of view of the actors, they are clearly not very effective when the system has only one, or even zero, actors. Use cases capture functional requirements, and so they are not effective for systems dominated by non-functional requirements. Use cases are the best choice for requirements capture when:

- the system is dominated by functional requirements;
- the system has many types of users to which it delivers different functionality (there are many actors);
- the system has many interfaces (there are many actors).

Use cases would be a poor choice when:

- the system is dominated by non-functional requirements;
- the system has few users;
- the system has few interfaces.

Examples of systems where use cases may not be appropriate are embedded systems, and systems that are algorithmically complex but with few interfaces. For these systems, you may well be much better off falling back on more conventional requirements engineering techniques. It is really just a matter of choosing the right tool for the job in hand.

## 4.7    What we have learned

This chapter has been all about capturing system requirements using use case modeling. You have learned the following.

- The use case modeling activity is part of the requirements workflow.
- Most of the work in the requirements workflow occurs in the Inception and Elaboration phases of the UP project lifecycle.
- The key UP activities are "Find actors and use cases" and "Detail a use case".
- Use case modeling is another form of requirements engineering that proceeds as follows:
  — find the system boundary;
  — find actors;
  — find use cases.
- Actors are roles played by things external to the system that interact directly with the system.
  — You can find actors by considering who or what uses or interacts directly with the system.
  — Time is often an actor.
- Use cases are functions that the system performs on behalf of, and to deliver benefit to, specific actors. You can find use cases by considering how each actor interacts with the system.

- The use case diagram shows:
  — the system boundary;
  — actors;
  — use cases;
  — interactions.

- The Project Glossary provides definitions of key business terms – it resolves synonyms and homonyms.

- The use case specification contains:
  — a use case name;
  — a unique identifier;
  — preconditions – system constraints that affect the execution of a use case;
  — flow of events – the sequence of declarative, time-ordered steps in the use case;
  — postconditions – system constraints arising from the execution of a use case.

- You can reduce the number of use cases by allowing a limited amount of branching within the flow of events:
  — use the keyword If for branches that occur at a particular step in the flow;
  — use Alternative Flow sections in the use case to capture branches that may occur at any point in the flow.

- You can show repetition within a flow by using the keywords:
  — For (iteration expression);
  — While (Boolean condition).

- Requirements in a System Requirements Specification may be traced to use cases using a Requirements Traceability Matrix.

- Complex use cases may be decomposed into several scenarios – a scenario is one specific path through a use case.

- Each complex use case has one primary scenario – this is the "happy day" scenario where everything goes as planned.

- Each complex use case may have one or more secondary scenarios – these are alternative paths that represent exceptions, branches, and interrupts.

- You find secondary scenarios by examining the primary scenarios and looking for:
  — alternatives;
  — errors;
  — interrupts.

- Only decompose a use case into scenarios when it adds value to the model.

- Use case modeling is most appropriate for systems that:
  — are dominated by functional requirements;
  — have many types of user;
  — have many interfaces to other systems.

- Use case modeling is least appropriate for systems that:
  — are dominated by non-functional requirements;
  — have few users;
  — have few interfaces.

# chapter 5

# Advanced use case modeling

## 5.1 Chapter roadmap

In this chapter, we're going to discuss some advanced aspects of use case modeling.

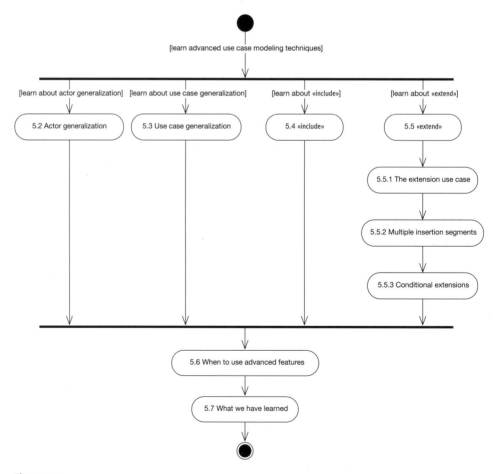

[learn advanced use case modeling techniques]

[learn about actor generalization]  [learn about use case generalization]  [learn about «include»]  [learn about «extend»]

5.2 Actor generalization

5.3 Use case generalization

5.4 «include»

5.5 «extend»

5.5.1 The extension use case

5.5.2 Multiple insertion segments

5.5.3 Conditional extensions

5.6 When to use advanced features

5.7 What we have learned

**Figure 5.1**

We will discuss the relationships that are possible between actors and actors, and between use cases and use cases. These relationships are as follows.

- Actor generalization – a generalization relationship between a more general actor and a more specific actor.
- Use case generalization – a generalization relationship between a more general use case and a more specific use case.
- «include» – a relationship between use cases that lets one use case include behavior from another.
- «extend» – a relationship between use cases that lets one use case extend its behavior with one or more behavior fragments from another.

It is very important to keep all models as simple as possible, so these relationships should be used with discretion and only where they improve the overall clarity of the use case model. It is easy to go overboard with «include» and «extend» in particular, but you must avoid this.

## 5.2  Actor generalization

Actor generalization factors out behavior common to two or more actors into a parent actor.

In the example in Figure 5.2, you can see that there is quite a lot of commonality between the two actors, Customer and SalesAgent, in the way that they interact with the Sales system (here, the SalesAgent can handle a sale on behalf of a Customer). Both actors trigger the use cases ListProducts, OrderProducts, and AcceptPayment. In fact, the only difference between the two actors is that the SalesAgent also triggers the CalculateCommission use case. Apart from the fact that this similarity in behavior gives lots of crossed lines on

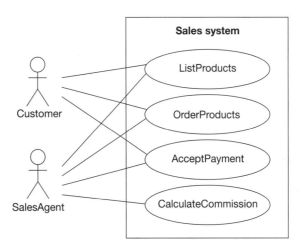

**Figure 5.2**

the diagram, it seems to indicate that there is some common actor behavior that could be factored out into a more *generalized* actor.

You can factor out this common behavior using actor generalization as shown in Figure 5.3. You create an abstract actor called Purchaser that interacts with the use cases ListProducts, OrderProducts, and AcceptPayment. Customer and SalesAgent are known as concrete actors because real people (or other systems) could fulfill those roles. However, Purchaser is an abstract actor as it is an abstraction introduced simply to capture the common behavior of the two concrete actors. Customer and SalesAgent inherit all of the roles and relationships to use cases of their abstract parent. So, interpreting Figure 5.3 – both Customer and SalesAgent have interactions with the use cases ListProducts, OrderProducts, and AcceptPayment that they inherit from their parent, Purchaser. In addition, SalesAgent has another interaction with the use case CalculateCommission that is not inherited – it is specific to the SalesAgent actor. You can see that judicious use of abstract actors can simplify use case diagrams.

It is worth pointing out that the parent actor in actor generalization does not always have to be abstract – it may be a concrete role that a person or system could play. However, good style dictates that parent actors are usually abstract.

> We can use a descendent anywhere the ancestor actor is expected.

What we have seen is that if two actors communicate with the same set of use cases in the same way, we can express this as a generalization to another (possibly abstract) actor. The descendent actors inherit the roles and relationships to use cases held by the parent actor. You can substitute a descendent actor anywhere the ancestor actor is expected. This is the substitutability principle, which is an important test for correct use of generalization with *any* classifier.

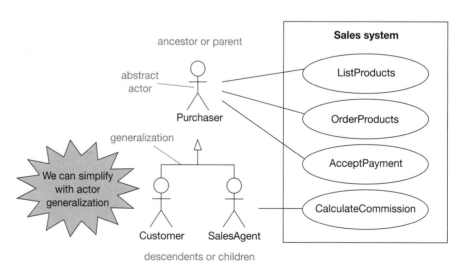

**Figure 5.3**

In this example, it is reasonable that you can substitute a SalesAgent or a Customer anywhere a Purchaser is expected (i.e. interacting with use cases ListProducts, OrderProducts, and AcceptPayments), so actor generalization is the correct strategy.

## 5.3   Use case generalization

Use case generalization is used when you have one or more use cases that are really specializations of a more general case. Just like actor generalization, you should only use this when it simplifies your use case diagrams.

In use case generalization, the child use cases represent more specific forms of the parent. The children may:

● inherit features from their parent use case;

● add new features;

● override (change) inherited features.

> Use case generalization factors out behavior common to one or more use cases into a parent use case.

The child use case automatically inherits *all* features from its parent. However, not every type of use case element may be overridden – the restrictions are summarized in Table 5.1.

**Table 5.1**

| Use case element | Inherit | Add | Override |
|---|---|---|---|
| Relationship | Y | Y | N |
| Precondition | Y | Y | Y |
| Postcondition | Y | Y | Y |
| Step in main flow | Y | Y | Y |
| Alternative flow | Y | Y | Y |
| Attribute | Y | Y | N |
| Operation | Y | Y | Y |

How is use case generalization documented in use case specifications? The UML specification remains silent on this point, but there are several fairly standard techniques. We prefer to use simple typographical conventions to highlight the three possibilities in a child use case – these are summarized in Table 5.2.

As well as highlighting inherited, overridden, and added features, you also have to be very careful to relate the elements in the child use case to the corresponding elements in the parent in some way. This is so you can

**Table 5.2**

| Feature is ... | Typographical convention |
|---|---|
| Inherited without change from the parent | Normal text |
| Overridden | *Italic text* |
| Added | **Bold text** |

trace an inherited or overridden element in the child back to the original element in the parent.

Sometimes, an inherited or overridden element in the child has the same number as the corresponding element in the parent and, in this case, no action is needed. But where an inherited or overridden element in the child needs to have a *different* number than in the parent, you must record the corresponding parent number in parentheses directly after the child number.

Figure 5.4 shows an extract from the use case diagram of a Sales system. We have the parent use case FindProduct, and then two specializations of this, FindBook and FindCD.

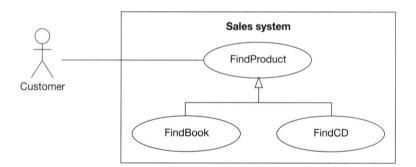

**Figure 5.4**

Figure 5.5 shows the specification for the parent use case FindProduct – notice that it is expressed at a very high level of abstraction.

The two child use cases are shown in Figure 5.6. This illustrates the application of our typographical standard for highlighting overridden or new features.

These child use cases are much more concrete – each is specialized from the more abstract parent to deal with a specific type of product.

If the parent use case has no flow of events, or a flow of events that is incomplete, then it is an abstract use case. Abstract use cases are quite common as they are useful for capturing behavior at the highest levels of abstraction. Because abstract use cases have a missing or incomplete flow of

| Use case: FindProduct |
| --- |
| **ID: UC12** |
| **Actors:**<br>Customer |
| **Preconditions:** |
| **Flow of events:**<br>1.  The Customer selects "find product".<br>2.  The system asks the Customer for search criteria.<br>3.  The Customer enters the requested criteria.<br>4.  The system searches for products that match the<br>    Customer's criteria.<br>5.  If the system finds some matching products then<br>        5.1. The system displays a list of the matching<br>             products.<br>6.  Else<br>        6.1. The system tells the Customer that no matching<br>             products could be found. |
| **Postconditions:** |
| **Alternative flow:**<br>1.  At any point the Customer may move to a different page. |
| **Postconditions:** |

**Figure 5.5**

events, they can never be executed by the system. Rather than a flow of events, abstract use cases may just have a plain text summary of the high-level behavior that their children will be expected to implement.

Use cases are UML classifiers (as are classes) and so have attributes and operations (see Section 1.8.3.1 for more information on the different types of classifier). But why are use cases modeled in UML as classifiers? Well, you can think of each use case as describing a set of use case instances, each of which is a specific execution of the use case. To be frank, this is a piece of UML esoterica which seems to be of little practical importance. In fact, we could make a very good case for suggesting that use cases should *not* be modeled as UML classifiers at all!

The use case attribute values represent the state of a use case instance when it is executing, and the operations represent a piece of work that the use case can perform. Again, the use case attributes and operations don't seem to add any real value and they are not even supported in most CASE tools. According to the UML specification, the operations of a use case are not even callable externally, so it is quite hard to imagine why they are there at all. Our advice is to simply ignore this feature of use cases until there is more clarity on how it should be used.

| Child use case: FindBook | Child use case: FindCD |
|---|---|
| **ID: UC16** | **ID: UC17** |
| **Parent Use Case ID:**<br>UC12 | **Parent Use Case ID:**<br>UC12 |
| **Actors:**<br>Customer | **Actors:**<br>Customer |
| **Preconditions:** | **Preconditions:** |
| **Flow of events:**<br>1.  *The Customer selects "find book".*<br>2.  *The system asks the Customer for book search criteria consisting of author name, title, ISBN, or topic.*<br>3.  *The Customer enters the requested criteria.*<br>4.  *The system searches for books that match the Customer's criteria.*<br>5.  *If the system finds some matching books then*<br>    5.1.  *The system displays a page showing details of a maximum of five books.*<br>    **5.2.  For each book on the page the system displays the title, author, price, and ISBN.**<br>    **5.3.  While there are more books**<br>        **5.3.1.  The system gives the Customer the option to display the next page of books.**<br>6.  Else<br>    **6.1.  The system redisplays the "find book" search page.**<br>    6.2.  The system tells the Customer that no matching products could be found. | **Flow of events:**<br>1.  *The Customer selects "find CD".*<br>2.  *The system asks the Customer for CD search criteria consisting of artist, title, or genre.*<br>3.  *The Customer enters the requested criteria.*<br>4.  *The system searches for CDs that match the Customer's criteria.*<br>5.  *If the system finds some matcing CDs then*<br>    5.1.  *The system displays a page showing details of a maximum of ten CDs.*<br>    **5.2.  For each CD on the page the system displays the title, artist, price, and genre.**<br>    **5.3.  While there are more CDs**<br>        **5.3.1.  The system gives the Customer the option to display the next page of CDs.**<br>6.  Else<br>    **6.1.  The system redisplays the "find CD" search page.**<br>    6.2.  The system tells the Customer that no matching products could be found. |
| **Postconditions:** | **Postconditions:** |
| **Alternative flow:**<br>1.  At any point the Customer may move to a different page. | **Alternative flow:**<br>1.  At any point the Customer may move to a different page. |
| **Postconditions:** | **Postconditions:** |

**Figure 5.6**

## 5.4   «include»

Writing use cases can be very repetitive at times. Suppose you are writing a Personnel system (see Figure 5.7). Almost anything we ask the system to do will first involve locating the details of a specific employee. If you had to write this sequence of events (involving user authentication, entering a user ID or some other unique identifier, etc.) every time you needed employee details, then your use cases would become quite repetitive. The «include» relationship between use cases allows you to include the behavior of a supplier use case into the flow of a client use case.

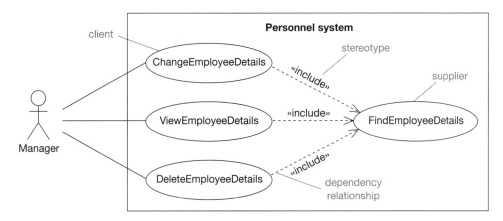

**Figure 5.7**

> «include» factors out steps common to several use cases into a separate use case which is then included.

We refer to the *including* use case as the *client* use case, and to the *included* use case as the *supplier* use case. This is because the included use case supplies behavior to its client use case.

You must specify the *exact* point in the client use case where you need the behavior of the supplier use case to be included. The syntax for «include» is a bit like a function call, and indeed it has somewhat similar semantics.

The semantics of «include» are very simple (see Figure 5.8). The client use case executes until the point of inclusion is reached, then execution passes over to the supplier use case. When the supplier finishes, control returns to the client again.

The client use case is not complete without all of its supplier use cases. The supplier use cases form integral parts of the client use case. However, the supplier use cases may or may not be complete. If a supplier use case is *not*

| ChangeEmployeeDetails |
| --- |
| **ID: UC1** |
| **Actors:**<br>Manager |
| **Preconditions:**<br>1.  A valid Manager is logged on to the system. |
| **Flow of events:**<br>1.  The Manager enters the employee's ID number.<br>2.  include (FindEmployeeDetails).<br>3.  The Manager selects the part of the employee details to change.<br>4.  ... |
| **Postconditions:** |

| ViewEmployeeDetails |
| --- |
| **ID: UC2** |
| **Actors:**<br>Manager |
| **Preconditions:**<br>1.  A valid Manager is logged on to the system. |
| **Flow of events:**<br>1.  The Manager enters the employee's ID number.<br>2.  include (FindEmployeeDetails).<br>3.  The system displays the employee details.<br>4.  ... |
| **Postconditions:** |

| DeleteEmployeeDetails |
| --- |
| **ID: UC3** |
| **Actors:**<br>Manager |
| **Preconditions:**<br>1.  A valid Manager is logged on to the system. |
| **Flow of events:**<br>1.  The Manager enters the employee's ID number.<br>2.  include (FindEmployeeDetails).<br>3.  The system displays the employee details.<br>4.  The Manager deletes the employee details.<br>5.  ... |
| **Postconditions:** |

**Figure 5.8**

complete, then it just contains a partial flow of events that will only make sense when it is included into a suitable client. We often refer to this as a behavior fragment. In this case, we say that the supplier use case is not instantiable – this means that it can't be triggered directly by actors, it can only execute when included in a suitable client. If, however, the supplier use cases *are* complete in themselves, then they act just like normal use cases and are instantiable. It is then quite reasonable to trigger them by actors.

## 5.5   «extend»

«extend» is a way of inserting new behavior into an existing use case.

«extend» provides a way to add new behavior to an existing use case (see Figure 5.9). The base use case provides a set of extension points which are hooks where new behavior may be added, and the extension use case provides a set of insertion segments that can be inserted into the base use case at these hooks. The «extend» relationship itself can, as you will see shortly, be used to specify *exactly* which extension points in the base use case are being extended.

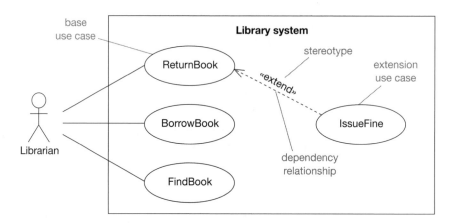

**Figure 5.9**

What is interesting about «extend» is that the base use case does not know anything about the extending use cases – it just provides hooks for them. In fact, the base use case is perfectly complete without its extensions. This is *very* different to «include» where the client use cases were incomplete without their included use cases. Furthermore, the extension points are not actually inserted into the flow of events of the base use case, rather they are added to an overlay on top of the flow of events.

Extension points are indicated in the flow of events of the base use case as shown in Figure 5.10. You can also show extension points on the use case diagram by listing them in a new compartment in the base use case icon.

Notice that extension points in the main flow are not numbered. Instead, they appear *between* the numbered steps of the flow. In fact, UML explicitly states that extension points actually exist on an overlay on top of the main flow. They are therefore not part of the main flow at all. You can think of this overlay as being like an acetate film over the main flow where the extension points are recorded. The point of this idea of an overlay is to make the base use case flow completely independent of the extension points. In other words, the base use case flow doesn't know (or care) where it is being extended. This allows you to use «extend» to make arbitrary and ad hoc extensions to a base use case flow.

When you use «extend», the base use case acts as a modular framework into which you can plug extensions at predefined extension points. In the example in Figure 5.10, you can see that the ReturnBook base use case has an extension point called <overdueBook> between steps 3 and 4 in its flow of events.

You can see that «extend» provides a good way of dealing with exceptional cases, or cases in which you need a flexible framework because you can't predict (or just don't know) all of the possible extensions in advance.

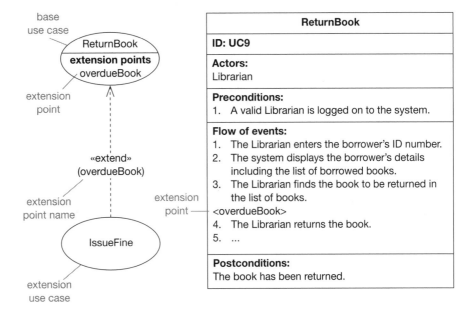

**Figure 5.10**

### 5.5.1   The extension use case

Extension use cases are *generally* not complete use cases and therefore can't usually be instantiated. They normally just consist of one or more behavior fragments known as insertion segments. The «extend» relationship specifies the extension point in the base use case where the insertion segment will be inserted. The following rules apply.

- The «extend» relationship must specify one or more of the extension points in the base use case or it is assumed that the «extend» relationship refers to *all* extension points.

- The extension use case must have the same number of insertion segments as there are extension points specified in the «extend» relationship.

- It is legal for two extension use cases to «extend» the same base use case at the same extension point – but if this happens, the order in which the extensions execute is indeterminate.

In the example in Figure 5.11, there is an insertion segment in the IssueFine extending use case.

The extension use case may also have preconditions and postconditions. The preconditions must be fulfilled otherwise the insertion segment does not execute. The postconditions constrain the state of the system after the insertion segment has executed.

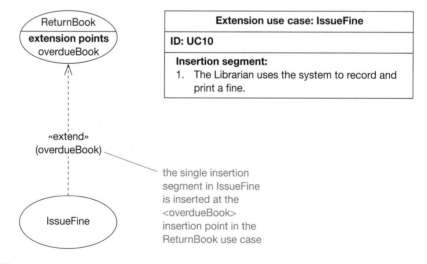

**Figure 5.11**

## 5.5.2   Multiple insertion segments

You can have multiple insertion segments in an extension use case. This is useful when you can't capture the extension cleanly in a single insertion segment because of the need to go back to the main flow of the base use case to do something. In the example in Figure 5.12, you can imagine that after recording and printing a fine, we go back to the main flow to process any more overdue books and then, finally, at extension point <payFine>, we give the borrower the option to pay the total fine. This is clearly more efficient than having to print and accept payment for each fine individually, which would have been the case if we had combined the two segments in IssueFine.

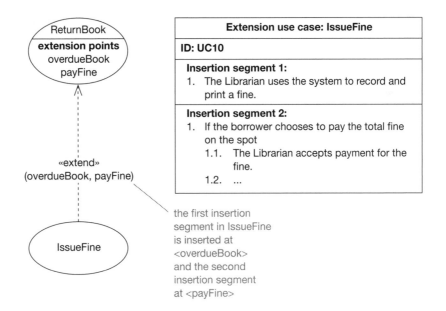

**Figure 5.12**

This example is interesting because you can see that the second insertion segment begins with an If statement. As such it is a conditional flow, and is itself a good candidate for becoming an extension use case. This would be OK – extension use cases may themselves have extensions as well as includes. In this specific case, we have chosen to use conditional logic as that particular insertion segment really doesn't seem to warrant becoming a whole new use case. If, however, we were building a system where a payment insertion segment could be reused in other use cases, it might be a different matter, and then it might be a good strategy to factor this behavior out into a separate extension use case. But please be careful about this sort of thing – it is very bad style to have too many «include» or «extend» relationships on a use case model.

### 5.5.3  Conditional extensions

The example in Figure 5.13 shows a slightly more benign library system in which borrowers are given a warning the first time a book is returned overdue and are only fined subsequently. We can model this by adding a new extension use case, IssueWarning, and then placing conditions on the «extend» relationships. The conditions are Boolean expressions, and the insertion is made if, and only if, the expression evaluates to true.

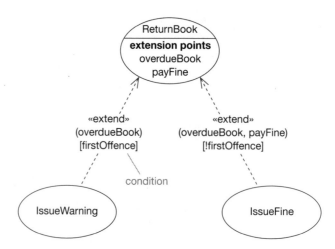

**Figure 5.13**

Notice that the IssueWarning extension use case only extends at the <overdueBook> extension point. However (as before), the IssueFine extension use case extends both at <overdueBook> and at <payFine>. This immediately tells you that IssueWarning must contain exactly one insertion segment, whereas IssueFine must (as we have already seen) contain two.

## 5.6  When to use advanced features

Use advanced features when they simplify the use case model. We have found time and again that the best use case models are simple. Remember that the use case model is a statement of requirements and, as such, must

> Use advanced features only when they simplify the model and make it easier to understand.

be accessible to the stakeholders as well as the modelers. A simple use case model that only uses advanced features sparingly, if at all, is in every respect preferable to one that overuses advanced features, even if that model is in some ways more elegant from a modeler's perspective.

Based on our experience in use case modeling in many different companies, we have found that:

- generally, stakeholders can easily understand actors and use cases with just a little training/mentoring;

- stakeholders find actor generalization more difficult to grasp;

- heavy use of «include» can make use case models harder to understand – stakeholders and modelers have to look at more than one use case to get the complete picture;

- stakeholders have great difficulty with «extend» – this can be true even with careful explanation;

- a surprising number of object modelers misunderstand the semantics of «extend»;

- use case generalization should be avoided unless abstract (rather than concrete) parent use cases are used – otherwise, it adds too much complexity to the child use cases.

## 5.7  What we have learned

You have learned about techniques for advanced use case modeling.

- Actor generalization allows you to factor out behaviors that are common to two or more actors into a parent actor.
  - The parent actor is more generalized than its children and the children are more specialized than their parent.
  - You can substitute a child actor anywhere a parent actor is expected – this is the substitutability principle.
  - The parent actor is often abstract – it specifies an abstract role.
  - The child actors are concrete – they specify concrete roles.
  - Actor generalization can simplify use case diagrams.

- Use case generalization allows you to factor out features that are common to two or more use cases into a parent use case.
  - The child use cases inherit all features of their parent use case (actors, relationships, preconditions, postconditions, flow of events, alternative flows).

— The child use cases may add new features.
— The child use cases may override parent features:
  – relationships to actors or other use cases may be inherited, or added;
  – preconditions and postconditions may be inherited, overridden, or added;
  – steps in the main flow and alternative flows may be inherited, overridden, or added;
  – attributes may be inherited or added;
  – operations may be inherited, overridden, or added.
— We use a simple typographical convention in the child use cases:
  – inherited – normal text;
  – added – **bold face text**;
  – overridden – *italic text*.
— Good style indicates that the parent use cases should normally be abstract.

- «include» allows you to factor steps repeated in several use case flows into a separate use case which you include where you need to.
  — The keyword include(use case name) is used to include the behavior of another use case.
  — The including use case is the client use case.
  — The included use case is the supplier use case.
  — The client is not complete without all of its suppliers.
  — Suppliers may:
    – be complete – they are just normal use cases and are instantiable;
    – be incomplete – they only contain a behavior fragment and are not instantiable.

- «extend» adds new behavior to an existing (base) use case.
  — The base use case has extension points in an overlay on its flow of events – extension points occur between the steps in the flow of events.
  — Extension use cases provide insertion segments – these are behavior fragments that may be "plugged into" extension points.
  — The «extend» relationship between the extension use cases and the base use case specifies the extension points that the extension use case insertion segments are plugged into.
  — The base use case is complete without the insertion segments – the extended use case does not know anything about possible insertion segments, it just provides hooks for them.

— The extension use case is generally not complete – usually, it just consists of one or more insertion segments; it may also be a complete use case, but this is rare.

— If the extension use case has preconditions, these must be fulfilled, otherwise the extension use case does not execute.

— If the extension use case has postconditions, these constrain the state of the system after the extension use case has executed.

— An extension use case may contain many insertion segments.

— Two or more extension use cases may extend the same base use case at the same extension point – the order of execution of each extension use case is indeterminate.

— Conditional extensions – Boolean guard conditions on the «extend» relationship allow an insertion if true, and prevent an insertion if false.

● Use advanced features as follows:

— actor generalization – use only where it simplifies the model;

— use case generalization – consider *not* using, or only using with abstract parents;

— «include» – use only where it simplifies the model; beware of overuse, as this makes a use case model turn into a functional decomposition;

— «extend» – consider *not* using; but if you do use it, be careful to ensure that all modelers and stakeholders exposed to the model understand and agree on its semantics.

Your goal should always be to produce a simple, easy to understand use case model that captures the necessary information in as clear and concise a way as possible. Personally, we would always prefer to see a use case model that did not use any of the advanced features rather than one where there is so much generalization, «include» and «extend» that it is hard to figure out what's going on. A good rule of thumb here is, "if in doubt – leave it out".

part 3

# Analysis

Chapter **6**

# The analysis workflow

## 6.1 Chapter roadmap

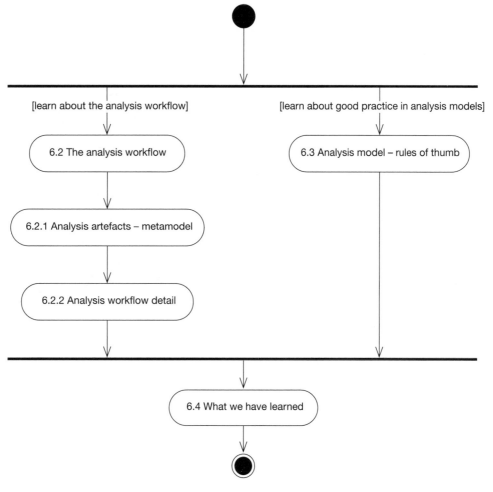

**Figure 6.1**

This chapter begins our investigation of the process of OO analysis. It provides a brief overview of the UP analysis workflow and then some "rules of thumb" for analysis models, which sets the scene for more detailed discussions in the other chapters in this part of the book.

## 6.2   The analysis workflow

Analysis modeling is strategic as we are trying to model the system's essential behavior.

The main work in analysis begins toward the end of the Inception phase and is the main focus of the Elaboration phase, along with requirements.

Most of the activity in Elaboration is about creating models that capture the desired behavior of the system. Notice in Figure 6.2, that analysis work overlaps to a great extent with requirements capture. In fact, these two activities often go hand-in-glove – you often need to perform some analysis on your requirements in order to clarify them and uncover any missing or distorted requirements.

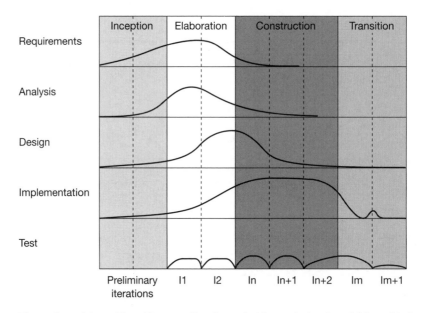

**Figure 6.2**   Adapted from Figure 1.5 [Jacobson 1] with permission from Addison-Wesley

The aim of the analysis workflow (from the point of view of the OO analyst) is to produce an analysis model. This model focuses on *what* the system needs to do, but leaves the details of *how* it will do it to the design workflow.

The boundary between analysis and design can be quite vague, and to some extent it is up to the individual analyst to draw the line where they see fit. See Section 6.3 for some rules of thumb that can help in the production of successful analysis models.

### 6.2.1   Analysis artefacts – metamodel

In the analysis workflow, two key artefacts are produced:

- analysis classes – these model key concepts in the business domain;
- use case realizations – these illustrate how instances of the analysis classes can interact to realize system behavior specified by a use case.

We can model the analysis model itself using UML. A metamodel of the analysis model is shown in Figure 6.3.

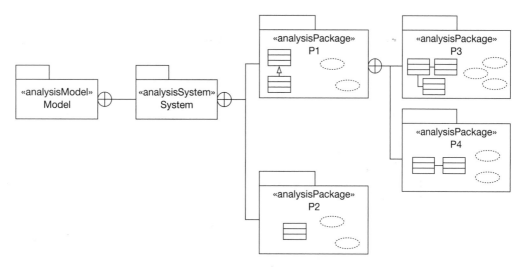

**Figure 6.3**

You've seen class syntax already, but the package syntax (the things that look like folders) is new. For now, just think of a package as a container for UML modeling elements and diagrams. Each element (or diagram) is owned by exactly one package.

The analysis model is a collection of UML modeling elements and diagrams, so we can model this as a package stereotyped «analysisModel». This package contains exactly one analysis system (which we model as a package with the standard stereotype «analysisSystem») and this system is composed of one or more analysis packages.

In Figure 6.3, we have shown four analysis packages. However, the analysis system may actually contain many analysis packages and each package may in turn contain nested analysis packages.

### 6.2.2 Analysis workflow detail

Figure 6.4 shows the UP analysis workflow. We will look at the relevant activities in turn in later chapters, but before we can understand these activities, we first have to understand classes and objects. We'll look at this topic in Chapter 7.

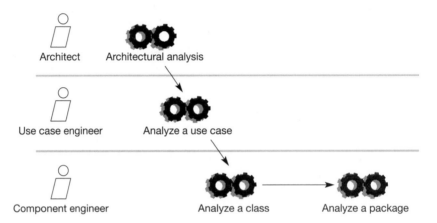

**Figure 6.4** Reproduced from Figure 8.18 [Jacobson 1] with permission from Addison-Wesley

## 6.3 Analysis model – rules of thumb

Every system is different, and so it is hard to generalize about analysis models. Still, for a system of moderate size and complexity there are probably about 50 to 100 analysis classes in the analysis model. Remember that, when constructing the analysis model, it is vitally important to restrict yourself *only* to those classes that are part of the vocabulary of the problem domain. It is always tempting to put design classes (such as communications or database access classes) in an analysis model, but this should be avoided (unless the problem domain is actually about communications or databases!) We restrict ourselves in this way to try to keep the analysis model a concise and simple statement of the system structure and behavior. All implementation decisions should be left to the design and implementation workflows.

Here are some rules of thumb for successful analysis modeling.

- The analysis model is *always* in the language of the business. The abstractions found in the analysis model should form part of the vocabulary of the business domain.

- Create models that "tell a story". Each diagram produced should elucidate some important part of the system's desired behavior. If it doesn't, then what purpose does it serve? You'll see good ways of producing such diagrams when we consider use case realizations.

- Concentrate on capturing the big picture. Don't get bogged down in the details of how the system will work – there is plenty of time for this in design.

- Distinguish clearly between the problem domain (the business requirements) and the solution domain (detailed design considerations). Always focus on abstractions that exist in the problem domain. So, for example, if you are modeling an e-commerce system, you would expect to see classes like Customer, Order and ShoppingBasket in the analysis model. You would *not* expect to see database access classes or communications classes, as these are clearly artefacts arising from the solution domain.

- Always try to minimize coupling. Each association between classes creates coupling between them. You will see in Chapter 9 how you can apply multiplicities and navigation to associations to minimize this coupling.

- Explore inheritance *if* there seems to be a natural and compelling hierarchy of abstractions. In analysis, never apply inheritance just to reuse code. Inheritance is the strongest form of coupling between classes, as you will see in Section 15.5.

- Always ask, "is the model useful to all the stakeholders?" There's nothing worse than producing an analysis model that is ignored by the business users, or the designers and developers. Yet this happens all too often, particularly to inexperienced analysts. The key preventive strategies are to make the analysis model and modeling activity as visible as possible, to incorporate stakeholders into the process wherever possible, and to hold frequent and open reviews.

Finally – keep the model simple! This is easier said than done of course, but it has certainly been our experience that inside every complex analysis model is a simple analysis model struggling to get out. One of the ways of creating simplification is to look at the general case rather than specifics. As a case in point, a system we recently reviewed had completely separate models for how tickets, hotel reservations, and car hire were to be sold. Clearly there is a generic "selling system" model implicit in that system that could handle the different cases using a relatively simple combination of inheritance and polymorphism.

## 6.4   What we have learned

- Analysis is about creating models that capture the essential requirements and characteristics of the desired system – analysis modeling is
strategic.

- Most of the work in the analysis workflow occurs towards the end of the
Inception phase and throughout the Elaboration phase.

- Analysis and requirements workflows overlap, especially in the Elaboration
phase – it is often advantageous to analyze requirements as we find them
to uncover missing or distorted requirements.

- The analysis model:
  — is always in the language of the business;
  — captures the big picture;
  — contains artefacts that model the problem domain;
  — tells a story about the desired system;
  — is useful to as many of the stakeholders as possible.

- Analysis artefacts are:
  — analysis classes – model key concepts in the business domain;
  — use case realizations – illustrate how instances of the analysis classes
  can interact to realize system behavior specified by a use case.

- UP analysis workflow comprises the following activities:
  — Architectural analysis;
  — Analyze a use case;
  — Analyze a class;
  — Analyze a package.

- Analysis model – rules of thumb:
  — about 50 to 100 analysis classes in the analysis model of an average
  system;
  — only include classes that model the vocabulary of the problem
  domain;
  — do *not* make implementation decisions;
  — focus on classes and associations – minimize coupling;
  — use inheritance where there is a natural hierarchy of abstractions;
  — keep it simple!

chapter 7

# Classes and objects

## 7.1 Chapter roadmap

This chapter is all about objects and classes. These are the basic building blocks of OO systems. If you are already familiar with the notion of objects and classes, then you may choose to skip Sections 7.2 and 7.4. You will, however, want to learn UML object notation (Section 7.3) and class notation (Section 7.5).

The chapter finishes with a discussion of the related topics of method and attribute scope (Section 7.6) and object construction and destruction (Section 7.7).

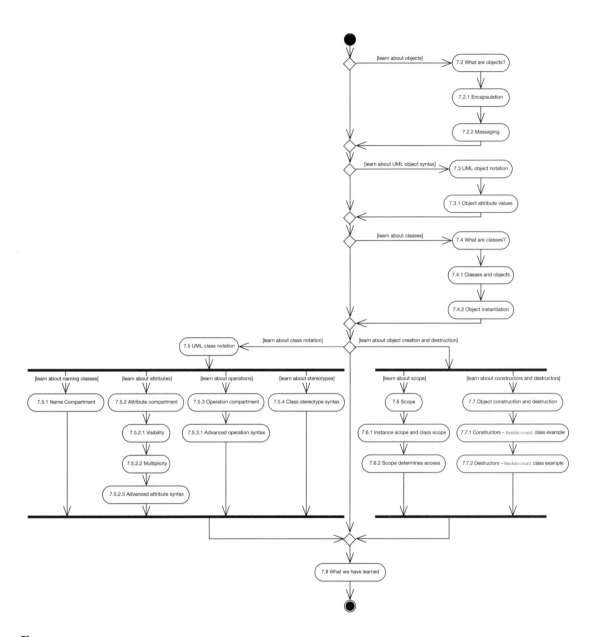

**Figure 7.1**

## 7.2   What are objects?

*The UML Reference Manual* [Rumbaugh 1] defines an object as, "A discreet entity with a well-defined boundary that encapsulates state and behavior; an instance of a class."

We can think of an object as a cohesive packet of data and function. Generally speaking, the only way to get to the data part of an object is by calling one of the functions that the object makes available. We refer to these functions as operations in analysis, and as methods in design. This is a useful distinction to make because in analysis we are describing an abstract specification of a function (an operation), but in design we are describing the actual, physical implementation of a function (a method). Hiding the data part of an object behind this layer of functions is known as encapsulation or data-hiding. Encapsulation is not enforced in UML as some OO languages do not demand it. However, to hide the data part of an object behind its set of operations or methods is always good OO style.

Every object is itself an instance of some class that defines the common set of features (attributes, and operations or methods) that are shared by all instances of that class. The idea of classes and classifiers is really very simple. Think of a printer of type "Epson Photo 1200." This describes the properties of all specific instances of this class such as the particular "Epson Photo 1200 S/N 34120098" sitting on our desk. A specific instance of a class is called an object.

Thinking about this example of an Epson printer object a bit more, we see that it has certain properties that are common to all objects.

- Identity – this is the object's unique existence in time and space. It is what makes it different from all other objects. In our example, the printer's serial number can be used as the identifier to point to this particular printer on our desk and represent the unique identity of that object. A serial number is a great way to specify the identity of a physical object, and we use a similar principle, the idea of an object reference, to specify the identity of every one of the software objects we will be working with in OO analysis and design. Of course, in the real world not every object has a serial number, but they still have unique identities because of their particular spatial and temporal coordinates. Similarly, in OO software systems every object has some sort of object reference.

- State – this is determined by the attribute values of an object at a particular point in time. Table 7.1 gives a non-exhaustive list of the states the printer can go through. You can see from this how an object's state depends on the values of its attributes.

Objects combine data and function in a cohesive unit.

Objects hide data behind a layer of functions.

Every object is uniquely identifiable.

Attribute values hold an object's data.

**Table 7.1**

| Object state | Class attribute | Attribute value for object |
|---|---|---|
| On | power | on |
| Off | power | off |
| OutOfBlackInk | blackInkCartridge | empty |
| OutOfColourInk | colourInkCartridge | empty |

● Behavior – there are certain things the printer can do for me:

switchOn()
switchOff()
printDocument()
pageFeed()
clearInkJetNozzles()
changeInkCartridge()

> An object's functions are called operations in analysis, and methods in design.

These behaviors are modeled as operations in analysis, and as methods in design. Invoking an operation or method on an object will often cause a change in the values of one or more of its attributes, and this may constitute a state transition. This is a meaningful movement of the object from one state to another state. Considering Table 7.1 again, it is clear that an object's state can also affect its behavior. For example, if the printer is out of ink (object state = OutOfBlackInk), then invoking the operation printDocument() will cause it to signal an error. The actual behavior of printDocument() is therefore *state dependent*.

## 7.2.1 Encapsulation

As we have already mentioned, the identity of an object is some unique handle, usually an address in memory, provided by the implementation language. We will always refer to these handles as object references from now on. You don't need to worry about how these are implemented in OO analysis – you can simply assume that each object has a unique identity that is managed by the implementation technology. In design you may need to consider the implementation of object references if you are targeting an OO language, such as C++, that allows the direct manipulation of special types of object references known as pointers.

In Figure 7.2 we show a conceptual picture of an object that emphasizes encapsulation. Note that Figure 7.2 is *not* a UML diagram. You'll see what the UML syntax for objects is shortly.

> An object's state is determined by its attribute values.

The state of this object is the set of attribute values (in this case 1234567801, "Jim Arlow", 300.00) held by the object at any point in time. Typically, some of these data values will remain fixed, and some will change over time. For example, it is highly unlikely that the account number and name will change over time, but we hope that the balance goes up steadily!

As the balance changes with time, we see that the object's state also changes with time. For example, if the balance is negative, then we may say that object is in the state overdrawn. As the balance changes from negative to zero, the object makes a significant change in its nature – it makes the state transition from the state overdrawn to the state empty. Furthermore, as the

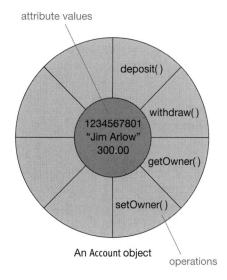

attribute values

1234567801
"Jim Arlow"
300.00

deposit( )

withdraw( )

getOwner( )

setOwner( )

An Account object

operations

**Figure 7.2**

> An object's behavior is "what it can do for us" – its operations.

Account object's balance becomes positive, it makes another state transition from the state empty to the state inCredit. There may be many more possible state transitions than this. In fact, any method invocation that leads to a substantive change in the object's nature creates a state transition. UML provides a powerful set of modeling techniques called statecharts for modeling state changes – we'll look at those in Chapter 19.

The behavior of any object is basically "what it can do" for us, and you can see that the object in Figure 7.2 provides the operations listed in Table 7.2.

This set of operations specifies the object's behavior. Notice that invoking some of these operations (deposit(), withdraw(), setOwner()) change attribute values and *may* generate state transitions. The other operation (getOwner()) does not change any attribute values and thus will *not* cause a state transition.

**Table 7.2**

| Operation | Semantics |
|---|---|
| deposit() | Deposit some money in the Account object |
| | Increment the balance attribute value |
| withdraw() | Withdraw some money from the Account |
| | Decrement the balance attribute value |
| getOwner() | Returns the owner of the Account object |
| setOwner() | Change the owner of the Account object |

Encapsulation, or data-hiding, is one of the primary benefits of OO programming and it can lead to more robust and extendible software. In this simple Account example, a user of this object need not be concerned with the structure of the data hidden inside the object, only with what the object can do – in other words with the *services* it offers to other objects.

## 7.2.2   Messaging

Objects generate system behavior by sending messages to each other over links. This is collaboration.

Objects have attribute values and behavior, but how do you put objects together to create software systems? Objects collaborate to perform the functions of the system. What this means is that objects form links to other objects and send messages back and forth along those links. When an object receives a message, it looks at its set of operations (or methods if you are in design) to see if there is an operation whose signature matches the message signature. If there is, then it invokes that operation (see Figure 7.3). These signatures comprise the message (or operation) name, parameter types, and return value.

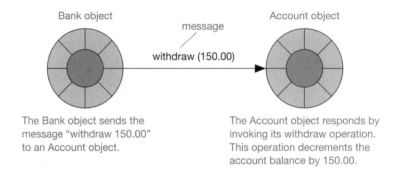

**Figure 7.3**

The run-time structure of an OO system consists of many objects being created, abiding for a time, and then perhaps being destroyed. These objects send messages to each other to invoke each other's services. This is a radically different structure to procedural software systems that evolve over time by the progressive application of functions to data.

## 7.3   UML object notation

The UML object icon is a box with two compartments – an example is shown in Figure 7.4. The top compartment contains the object identifier, which is *always* underlined. This is very important, as the UML notation for

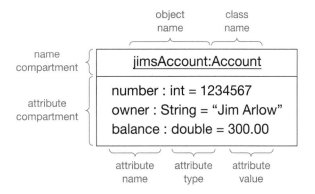

**Figure 7.4**

classes is very similar to that for objects. Being rigorous about using the underline correctly removes any confusion as to whether a modeling element is a class or an object.

UML is very flexible about how objects may be represented on object diagrams. The object identifier can consist of any of the following.

- The class name alone – e.g. :Account. This signifies that you have an anonymous object, or instance of that class (i.e. you are looking at an instance of an Account but haven't identified, or don't really care, which specific instance it is). Anonymous objects are often used when there is only one object of a particular class on a given diagram. If you need to show two objects of the same class, then you should give each a name to distinguish them from each other.

- The object name alone – e.g. jimsAccount. This identifies a specific object but doesn't identify which class it belongs to. This notation can be useful in very early analysis when you haven't yet discovered all the classes.

- The object name concatenated with the class name, separated from each other by a colon. You may read the colon as, "is an instance of class". So, in Figure 7.4, you could read the diagram as follows – there is an object called jimsAccount that is an instance of class Account.

Objects are usually named in mixed upper and lowercase, starting with a lowercase letter. Special characters, such as spaces and underscores, are avoided. This is known as CamelCase, as the resulting words appear to have humps.

From Section 7.2, you will know that a class defines the attributes and operations of a set of objects. As all objects of the *same* class have exactly the *same* set of operations, the operations are listed on the class icon not the object icon.

> Objects of the same class have the same operations and the same attributes, but may have different attribute values.

Attributes may be optionally shown in the lower compartment of the object icon. Those attributes that you choose to show *must* be named, and may have an optional type and value. Attributes are also named in CamelCase starting with a lowercase letter.

### 7.3.1   Object attribute values

Each object attribute value has the following form:

name : type = value

You may choose to show all, some, or none of the object attribute values, depending on the purpose of the diagram.

To keep object diagrams simple and clear, you may choose to omit attribute types as they are already defined in the class of the object. When you see how object diagrams are used in analysis in Chapter 12, it will be clear why you might choose to show only some of the information in an object icon.

## 7.4   What are classes?

> A class describes the features of a set of objects.

*The UML Reference Manual* [Rumbaugh 1] defines a class as, "The descriptor for a set of objects that share the same attributes, operations, methods, relationships, and behavior." We could summarize this by saying that a class is a descriptor for a set of objects that have the same features.

Every object is an instance of exactly one class. Here are some useful ways to think about classes.

- Think of a class as being a template for objects – a class determines the structure (set of features) of all objects of that class. All objects of the *same* class must have the *same* set of operations, the *same* set of attributes, and the *same* set of relationships, but may have *different* attribute values.

- Think of a class as being like a rubber stamp, and objects as actual stamp marks on a piece of paper; or think of a class as being like a cookie cutter, and the objects as being the cookies.

> Every object is an instance of exactly one class.

Classifier and instance are one of UML's common divisions (see Chapter 1) and the most common example of this division is class and object. A class is a specification or template that all objects of that class (instances) must follow. Each object of the class has specific values for the attributes defined by the class, and will respond to messages by invoking the operations defined by the class.

Depending on their state, different objects may respond to the same message in different ways. For example, if you try to withdraw $100 from a bank account object that is already overdrawn, this will give a different result from trying to withdraw $100 from a bank account object that is several hundred dollars in credit.

Classification is possibly the single most important way that human beings have of ordering information about the world. As such, it is also one of the most important OO concepts. Using the notion of classes, you can talk about a particular type of car, or a type of tree, without ever mentioning a specific instance. It is the same for software. Classes allow us to describe the set of features that every object of the class *must* have without having to describe every one of those objects.

Take a look at Figure 7.5 and think about classes for a minute or two. How many classes are there in this figure?

**Figure 7.5**

In fact, there's no answer to that question! There is an almost infinite number of ways of classifying objects in the real world. A few classes we can see are:

- the class of cats;
- the class of fat food-loving cats (we have a cat who is an instance of this class!);
- the class of trees;
- the class of leaves;
- etc., etc., etc.

Finding the right classification scheme is one of the keys to successful OO analysis.

Given that there are so many options, choosing the most appropriate classification scheme is one of the most important aspects of OO analysis and design. You'll see how to do this in Chapter 8.

Looking at Figure 7.5 very closely, you might begin to see other types of relationships apart from classifier/instance. For example, you might see multiple levels of classification. We have the class of cats, and we could classify things further into the subclasses "house cat" and "wild cat" – or even the subclasses "modern cat" and "prehistoric cat". This is a relationship between classes – one class is a subclass of another. Conversely, the class "cat" is a superclass of "house cat" and "wild cat". We'll look at this in much more detail when we study inheritance in Chapter 10.

Also, if you consider the leaves and trees in Figure 7.5, you can see that tree objects have collections of leaf objects. There is a very strong kind of relationship between trees and leaves. Each leaf object belongs to a specific tree object and can't be swapped or shared between them, and the lifecycle of the leaf is intimately tied to, and controlled by, the tree. This is a relationship between objects and is known in UML as composition.

If, however, you consider the relationship between computers and peripherals, the object relationship is very different. One peripheral, such as a pair of speakers, can be swapped between different computers – different computers can even share some peripherals. Also, even if a computer is thrown away, its peripherals may well survive it and be used by a new machine. The lifecycle of the peripherals is typically independent of the lifecycle of the computer. In UML this type of object relationship is known as aggregation. We'll discuss object relationships, and in particular composition and aggregation, in much more depth in Chapter 16.

## 7.4.1 Classes and objects

The relationship between a class and objects of that class is an «instantiate» relationship. This is the first example of a relationship that we have come across. *The UML Reference Manual* [Rumbaugh 1] defines a relationship as, "a connection between modeling elements." There are many types of relationship in UML and we will eventually explore them all.

> Relationships connect things together.

The «instantiate» relationship between objects and classes is shown in Figure 7.6. The dotted arrow is actually a dependency relationship that has been given a special meaning by the stereotype «instantiate». As you saw in Chapter 1, anything inside guillemots («...») is known as a stereotype, and stereotypes are one of the three UML extensibility mechanisms. A stereotype is a way of customizing modeling elements – a way of creating variants with new semantics. In this case, the stereotype «instantiate» turns an ordinary dependency into an instantiation relationship between a class and objects of that class.

> A dependency relationship means that a change to the supplier thing affects the client thing.

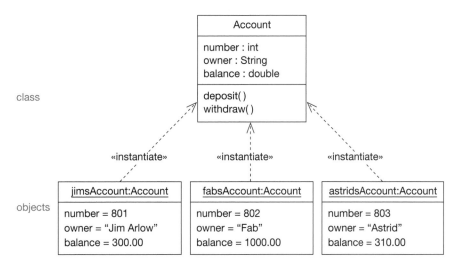

**Figure 7.6**

*The UML Reference Manual* [Rumbaugh 1] defines a dependency as, "A relationship between two elements in which a change to one element (the supplier) may affect or supply information needed by the other element (the client)." It is quite clear in Figure 7.6, that the class Account must be the supplier, as it determines the structure of all objects of that class, and that the objects are the clients.

## 7.4.2  Object instantiation

Instantiation is the creation of new instances of model elements. In this case we are instantiating objects from classes – we are creating *new instances* of classes.

UML tries to be very general, and so instantiation applies to other modeling elements as well as classes and objects. In fact, instantiation captures the general notion of creating a specific instance of something from a template.

> Object instantiation creates a new object using its class as the template.

In most OO programming languages, there are special operations, called constructors, which really belong to the class itself rather than the objects of that class. We say that these special operations have class scope and we'll say a bit more about scope in Section 7.6. The purpose of constructor operations is to create new instances of the class. The constructor allocates memory for the new object, gives it a unique identity, and sets the initial attribute values for the object. It also sets any links to other objects.

## 7.5    UML class notation

The visual UML syntax for a class is very rich, and to make it manageable it is important to apply the UML notion of optional adornments. The only mandatory part of the visual syntax is the name compartment with the class name in it. All the other compartments and adornments are optional. However, we've shown the whole thing in Figure 7.7 for your reference.

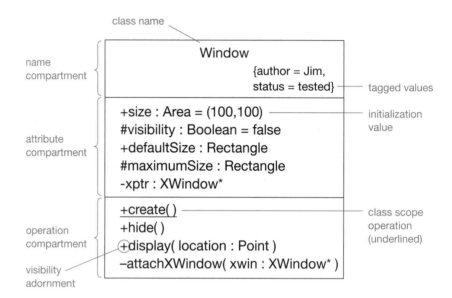

**Figure 7.7**

Which compartments and adornments you actually include on a class in a class diagram depends entirely on the purpose of the diagram. If you are only interested in showing the relationships between various classes, then you may be content with just the name compartment. If the diagram is trying to illustrate the behavior of the classes, then you will probably add the operation compartment and the key operations on each class. On the other hand, the diagram might be more "data oriented", perhaps trying to show the mapping of classes on to relational tables. In this case, you would show the name compartment and the attribute compartment, perhaps also showing attribute types. You should aim to use this UML flexibility to show just the right amount of information on class diagrams to make your point clearly and concisely.

Only show the compartments and adornments that make a point.

## 7.5.1 Name compartment

While UML does not mandate any naming convention for classes, there is a convention that is almost universally followed.

● Class name is in CamelCase – it begins with an uppercase letter, and then is in mixed upper and lowercase, with each word beginning in uppercase. Special symbols such as punctuation marks, dashes, underscores, ampersands, hashes, and slashes are *always* avoided. There is a good reason for this – these symbols are used in languages such as HTML, XML, and by operating systems. Including them in class names, or the names of any other modeling element for that matter, can lead to unexpected consequences when code or HTML/XML documentation is generated from the model.

● Avoid abbreviations *at all costs*. Class names should always reflect the names of real-world entities *without* abbreviation. For example, FlightSegment is always preferable to FltSgmnt, DepositAccount is always preferable to DpstAccnt. Again, the reason for this is very simple – abbreviations make the model (and resulting code) harder to read. Any time saved typing is lost many times over when the abbreviated model or code needs to be maintained.

> Never abbreviate class, attribute, or operation names.

## 7.5.2 Attribute compartment

The only mandatory part of the UML attribute syntax (Figure 7.8) is the attribute name:

**Figure 7.8**

It is possible to define the value an attribute will take when an object is instantiated from the class. This is known as the initial value of the attribute because it is the value that the attribute takes at the point of object creation. In design, use of initial values wherever possible is very good style as it helps to ensure that objects of the class are always created in a valid and useful state. Initial values are only used in analysis when they can express or highlight an important business constraint. This tends to be quite rare.

## 7.5.2.1    *Visibility*

Visibility controls access to the features of a class.

The visibility adornment (Table 7.3) applies to attributes and operations within the class. It may also be applied to role names on relationships (Chapter 9). In analysis, you typically don't clutter the diagrams with visibility as this is really a statement of "how" rather than "what".

**Table 7.3**

| Adornment | Visibility Name | Semantics |
|---|---|---|
| + | Public visibility | Any element that can access the class can access any of its features with public visibility |
| – | Private visibility | Only operations within the class can access features with private visibility |
| # | Protected visibility | Only operations within the class, or within children of the class, can access features with protected visibility |
| ~ | Package visibility | Any element that is in the same package as the class, or in a nested subpackage, can access any of its features with package visibility |

All types of visibility, except public, are implementation language dependent. This is an important point – in fact different languages may define additional types of visibility that UML does not support by default.

*The UML Reference Manual* [Rumbaugh 1] leaves *how* these language specific types of visibility are captured in CASE tools wide open: "The use of additional choices (for visibility) must be by convention between the user and any modeling tools and code generators". So, UML can, in principle, support visibility as defined by any language, but it does not define a standard way of doing that! Typically, this is not really a problem. The most common OO languages, C++ and Java, and even common semi-OO languages such as Visual Basic, get along just fine with public, private, protected and package visibility, at least as a first approximation.

Let's look at two OO languages in detail – Table 7.4 compares UML visibility semantics with those of Java and C#.

As you can see, visibility is entirely implementation language dependent, and can become quite complex. The exact type of visibility used is really a very detailed implementation decision that would usually be made by the programmer rather than by the analyst/designer. For general modeling, the UML standard definitions of public, private, protected, and package are quite adequate and we encourage you to restrict yourself to these.

**Table 7.4**

| Visibility | UML semantics | Java semantics | C# semantics |
|---|---|---|---|
| public | Any element that can access the class, can access any of its features with public visibility | Same as UML | Same as UML |
| private | Only operations within the class can access features with private visibility | Same as UML | Same as UML |
| protected | Only operations within the class, or within children of the class, can access features with protected visibility | As UML but is also accessible to all classes in the same Java package as the defining class | Same as UML |
| package | Any element that is in the same package as the class, or in a nested subpackage, can access any of its features with package visibility | The default visibility in Java – nested classes in nested subpackages don't automatically have access to elements in their parent package | – |
| private protected | – | Same as UML protected | – |
| internal | – | – | Accessible by any element in the same program |
| protected internal | – | – | Combines the semantics of protected and internal – only applicable to attributes |

### 7.5.2.2 *Multiplicity*

> Multiplicity allows you to model null values or arrays of things.

Multiplicity is widely used in design, but may also be used in analysis models as it can provide a concise way to express certain business constraints relating to the "number of things" participating in a relationship. In fact, multiplicity allows you to model two distinctly different things by using a multiplicity expression (see Figure 7.9).

● Arrays – if the multiplicity expression results in an integer greater than 1, then you are specifying an array of the type. For example, colors [7]: Color would model an array of seven Color objects which you could use to model the colors of the rainbow.

● Null values – there is a difference in many languages between an attribute that contains an empty or uninitialized object, such as the empty String, "", and an attribute that points nowhere, i.e. to the null object reference. When an attribute references null, this means that the object it will point to has not yet been created or has ceased to exist. It can sometimes be important in detailed design to distinguish when null is a possible value for an attribute, and you can model the fact that an attribute can be null by using the special multiplicity expression [0..1]. Take the emailAddress example in Figure 7.9 – if the attribute emailAddress has the value "" (the empty String), you might take this to mean that you have asked the person for their e-mail address and they have told you that they do not have e-mail. On the other hand, if the attribute emailAddress points to null, you might take this to mean that you have not yet asked for the e-mail address, and so its value is unknown. As you can see, this is a fairly detailed design consideration, but it can be important and useful.

Figure 7.9 gives some examples of multiplicity syntax.

multiplicity expression

address [3]: String                     an address is composed of an
                                        array or three Strings

name [2..*] : String                    a name is composed of two or
                                        more Strings

emailAddress [0..1] : String            an emailAddress is composed
                                        of one String or null

**Figure 7.9**

### 7.5.2.3   Advanced attribute syntax

Like any other UML modeling element, you can extend the semantics of attributes by prefixing them with stereotypes to indicate special semantics. You can also extend the specification of an attribute by postfixing the attribute with tagged values – for example,

«stereotype» attribute { tag1 = value1, tag2 = value2, ...}

In practice, neither of these techniques seems to be in wide use, and CASE support for them may be limited.

You can store whatever information you choose in tagged values. They are often used to store version information as shown here:

address {addedBy=Jim Arlow, date=20MAR2001}

In this example, we have recorded that Jim Arlow added the address attribute to some class on 20 March 2001.

### 7.5.3    Operation compartment

Operations are functions that are bound to a particular class. As such, they have all of the characteristics of functions:

- name;
- parameter list;
- return type.

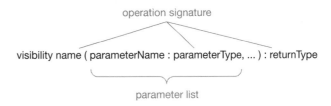

**Figure 7.10**

An operation signature comprises its name, the type of all its parameters, and its return type.

The combination of the operation name, types of all the parameters, and the return type is the operation signature (Figure 7.10). Every operation of a class must have a unique signature, as it is this signature that gives the operation its identity. When a message is sent to an object, the message signature is compared to the operation signatures defined in the object's class, and if a match is found the appropriate operation is invoked on the object.

Different implementation languages have slightly different interpretations as to what constitutes an operation signature. For example, in C++ and Java the return type is ignored. This means that two operations on a class which only differ by return type will be considered to be the same operation and will generate a compiler/interpreter error. In Smalltalk, which is a very weakly typed language, the parameters and return type are all of type Object, and so it is only the operation name that constitutes the signature.

Operations are named in CamelCase. Unlike class names, they always start with lowercase, and then continue in mixed upper and lowercase. Special symbols and abbreviations are avoided. Operation names are usually a verb or verb phrase.

#### 7.5.3.1    *Advanced operation syntax*

You can extend the semantics of operations by prefixing them with stereotypes and postfixing them with tagged values.

«stereotype» operation(...){ tag1 = value1, tag2 = value2, ...}

This doesn't seem to be a commonly used technique however.

### 7.5.4  Class stereotype syntax

There is a lot of flexibility in how stereotypes can be displayed (Figure 7.11). However, most modelers just use the name in guillemots («stereotypeName») or the icon. The other variants don't tend to be used as much and the CASE tool you are using often imposes limits.

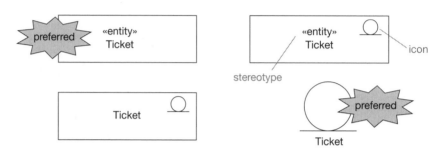

**Figure 7.11**

Stereotypes can also be associated with colors or textures – but this is very bad practice. Some readers, the visually impaired or the color blind, may have difficulty interpreting such diagrams. Also, diagrams often have to be printed in black and white.

## 7.6  Scope

> Instance scope attributes and operations belong to, or operate on, specific objects.

> Class scope attributes and operations belong to, or operate on, the whole class of objects.

Up to now you have seen that objects have their own copies of the attributes defined in their class, so that different objects can have different attribute values. Similarly, the operations that you have seen so far all act on specific objects. This is the normal case, and we say that these attributes and operations have instance scope.

However, sometimes it is useful to define attributes that have a single, shared value for every object of the class, and to have operations (like object creation and destruction operations) that don't operate on any particular class instance. We say that these attributes and operations have class scope. Class scope features provide a set of global features for an entire class of objects.

### 7.6.1  Instance scope and class scope

The notation for instance scope and class scope attributes and operations is shown in Figure 7.12. The semantics for instance scope and class scope attributes and operations is summarized in Table 7.5.

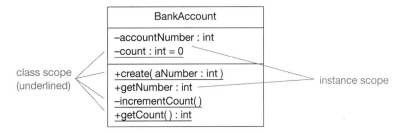

**Figure 7.12**

**Table 7.5**

| | Instance scope | Class scope |
|---|---|---|
| Attributes | By default, attributes have instance scope | Attributes may be defined as class scope |
| | Every object of the class gets its own copy of the instance scope attributes | Every object of the class shares the same, single copy of the class scope attributes |
| | Each object may therefore have different instance scope attribute values | Each object will therefore have the same class scope attribute values |
| Operations | By default, operations have instance scope | Operations may be defined as class scope |
| | Every invocation of an instance scope operation applies to a specific instance of the class | Invocation of a class scope operation does not apply to any specific instance of the class – instead, you can think of class scope operations as applying to the class itself |
| | You can't invoke an instance scope operation unless you have an instance of the class available – clearly, this means that you *can't* use an instance scope operation of a class to create objects of that class, as you could never create the first object | You can invoke a class scope operation even if there is no instance of the class available – this is ideal for object creation operations |

## 7.6.2  Scope determines access

Whether an operation can access another feature of the class or not is determined by the scope of the operation and the scope of the feature it is trying to access.

Instance scope operations can access other instance scope attributes and operations, and also all of the class scope attributes and operations.

Class scope operations may *only* access other class scope operations and attributes. Class scope operations can't access instance scope operations because:

● there might not be any class instances created yet;

● even if class instances exist, you don't know which one to use.

## 7.7  Object construction and destruction

> Constructors are special methods that create new objects. They have class scope.

Constructors are special operations that create new instances of classes – these operations *must* be class scope. If they were instance scope, you obviously couldn't invoke them to create the first instance as you would not yet have created any instances.

Different languages have different standards for naming constructors. A completely generic approach is just to call the constructor create(...). This makes the intention of the operation clear. Java, C#, and C++ all demand that the constructor name is the same as the class name.

A class may have many constructors, all with the same name, but each distinguished by a different parameter list. The constructor with no parameters is known as the default constructor. We can use constructor parameters to initialize attribute values at the point of object construction.

Figure 7.13 shows a simple BankAccount example. Every time you create a new BankAccount object, you have to pass in a number as a parameter to the constructor. This number is used to set the accountNumber attribute. The fact that the BankAccount constructor needs a parameter means that there is *no way* to create a BankAccount object *without* specifying this parameter. This ensures that every BankAccount object has the accountNumber attribute value set at the point of creation – this is very good style.

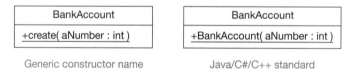

Figure 7.13

In analysis-level models, you generally don't bother specifying constructors at all. They usually have no impact on, or relationship to, the business semantics of the class. If you *do* want to show constructor operations, you can put in a create() operation with no parameters as a placeholder. Alternatively, you can specify just those parameters that are important from a business perspective.

In detailed design, you need to specify the name, parameter types and return type of *every* operation – we will therefore look at object construction again when we reach the design workflow in Part 4.

Object destruction is not as straightforward as object construction. Different OO languages have different semantics for object destruction. We'll explore object construction and destruction in the next two sections using a simple BankAccount class as an example.

## 7.7.1  Constructors – **BankAccount** class example

The BankAccount example in Figure 7.14 shows a typical use of class scope attributes and operations. The count attribute is a private class scope attribute of type int. This attribute is therefore shared by all objects of the BankAccount class, and will have the same value for each of those objects.

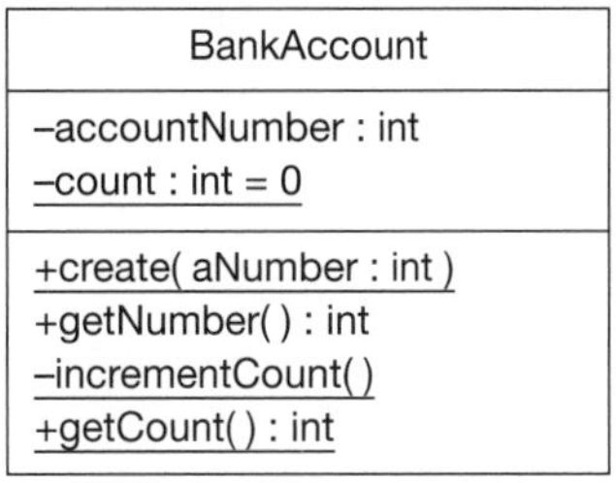

```
┌─────────────────────────────┐
│         BankAccount         │
├─────────────────────────────┤
│ –accountNumber : int        │
│ –count : int = 0            │
├─────────────────────────────┤
│ +create( aNumber : int )    │
│ +getNumber( ) : int         │
│ –incrementCount( )          │
│ +getCount( ) : int          │
└─────────────────────────────┘
```

**Figure 7.14**

At the point at which the count attribute is created, it is initialized to zero. Now, if this were an instance scope attribute, each object would get its own copy of it when the object was created. However, it is class scope – this means that there is only one copy, and this single copy is only initialized once. Exactly *when* that happens is implementation language dependent but, as far as we are concerned, all we have to know is that it initialized to the value zero when the program started.

Suppose that in the create() operation you invoke the class scope operation incrementCount(). This operation increments the value of the class scope attribute count. Every time an instance of the class is created, count is incremented – a counter has been added to the class! You can query the value of count by using the class scope operation getCount(). This returns a number that is equal to the number of BankAccount objects created.

## 7.7.2  Destructors – **BankAccount** class example

What happens if the program creates *and* destroys BankAccount objects? Obviously the value of count would rapidly become meaningless. You can fix this by introducing an operation to the class to decrement count and then ensuring that this operation is called every time an instance of BankAccount is destroyed.

Destructors are special class scope methods that "clean up" when objects are destroyed.

Some OO languages have special class scope methods called destructors that are automatically called at the point of object destruction. In C++, for example, the destructor is always of the form ~ClassName( parameterList ). In C++ the destructor method is *guaranteed* to be called at the point at which an object is deleted.

Java has a similar capability – every class has a method called finalize() that is called when the object is finally deleted. However, objects are not explicitly deleted by the program itself, but rather are left to an automatic garbage collector. As such, you know that finalize() will be called, but you just don't know *when*! This is obviously not going to work for our simple counter application, and you would have to explicitly decrement count yourself (perhaps by calling a class or instance scope method called decrementCount() ) whenever you were finished with an object and were letting it go to garbage collection.

C# has identical destruction semantics to Java, except the method is called Finalize().

## 7.8  What we have learned

This chapter has presented the basic groundwork on classes and objects that will be used throughout the rest of the book. Classes and objects are the building blocks of OO systems, so it is very important to have a thorough and detailed understanding of them.

You have learned the following.

- Objects are cohesive units that combine data and function.

- Encapsulation is where the data inside an object is hidden and can only be manipulated by invoking one of the object's functions:
  — operations are abstract specifications for object functions created in analysis;
  — methods are concrete specifications for object functions created in design.

- Every object is an instance of a class – a class defines the common features shared by all objects of that class.

- Every object has the following features.
  — Identity – its unique existence – you use object references to uniquely refer to specific objects.
  — State – a meaningful set of attribute values for the object at a point in time.
    - Only those sets of attribute values that constitute a semantically important distinction from other possible sets constitute a state. For example,  BankAccount object – balance < 0, state = overdrawn; balance > 0, state = inCredit.
    - State transition – the movement of an object from one meaningful state to another.

— Behavior – services the object offers to other objects:
  - modeled as a set of operations in analysis;
  - modeled as a set of methods in design;
  - invoking operations or methods *may* generate a state transition.

- Objects interact together to generate the behavior of the system. Interaction involves objects sending messages back and forth – when a message is received, the corresponding method is invoked; this *may* cause a state transition.

- UML object notation – every object icon has two compartments.
  — The top compartment contains the object name and/or the class name, *all* of which must be underlined.
    - Object and class names are in CamelCase. Object names start with a lowercase letter, and class names start with an uppercase letter – the rest of the name is in mixed upper and lowercase with no special symbols.
    - Object name is separated from class name by a single colon.
  — The bottom compartment contains the attribute names and values separated by an equals sign.
    - Attribute types are generally omitted from the diagram.
    - Attribute names and values are in CamelCase and start with a lowercase letter.

- A class defines the features (attributes, operations, methods, relationships, and behavior) of a set of objects.
  — Each object is an instance of exactly one class.
  — Different objects of the same class have the same set of attributes, but may have different values for those attributes. Different attribute values cause objects of the same class to behave differently – for example, compare trying to withdraw $100 from a BankAccount object that is overdrawn with trying to withdraw $100 from a BankAccount object that is $200 in credit.
  — There are many ways of classifying the world – finding the right classification scheme is one of the keys to successful OO analysis.
  — You can show the instantiate relationship between a class and one of its objects by using a dependency stereotyped as «instantiate»:
    - relationships connect things together;
    - a dependency relationship indicates that a change to the supplier affects the client.
  — Object instantiation creates a new object using its class as a template.
    - Most OO languages provide special methods called constructors that are called when an object needs to be created – constructors set up or initialize objects; constructors are class scope (they belong to the class).
    - Some OO languages provide special methods called destructors that are called when an object is destroyed – destructors clean up after objects; destructors are class scope.

- UML class notation.
  - Name compartment has the class name in CamelCase beginning with uppercase; there are no abbreviations.
  - Attribute compartment – each attribute has:
    - visibility – this controls access to features of a class;
    - name (mandatory) – CamelCase beginning with lower-case;
    - multiplicity – arrays, e.g. [10]; null values e.g. [0..1];
    - type;
    - attributes may have stereotypes and tagged values.
  - Operation compartment – each operation may have:
    - visibility;
    - name (mandatory) – CamelCase beginning with uppercase;
    - parameter list (name and type for each parameter);
    - return type;
    - stereotype;
    - tagged values.
  - An operation signature comprises:
    - name;
    - parameter list (types of all parameters);
    - return type.
  - Every operation or method of a class must have a unique signature.
- Scope.
  - Instance scope attributes and operations belong to or operate on specific objects.
    - Instance scope operations can access other instance scope operations or instance scope attributes.
    - Instance scope operations can access all class scope attributes or operations.
  - Class scope attributes and operations belong to, or operate on, the whole class of objects.
    - Class scope attributes and operations can only access other class scope operations.
    - Constructors – special class scope methods that create new objects.
    - Destructors – special class scope methods that clean up when objects are destroyed.

# chapter 8

# Finding analysis classes

## 8.1 Chapter roadmap

This chapter is all about the core activity of OO analysis, finding the analysis classes. If you want to understand the UP activity in which analysis classes are found, go to Section 8.2. If you need to know what an analysis class is, go to Section 8.3.

In Section 8.4 we describe how to find analysis classes. We present two specific techniques – noun/verb analysis (8.4.1) and CRC analysis (8.4.2) – and also a general consideration of other possible sources for classes (8.4.3).

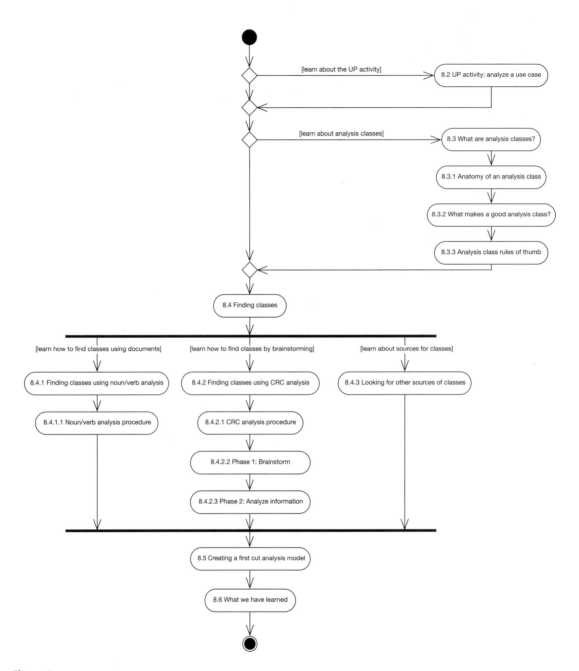

**Figure 8.1**

## 8.2 UP activity: analyze a use case

The outputs from the UP workflow "Analyze a use case" (see Figure 8.2) are analysis classes and use case realizations. In this chapter we focus on analysis classes. We consider use case realizations in Chapter 12 – these are collaborations between objects that show how systems of interacting objects can realize the system behavior expressed in the use cases.

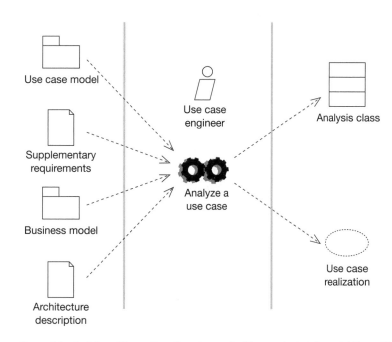

The UP activity "Analyze a use case" involves creating analysis classes and use case realizations.

**Figure 8.2** Adapted from Figure 8.25 [Jacobson 1] with permission from Addison-Wesley

## 8.3 What are analysis classes?

Analysis classes model important aspects of the problem domain such as "customer" or "product".

Analysis classes are classes that:

● represent a crisp abstraction in the problem domain;
● should map on to real-world business concepts (and be carefully named accordingly).

The problem domain is the domain in which the need for a software system (and hence a software development activity) first arises. This is usually a specific area of the business such as online selling or customer relationship management. However, it is important to note that the problem domain might not be any specific business activity at all, but might arise from a piece of physical hardware that needs software to operate it – this is an embedded system. Ultimately, all commercial software development serves some business need, be that automating an existing business process, or developing a new product that has a significant software component.

The most important aspect of an analysis class is that it should map in a clear and unambiguous way on to some real-world business concept such as customer, product, or account. However, this statement assumes that the business concepts themselves are clear and unambiguous and this is rarely the case. It is therefore the job of the OO analyst to try to clarify confused or inappropriate business concepts into something that can form the basis of an analysis class. This is why OO analysis can be difficult.

So the first step in building OO software is to clarify the problem domain. If it contains clearly defined business concepts and has a simple, functional structure, then the solution is virtually there for the taking. Much of this work will be done in the requirements workflow in the activities of capturing requirements, and creating a use case model and Project Glossary. However, much more clarification occurs in the construction of analysis classes and use case realizations.

It is important that *all* classes in the analysis model are analysis classes rather than classes arising from design considerations (the solution domain). When you get down to detailed design you may find that analysis classes are ultimately refined into one or more design classes.

Although, in the previous chapter, we necessarily began by considering specific objects, it will now be clear that the real goal of OO analysis is finding the classes of those objects. In fact, finding the right analysis classes is the key to OO analysis and design. If the classes are not right in analysis, then the rest of the software engineering process, which is predicated on the requirements and analysis workflows, will be in jeopardy. It is therefore crucial to spend sufficient time in the analysis workflow to ensure that the right set of analysis classes has been identified. This time will be well spent, as it will almost certainly save time later.

In this book, we focus on development of business systems, as that is what most OO analysts and designers are involved in. However, development of embedded systems is really just a special case of normal business development and all the same principles apply. Business systems are usually dominated by functional requirements and so it is generally the requirements and analysis activities that are the most difficult. In embedded systems, which tend to be dominated by non-functional requirements, the requirements are often a given and analysis tends to be straightforward, but design can be difficult.

> An analysis class should map in a clear and unambiguous way onto a real-world business concept.

## 8.3.1 Anatomy of an analysis class

Analysis classes should present a very "high level" set of attributes. They *indicate* the attributes that the resultant design classes will *probably* have. We might say that analysis classes capture candidate attributes for the design classes.

> Analysis classes only have key attributes and very high-level responsibilities.

Analysis class operations specify, at a high level, the key services that the class must offer. In design they will become actual, implementable methods. However, one high-level operation will often break down into more than one method.

We have already covered the UML syntax for classes in great detail in Chapter 7, but in analysis only a small subset of that syntax is actually used. Of course, the analyst is always free to add any adornments felt to be necessary to make the model clearer. However, the basic syntax of an analysis class *always* avoids implementation details. After all, in analysis we are trying to capture the big picture.

A minimal form for an analysis class consists of the following.

- Name – this is mandatory.
- Attributes – attribute names are mandatory although only an important subset of candidate attributes may be modeled at this point. Attribute types are considered optional.
- Operations – in analysis, operations might just be very high-level statements of the responsibilities of the class. Operation parameters and return types are only shown where they are important for understanding the model.
- Visibility – generally not shown.
- Stereotypes – may be shown if they enhance the model.
- Tagged values – may be shown if they enhance the model.

An example is given in Figure 8.3.

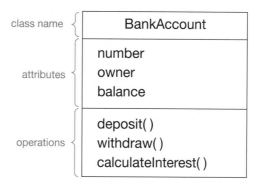

**Figure 8.3**

The idea of an analysis class is that you try to capture the *essence* of the abstraction, and leave the implementation details until you come to design.

## 8.3.2   What makes a good analysis class?

We can summarize what makes a good analysis class in the following points:

- its name reflects its intent;
- it is a crisp abstraction that models one specific element of the problem domain;
- it maps on to a clearly identifiable feature of the problem domain;
- it has a small, well-defined set of responsibilities;
- it has high cohesion;
- it has low coupling.

> The name of an analysis class should indicate its intent.

In analysis you are trying to model one aspect of the problem domain accurately and concisely from the perspective of the system you are trying to construct. For example, if you are modeling a customer in a banking system, you would want to capture the customer's name and address, etc. but you would be unlikely to be interested in their preference for window or aisle seats on an aircraft. You need to focus on the aspects of real-world things that are important from the perspective of the system you are building.

You can often get a first idea as to whether or not a class is a "good" class simply from its name. If you consider an e-commerce system, Customer would seem to refer to something quite precise in the real world, and would be a good candidate for a class. ShoppingBasket would also seem to be a good abstraction – we know, almost intuitively, what its semantics will be. However, something like WebSiteVisitor seems to have rather vague semantics, and in fact really sounds like a role that a Customer plays in relation to the e-commerce system. You should always be looking for a "crisp abstraction" – something that has clear and obvious semantics.

> Responsibilities describe cohesive sets of operations.

A responsibility is a contract or obligation that a class has to its clients. Essentially, a responsibility is a service that a class offers to other classes. It is crucial that your analysis classes have a very cohesive set of responsibilities that are in direct accord with the intent of the class (as expressed by its name) and with the real-world "thing" that the class is modeling. Going back to the ShoppingBasket example, you would expect this class to have responsibilities such as:

- add item to basket;
- remove item from basket;
- show items in basket.

This is a cohesive set of responsibilities, all about maintaining a collection of items that the customer has chosen. It is cohesive because all the responsibilities are working toward the same goal – maintaining the customer's shopping basket. In fact, we could summarize these three responsibilities as a very high-level responsibility called "maintain basket".

Now, you could also add the following responsibilities to the ShoppingBasket:

- validate credit card;
- accept payment;
- print receipt.

But these responsibilities do not seem to fit with the intent or intuitive semantics of shopping baskets. They are not cohesive and clearly should be assigned elsewhere – perhaps a CreditCardCompany class, a Checkout class, and a ReceiptPrinter class. It is important to distribute responsibilities appropriately over analysis classes to maximize cohesion within each class.

Finally, good classes have the minimum amount of coupling to other classes. We measure coupling between classes by the number of other classes that a given class has relationships to. An even distribution of responsibilities between classes will tend to result in low coupling. Localization of control or of many responsibilities in a single class tends to increase coupling to that class. We consider ways of maximizing cohesion and minimizing coupling in Chapter 15.

## 8.3.3   Analysis class rules of thumb

Here are some rules of thumb for creating well-formed analysis classes.

- About three to five responsibilities per class – typically, classes should be kept as simple as possible, and this usually limits the number of responsibilities that they can support to between three and five. Our previous example of a ShoppingBasket is a good example of a focused class with a small and manageable number of responsibilities.

- No class stands alone – the essence of good OO analysis and design is that classes collaborate with each other to deliver benefit to users. As such, each class should be associated with a small number of other classes with which it collaborates to deliver the desired benefit. Classes may delegate some of their responsibilities to other "helper" classes which are dedicated to that specific function.

- Beware of many very small classes – it can sometimes be hard to get the balance right. If the model seems to have lots and lots of very small classes with just one or two responsibilities each, then you should look at this very carefully with a view to consolidating some of the small classes into larger ones.

- Beware of few but very large classes – the converse of the above is a model that has few classes, where many of them have a large number (> 5) of responsibilities. The strategy here is to look at these classes in turn, and see if each can be decomposed into two or more smaller classes with the right number of responsibilities.

- Beware of "functoids" – a functoid is a really a normal procedural function disguised as a class. Grady Booch tells the amusing anecdote of a model of a very simple system that had thousands of classes. On closer inspection, each class had exactly one operation called dolt(). Functoids are always a danger when analysts, who are used to the technique of top-down functional decomposition, approach OO analysis and design for the first time.

- Beware of omnipotent classes – these are classes that seem to do everything. Look for classes with "system" or "controller" in their name! The strategy for dealing with this problem is to see if the responsibilities of the omnipotent class fall into cohesive subsets. If so, perhaps each of these cohesive sets of responsibilities can be factored out into a separate class. These smaller classes would then collaborate to implement the behavior offered by the original omnipotent class.

- Avoid deep inheritance trees – the essence of designing a good inheritance hierarchy is that each level of abstraction in the hierarchy should have a well-defined purpose. It is easy to add many levels that don't really serve any useful purpose. In fact, a common mistake is to use inheritance to implement a kind of functional decomposition where each level of abstraction has only one responsibility. This is, in every respect, pointless and just leads to a complex, difficult to understand model. In analysis, inheritance is only used where there is a clear, and obvious, inheritance hierarchy arising directly from the problem domain.

## 8.4  Finding classes

In the rest of this chapter we consider the core issue of OO analysis and design, finding the analysis classes.

As Meyer points out in *Object Oriented Software Construction* [Meyer 1], there is no simple algorithm for finding the right analysis classes. If such an algorithm did exist, then it would amount to an infallible way to design OO software and this is just as unlikely as finding an infallible way to prove mathematical theorems.

Still, there are tried and tested techniques that lead toward a good answer, and we present them here. They involve analyzing text, and interviewing users and domain experts. But ultimately, despite all the techniques, finding the "right" classes depends on the perspective, skill, and experience of the individual analyst.

## 8.4.1 Finding classes using noun/verb analysis

Noun/verb analysis is a very simple way of analyzing text to try to find classes, attributes, and responsibilities. In essence, nouns and noun phrases in the text indicate classes or attributes of classes, and verbs and verb phrases indicate responsibilities or operations of a class. Noun/verb analysis has been used for many years and works well as it is based on a direct analysis of the language of the problem domain. However, you have to be very aware of synonyms and homonyms as these can give rise to spurious classes.

> In noun/verb analysis you analyze text. Nouns and noun phrases indicate classes or attributes. Verbs and verb phrases indicate responsibilities or operations.

You also have to be very careful if the problem domain is poorly understood and defined. In this case, try to collect as much information about the domain from as many people as possible. Look for similar problem domains outside your organization.

Perhaps the trickiest aspect of noun/verb analysis is finding the "hidden" classes. These are classes which are intrinsic to the problem domain, but which might never be mentioned explicitly. For example, in a reservation system for a holiday company, you will hear the stakeholders talk about reservations, bookings, etc., but the single most important abstraction, Order, may never be mentioned explicitly if it does not exist in current business systems. You generally know when you have found a hidden class because the whole model seems to gel suddenly, with the introduction of this single, new abstraction. This happens surprisingly often – in fact, if we're ever having trouble with an analysis model, and it just doesn't seem to be making sense, we go on a search for hidden classes. If nothing else, this makes us ask some penetrating questions, and improves our understanding of the problem domain.

### 8.4.1.1 Noun/verb analysis procedure

The first step in noun/verb analysis is to collect as much relevant information as possible. Suitable sources of information are:

- the Supplementary Requirements Specification (if it exists);
- use cases;
- the project Glossary;
- anything else (architecture, vision documents, etc.).

After collecting the documentation, analyze it in a very simple way by highlighting (or recording in some other way) the following:

- nouns – e.g. flight;
- noun phrases – e.g. flight number;
- verbs – e.g. allocate;
- verb phrases – e.g. verify credit card.

Nouns and noun phrases may indicate classes or class attributes. Verbs and verb phrases may indicate responsibilities of classes.

If you come across any terms that you don't understand during this process, seek immediate clarification from a domain expert and add the term to the Project Glossary. Take the list of nouns, noun phrases, verbs, and verb phrases and use the Project Glossary to resolve any synonyms and homonyms. This creates a list of candidate classes, attributes, and responsibilities.

Once you have this list of candidate classes, attributes, and responsibilities, you make a tentative allocation of the attributes and responsibilities to the classes. You can do this by entering the classes into a CASE tool, and adding the responsibilities as operations to the classes. If you have found any candidate attributes, then you can tentatively assign these to classes as well. You might also have gained some idea of relationships between certain classes (the use cases are a good source of these) so you can add some candidate associations. This gives you a first cut class model that you can refine by further analysis.

## 8.4.2 Finding classes using CRC analysis

CRC is a brainstorming technique in which you capture the important things in the problem domain on sticky notes.

A very good (and fun) way to get user involvement in finding classes is to use CRC analysis – this stands for class, responsibilities, and collaborators. This technique uses the world's most powerful analysis tool, the sticky note! So popular is the CRC method that there is a (possibly apocryphal) story that at one point a company actually marketed sticky notes already marked out with class name, responsibilities, and collaborators.

You begin by marking up some sticky notes as shown Figure 8.4. The note is divided into three compartments – in the top compartment you record the

| **Class name:** BankAccount | |
|---|---|
| **Responsibilities:**<br>Maintain balance | **Collaborators:**<br>Bank |

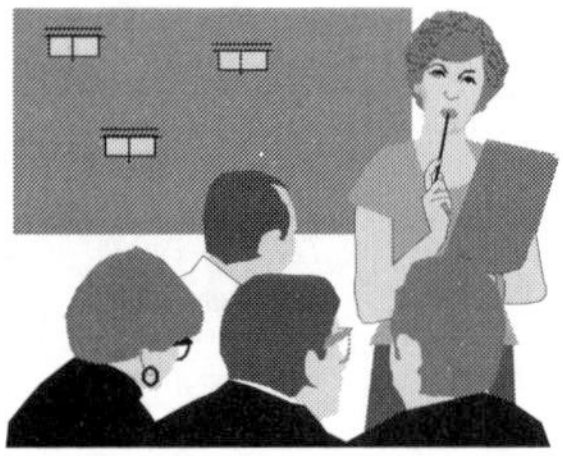

Figure 8.4

name of the candidate class; in the left compartment, the responsibilities; and in the right the collaborators. Collaborators are other classes that may collaborate with this class to realize a piece of system functionality. The collaborators compartment provides a way of recording relationships between classes. Another way to capture relationships (which we prefer) is to stick the notes on a whiteboard, and draw lines between the collaborating classes.

### 8.4.2.1  CRC analysis procedure

CRC analysis should always be used in conjunction with noun/verb analysis of use cases, requirements, glossary, and other relevant documentation, unless the system is very simple. The CRC analysis procedure is straightforward and the key is to separate information *gathering* from information *analysis*. CRC is therefore best run as a two-phase activity.

### 8.4.2.2  Phase 1: Brainstorm – gather the information

The participants are OO analysts, stakeholders, and domain experts. The procedure is as follows.

> Stakeholder involvement is essential for CRC success.

1   Explain that this is a true brainstorm.
    1.1   All ideas are accepted as good ideas.
    1.2   Ideas are recorded but *not* debated – never argue about something, just write it down and then move on. Everything will be analyzed later.

2   Ask the team members to name the "things" that operate in their business domain – e.g. customer, product.
    2.1   Write each thing on a sticky note – it is a candidate class, or attribute of a class.
    2.2   Stick the note on a wall or whiteboard.

3   Ask the team to state responsibilities that those things might have – record these in the responsibilities compartment of the note.

4   Working with the team, try to identify classes that might work together. Rearrange the notes on the whiteboard to reflect this organization and draw lines between them. Alternatively, record collaborators in the collaborators compartment of the note.

### 8.4.2.3  Phase 2: Analyze information

The participants are OO analysis, and domain experts. How do you decide which sticky notes should become classes and which should become attributes? Go back and look at Section 8.3.2 – analysis classes *must* represent a crisp abstraction in the problem domain. Certain sticky notes will represent key business concepts and clearly need to become classes. Other notes may become classes or attributes. If a note logically seems to be a *part* of another note, this is a good indication that it represents an attribute. Also, if a note

> Important business concepts generally become classes.

doesn't seem to be particularly important, or has very little interesting behavior, see if it can be made an attribute of another class.

If in doubt about a note just make it a class. The important point is to make a best guess and then drive this process to closure – you can always refine the model later.

### 8.4.3    Looking for other sources of classes

As well as the noun/verb analysis and CRC analysis, it is worth remembering that there are many other potential sources of classes that should be considered. As you are looking for crisp abstractions that map on to real-world things in the problem domain then, obviously, you can look to the real world for classes.

- Physical objects such as aircraft, people, and hotels may all indicate classes to you.

- Paperwork is another rich source of classes. Things like invoices, orders, and bankbooks may all indicate possible classes. However, you must be very careful when looking at paperwork. In many companies the paperwork has evolved over the years to support exactly the redundant business processes that the new system might be trying to replace! The last thing you want to do as an OO analyst/designer is to automate obsolete and pathological paper-based systems.

- Known interfaces to the outside world such as screens, keyboards, peripherals, and other systems can also be a source of candidate classes, especially for embedded systems.

- Conceptual entities are things that are crucial to the operation of the business but which are not manifest as concrete things. An example of this might be a LoyaltyProgram such as a reward card. Clearly, the program itself is not a concrete thing (you can't give it a kick!), but it is still a cohesive abstraction and so may warrant modeling as a class.

## 8.5    Creating a first cut analysis model

To create a first cut analysis model, you need to consolidate the outputs of noun/verb analysis, CRC analysis, and a consideration of other sources of classes into a single UML model in a CASE tool. You can do this as follows.

1    Compare all three sources of information – the CRC results, the results of noun/verb analysis, and the results of considering other sources of classes.

2    Consolidate the analysis classes, attributes, and responsibilities from the different sources and enter them into a CASE tool.

**2.1** Resolve synonyms and homonyms using the Project Glossary.

**2.2** Look for differences in the results of the three techniques – differences indicate areas where there is uncertainty, or where more work might be done. Resolve these differences now, or highlight for later work.

**3** Collaborators (or lines between sticky notes on the whiteboard) represent relationships between classes. You will see how to model these in Chapter 9.

**4** Improve the naming of classes, attributes, and responsibilities to follow any standard naming conventions that your company has, or follow the simple naming conventions described in Chapter 7.

The output from this activity is a set of analysis classes where each class *may* have some key attributes and *should* have between three to five responsibilities. This is your first cut analysis model.

## 8.6 What we have learned

In this chapter we have described what analysis classes are, and how to find these classes using the techniques of noun/verb analysis, CRC brainstorming, and an examination of other sources of classes.

You have learned the following.

- The UP activity "Analyze a use case" outputs analysis classes and use case realizations.

- Analysis classes represent a crisp, well-defined abstraction in the problem domain.
  — The problem domain is that domain in which the need for the software system has arisen.
  — Analysis classes should map in a clear, unambiguous way to a real-world business concept.
  — Business concepts often need to be clarified during analysis.

- The analysis model only contains analysis classes – any classes arising from design considerations (the solution domain) must be excluded.

- Analysis classes include:
  — a set of high-level candidate attributes;
  — a set of high-level operations.

- What makes a good analysis class?
  — Its name reflects its intent.
  — It is a crisp abstraction that models one specific element of the problem domain.

— It maps on to a clearly identifiable feature of the problem domain.
— It has a small, well-defined set of responsibilities:
  – a responsibility is a contract or obligation that a class has to its clients;
  – a responsibility is a semantically cohesive set of operations;
  – there should only be about three to five responsibilities per class.
— It has high cohesion – all features of the class should help to realize its intent.
— It has low coupling – a class should only collaborate with a small number of other classes to realize its intent.

- What makes a bad analysis class?
  — It is a functoid – a class with only one operation.
  — It is an omnipotent class – a class that does everything – look for classes with "system" or "controller" in their name.
  — It has a deep inheritance tree – in the real world inheritance trees tend to be shallow.
  — It has low cohesion.
  — It has high coupling.

- Noun/verb analysis.
  — Look for nouns or noun phrases – these are candidate classes or attributes.
  — Look for verbs or verb phrases – these are candidate responsibilities or operations.
  — The procedure is to collect relevant information and then to analyze it.

- CRC analysis is a powerful and fun brainstorming technique.
  — Important things in the problem domain are written on sticky notes.
  — Each note has three compartments:
    – class – contains the name of the class;
    – responsibilities – contains a list of the responsibilities of that class;
    – collaborators – contains a list of other classes with which this class collaborates.
  — Procedure – brainstorm:
    – ask the team members to name the "things" that operate in their business domain and write them on sticky notes;
    – ask the team to state the responsibilities of the things and record them in the responsibilities compartment of the note;
    – ask the team to identify classes that might work together and draw lines between them, or record this in the collaborators compartment of each note.

- Consider other sources of classes such as physical objects, paperwork, interfaces to the outside world, and conceptual entities.
- Create a first cut analysis model:
  — compare noun/verb analysis results with CRC results and the results of an examination of other sources of classes;
  — resolve synonyms and homonyms;
  — differences between the results of the different techniques indicate areas of uncertainty;
  — consolidate results into a first cut analysis model.

# chapter 9
# Relationships

## 9.1 Chapter roadmap

This chapter discusses relationships between objects, and relationships between classes. To find out what a relationship is, read Section 9.2. The chapter is then organized under three separate threads. We discuss links (relationships between objects) in Section 9.3, associations (relationships between classes) in Section 9.4 and finally dependencies (catch-all relationships) in Section 9.5.

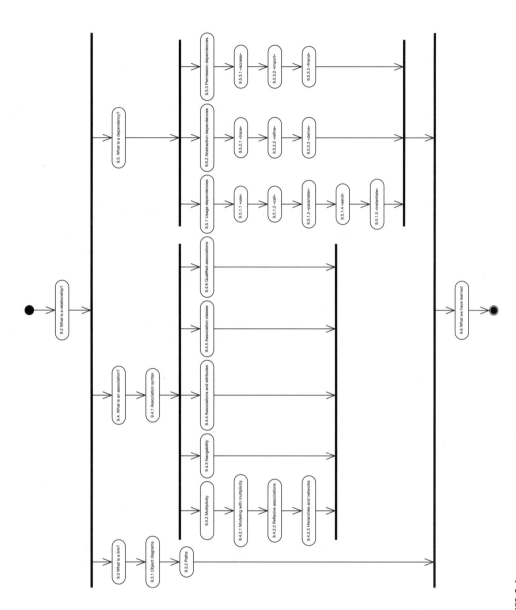

**Figure 9.1**

## 9.2   What is a relationship?

Relationships are semantic (meaningful) connections between modeling elements – they are the UML way of connecting things together. You have already seen a few types of relationship:

- between actors and use cases (association);
- between use cases and use cases (generalization, «include», «extend»);
- between actors and actors (generalization).

UML relationships connect things together.

In this chapter we will explore connections between objects and connections between classes. We start with links and associations, and then, in Chapter 10, look at generalization and inheritance.

In order to create a functioning OO system, you can't let the objects stand alone in glorious isolation. You need to connect them together so that they can perform useful work of benefit to the users of the system. Connections between objects are called links, and when objects work together, we say that they collaborate.

If there is a link between two objects, there must also be some semantic connection between their classes. This is really common sense – for objects to communicate directly with each other, the classes of those objects must know about each other in some way. Connections between classes are known as associations. Links between objects are actually instances of the associations between their classes.

## 9.3   What is a link?

To create an object-oriented program, objects need to communicate with each other. In fact, an executing OO program is a harmonious community of cooperating objects.

Objects send messages to each other over connections called links.

A link is a semantic connection between two objects that allows messages to be sent from one object to the other. An executing OO system contains many objects that come and go, and many links (that also come and go) that join those objects together. Messages are passed back and forth between objects over these links. On receipt of a message, an object will invoke the corresponding method.

Links are implemented in different ways by different OO languages. Java implements links as object references; C++ may implement links as pointers, references, or by direct inclusion of one object by another.

Whatever the approach, a minimal requirement for a link is that *at least one* of the objects must have an object reference to the other. This creates a unidirectional link from the object that owns the object reference (the source) to the referenced object (the target). An arrowhead is put on the end of a link to indicate navigability. If both objects have references to each other, this creates a bidirectional link which is shown as an unadorned line with no arrowheads.

## 9.3.1  Object diagrams

An object diagram is a diagram that shows objects and their relationships at a point in time. It is like a snapshot of part of an executing OO system at a particular instant, showing the objects and the links between them.

Objects that are connected by links may adopt various roles relative to each other. In Figure 9.2, you can see that the jim object adopts the role of chairman in its link with the downHillSkiClub object. You indicate this on the object diagram by placing the role name at the appropriate end of the link. You can put role names at either or both ends of a link. In this case, the downHillSkiClub object always plays the role of "club" and so there is no real point in showing this on the diagram – it would not really add anything to our understanding of the object relationships.

Object diagrams
are snapshots of an
executing OO system.

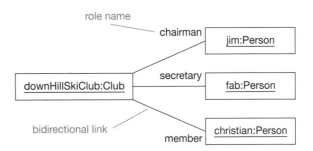

**Figure 9.2**

Figure 9.2 tells us that at a particular point in time, the object jim is playing the role of chairman. However, it is important to realize that links are *dynamic* connections between objects. In other words, they are not necessarily fixed over time. In this example, the chairman role may pass at some point to fab or christian, and we could easily create an object diagram to show this new state of affairs.

Normally, a single link connects exactly two objects as shown in Figure 9.2. However, UML does allow a single link to connect more than two objects. This is known as an n-ary link and is shown as a diamond with a path to each participating object. Many modelers (ourselves included) consider this idiom to be unnecessary. It is rarely used and UML CASE tools do not always support it, so we will not say anything more about it here.

Considering Figure 9.2 in more depth, you can see that there are three links between four objects:

- a link between downHillSkiClub and jim;
- a link between downHillSkiClub and fab;
- a link between downHillSkiClub and Christian.

In Figure 9.2, the links are bidirectional, so you can just as correctly say that the link connects jim to downHillSkiClub, or that the link connects downHillSkiClub to jim.

You can specify that the link only goes one way by placing an arrowhead on the appropriate end of the line. For example, Figure 9.3 shows that the link between :PersonDetails and :Address is unidirectional. This means that the :PersonDetails object has an object reference to the :Address object, but not vice versa. Messages can *only* be sent from :PersonDetails to :Address.

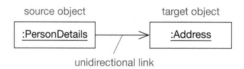

**Figure 9.3**

## 9.3.2 Paths

UML symbols, such as the object icon, use case icon, and class icon, are connected to other symbols by paths. A path is a "connected series of graphic segments" (in other words a line!) joining two or more symbols. There are two styles for drawing paths:

- orthogonal – where the path consists of a series of horizontal and vertical segments;
- oblique – where the path is a series of one or more sloping lines.

It is a matter of personal preference as to which style of path is used, and the two styles may even be mixed on the same diagram if this makes the diagram clearer and easier to read. We usually use the orthogonal style, as do many other modelers.

In Figure 9.4, we have adopted the orthogonal path style, and the paths have been combined into a tree. You can only combine paths that have the same properties. In this case, all the paths represent links and so we can legally combine them.

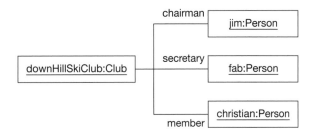

**Figure 9.4**

The visual neatness, readability, and general appeal of the diagrams is of crucial importance. Always remember that the majority of diagrams are drawn to be read by someone else. As such, no matter what style you adopt, neatness and clarity are vital.

## 9.4   What is an association?

Associations are relationships between classes. Just as links connect objects, associations connect classes. The key point is that for there to be a link between two objects, there *must* be an association between the classes of those objects. This is because a link is an instantiation of an association, just as an object is an instantiation of a class.

> Associations are connections between classes.

Figure 9.5 shows the relationship between classes and objects, and between links and associations. As you can't have a link without an association, it is clear that links *depend* on associations and you can model this with a dependency relationship (the dotted arrow) that we'll look at in more detail in Section 9.5. To make the semantics of the dependency between associations and links explicit, you stereotype the dependency «instantiate».

> Objects are instances of classes, and links are instances of associations.

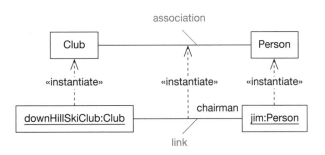

**Figure 9.5**

The semantics of the basic, unrefined association are very simple – an association between classes indicates that you can have links between objects of those classes. There are other more refined forms of association (aggregation and composition) that we'll look at in Chapter 16 in the design workflow.

### 9.4.1 Association syntax

Associations may have:

- an association name;
- role names;
- multiplicity;
- navigability.

Association names should be verb phrases as they indicate an action that the source object is performing on the target object. The name may also be prefixed or postfixed with a small black arrowhead to indicate the direction in which the association name should be read. Association names are in CamelCase starting with a lowercase letter.

In the example in Figure 9.6 you read the association as follows, "a Company employs many Persons." Although the arrow indicates the direction in which the association should be read, you can always read associations in the other direction as well. So in Figure 9.6 you can say, "each Person is employed by exactly one Company" at any point in time.

> Association names are verb phrases that indicate the semantics of the association.

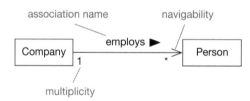

**Figure 9.6**

Alternatively, you may give role names to the classes on one or both ends of the association. These role names indicate the roles that objects of those classes play when they are linked by instances of this association. In Figure 9.7, you can see that a Company object will play the role employer, and Person objects will play the role employee when they are linked by instances of this association. Role names should be nouns or noun phrases as they name a role that objects can play.

**Figure 9.7**

> Role names are noun phrases that indicate the roles played by objects linked by instances of the association.

Associations can have *either* an association name, *or* role names – putting both role names *and* association names on the same association is theoretically legal, but this is very bad style – and overkill!

The key to good association names and role names is that they should read well. In Figure 9.6 a Company *employs* many Persons – this reads very well indeed. Reading the association the other way round, you can say that a Person *is employed* by exactly one Company at any point in time – it still reads very well. Similarly, the role names in Figure 9.7 clearly indicate the roles that objects of these classes will play when linked in this particular way.

## 9.4.2 Multiplicity

Constraints are one of the three UML extensibility mechanisms, and multiplicity is the first type of constraint that we have seen. It is also by far the most common type of constraint. Multiplicity constrains the number of objects of a class that can be involved in a particular relationship *at any point in time*. The phrase "at any point in time" is vital to understanding multiplicities. Considering Figure 9.8, you can see that at any point in time a Person object is employed by exactly one Company object. However, *over time* a Person object might be employed by a sequence of Company objects.

> Multiplicity specifies the number of objects that can participate in a relationship at any point in time.

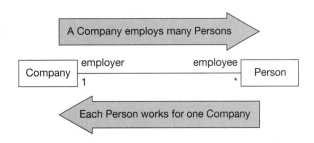

**Figure 9.8**

Looking at Figure 9.8, you can see something else that is interesting. A Person object can never be unemployed – it is always employed by exactly one Company object. The constraint therefore embodies two business rules of this model:

● that Person objects can only be employed by one Company at a time;

● that Person objects must *always* be employed.

Whether or not these are reasonable constraints depends entirely on the requirements of the system you are modeling – but this is what the model actually says.

You can see that multiplicity constraints are very important – they can encode key business rules in your model. However, these rules are "buried" in the details of the model. Literate modelers call this hiding of key business rules and requirements "trivialization". For a much more detailed discussion of this phenomenon, please see our Literate Modeling website at www.literatemodeling.com.

Multiplicity is specified as a comma-separated list of intervals, where each interval is of the form:

minimum..maximum

minimum and maximum may be integers or any expression that yields an integer result.

If multiplicity is not explicitly stated then it is undecided – there is no "default" multiplicity in UML. In fact it is a common UML modeling error to assume that an undecided multiplicity defaults to a multiplicity of 1. Some examples of multiplicity syntax are given in Table 9.1.

> If multiplicity is not explicitly stated then it is undecided.

**Table 9.1**

| Adornment | Semantics |
|---|---|
| 0..1 | Zero or 1 |
| 1 | Exactly 1 |
| 0..* | Zero or more |
| * | Zero or more |
| 1..* | 1 or more |
| 1..6 | 1 to 6 |
| 1..3,7..10,15, 19..* | 1 to 3 *or* 7 to 10 *or* 15 exactly *or* 19 to many |

> Always read the model exactly as written.

The example in Figure 9.9 illustrates that multiplicity is actually a very powerful constraint that often has a big effect on the business semantics of the model.

If you read the example carefully, you see that:

● a Company can have exactly seven employees;

● a Person can be employed by exactly one Company (i.e. in this model a Person can't have more than one job at a time);

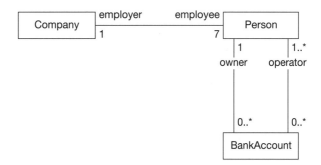

**Figure 9.9**

- a BankAccount can have exactly one owner;
- a BankAccount can have one or many operators;
- a Person may have zero to many BankAccounts;
- a Person may operate zero to many BankAccounts.

When reading a UML model, it is vital to figure out exactly what the model actually says, rather than making any assumptions, or hallucinating semantics. We call this "reading the model as written".

For example, Figure 9.9 states that a Company may have exactly seven employees, no more and no less. Most people would consider these semantics to be rather odd, or even incorrect (unless it is a very strange company), but this is what the model actually says. You must never lose sight of this.

### 9.4.2.1 *Modeling with multiplicity*

There is a certain amount of debate as to whether multiplicity should be shown on analysis models or not. We think that it should, because multiplicity describes business rules, requirements, and constraints, and can expose unwarranted assumptions made about the business. Clearly, such assumptions need to be exposed and challenged as early as possible.

As an illustrative example, consider Figure 9.10. The model states that a Person may never be unemployed and that the Company must employ exactly seven people at any point in time. But is this correct? Perhaps it is, and perhaps it isn't – it depends on the business system being modeled. However, unless you have stated multiplicities, the assumptions made may never be made explicit and may never be tested.

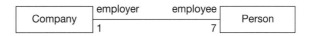

**Figure 9.10**

### 9.4.2.2   *Reflexive associations*

When class has an association to itself, it is a reflexive association.

It is quite common for a class to have an association to itself. This is called a reflexive association and it means that objects of that class have links to other objects of the same class. A good example of a reflexive association is shown in Figure 9.11. Each Directory object can have links to zero or more Directory objects that play the role subdirectory, and to zero or one Directory object that plays the role parent. In addition, each Directory object is associated with zero or more File objects. This models a directory structure quite well.

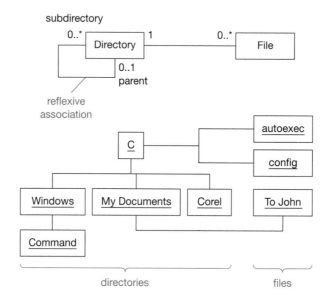

**Figure 9.11**

The top half of Figure 9.11 shows the class diagram, and the bottom half shows an example object diagram that accords with that class diagram.

### 9.4.2.3   *Hierarchies and networks*

When modeling, you'll find that objects often organize themselves into hierarchies or networks. A hierarchy has one root object, and every other node in the hierarchy has exactly one object directly above it. Directory trees naturally form hierarchies. So do part breakdowns in engineering, and elements in XML and HTML documents. The hierarchy is a very ordered, structured, and somewhat rigid way of organizing objects. An example is shown in Figure 9.12.

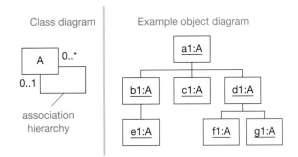

In a hierarchy an object may have zero or one object above it.

**Figure 9.12**

In the network, however, there is often no root object, although that is not precluded. In networks, each object may have many objects directly connected to it. There is no real concept of "above" or "below" in a network. It is a much more flexible structure in which it is possible that no node has primacy over another. The world wide web forms a complex network of nodes, as illustrated in a simple way in Figure 9.13.

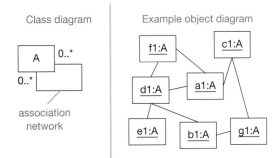

In a network an object may have zero or many objects above it.

**Figure 9.13**

As an example to illustrate hierarchies and networks, let's consider products – there are two fundamental abstractions:

- ProductType – this is a type of product, such as "Inkjet Printer";
- ProductItem – a specific ink jet printer, serial number 0001123430.

ProductTypes often tend to form networks – so a ProductType such as a computer package may consist of a CPU, screen, keyboard, mouse, graphics card and other ProductTypes. Each of these ProductTypes describes a *type* of product, not an individual item, and these types of product may participate in other composite ProductTypes, such as different computer packages.

However, if we consider the ProductItems, which are specific instances of a ProductType, any ProductItem, such as a specific CPU, can only be sold and delivered *once* as part of one package of goods. ProductItems, therefore, form hierarchies.

### 9.4.3  Navigability

Navigability
indicates that objects
of the source class
"know about" objects
of the target class.

Navigability shows us that it is possible to traverse from any object of the source class to one or more objects of the target class, depending on the multiplicity. You can think of navigability as meaning "messages can only be sent in the direction of the arrow". In Figure 9.14, Order objects can send messages to Product objects but not vice versa.

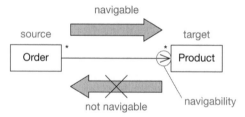

**Figure 9.14**

One of the goals of good OO analysis and design is to minimize coupling between classes, and using navigability is a good way to do this. By making the association between Order and Product unidirectional, you can navigate easily from Order objects to Product objects, but there is no navigability back from Product objects to Order objects. So Product objects *do not know* that they may be participating in a particular Order and therefore have no coupling to Order.

Even if a relationship is not navigable in a particular direction, it might *still* be possible to traverse the relationship in that direction. However, the computational cost of the traversal is likely to be very high. In the example in Figure 19.4, even though you can't navigate *directly* back from Product to Order, you could still find the Order object associated with a particular Product object by searching through all of the Order objects in turn. You have then traversed a non-navigable relationship, but the computational cost has been very high.

It is worth remembering that relationships without arrows are *always* bidirectional. Logic might suggest that if no arrows are shown then the relationship is not navigable in either direction – but then a relationship that is not navigable in any sense is not a relationship! Because of this, UML defines a relationship without any arrows as bidirectional, simply as a notational convenience.

If there is a role name on the target end of the relationship, then objects of the source class may reference objects of the target class using this role name.

In terms of implementation in OO languages, navigability implies that the source object holds an object reference to the target object. The source object may use this object reference to send messages to the target object. You could represent that on an object diagram as a unidirectional link with associated message.

> Even if an association is not navigable, it may still be possible to traverse the association but the cost will be high.

### 9.4.4 Associations and attributes

There is a close link between class associations and class attributes.

An association between a source class and a target class means that objects of the source class can hold an object reference to objects of the target class. Another way to look at this is that an association is equivalent to the source class having a pseudo-attribute of the target class. An object of the source class can refer to an object of the target class using this pseudo-attribute – see Figure 9.15.

If a navigable relationship has a role name, then it is as though the source class has a pseudo-attribute with the same name as the role name and the same type as the target class

**Figure 9.15**

There is no commonly used OO programming language that has a specific language construct to support associations. Therefore, when code is automatically generated from a UML model, one-to-one associations turn into attributes of the source class.

**Figure 9.16**

In Figure 9.16, the generated code has a House class that contains an attribute called address, which is of type Address. Notice how the role name provides the attribute name, and the class on the end of the association provides the attribute class. The Java code below was generated from the model above:

```
public class House
{
        private Address address;
}
```

You can see that there is a class House that has one attribute called address that is of type Address.

Multiplicities greater than 1 are implemented as either:

- an attribute of type array (a construct that is supported in most languages); or
- an attribute of some type that is a collection.

Collections are just classes whose instances have the specialized behavior of being able to store and retrieve references to other objects. A common Java example of a collection is a Vector, but there are many more.

This notion of pseudo-attributes is fine for one-to-one and one-to-many relationships, but it begins to break down when you consider many-to-many relationships. You will see how these are implemented in Chapter 16.

You use associations only when the target class is an important part of the model. Otherwise, you model the relationship using attributes. Important classes are business classes that describe part of the business domain. Unimportant classes are library components such as String classes, and Date and Time classes.

To some extent, the choice of explicit associations versus attributes is a matter of style – the best approach is always when the model and the diagrams express the problem clearly and precisely. Often it is clearer to show an association to another class, than to model the same relationship as an attribute which would be much harder to see. When the target multiplicity is greater than 1, this is a pretty good indication that the target is important to the model, and so you generally use associations to model the relationship.

If the target multiplicity is exactly 1, the target object may actually be just a part of the source, and so not worth showing as an association – it may be better modeled as an attribute. This is especially true if the multiplicity is exactly 1 at *both* ends of the relationship (as in Figure 9.16) where neither source nor target can exist alone.

## 9.4.5 Association classes

A common problem in OO modeling is that when you have a many-to-many relationship between two classes, there are sometimes some attributes that can't easily be accommodated in either of the classes. We can illustrate this by considering the simple example in Figure 9.17.

**Figure 9.17**

At first glance, this seems like a fairly innocuous model:

- each Person object can work for many Company objects;
- each Company object can employ many Person objects.

However, what happens if you add the business rule that each Person has a salary with each Company they are employed by? Where should the salary be recorded – in the Person class or in the Company class?

You can't really make the Person salary an attribute of the Person class as each Person instance may work for many Companies and may have a different salary with each Company. Similarly, you can't really make the Person salary an attribute of Company, as each Company instance employs many Persons all with potentially different salaries.

The answer is that the salary is actually a *property of the association itself*. For every employment association that a Person object has with a Company object, there is a specific salary for that particular employment.

UML allows you to model this situation using an association class as shown in Figure 9.18. It is important to understand this syntax – many people think that the association class is just the box hanging off the association. However, nothing could be further from the truth. The association class is actually the association line (including all role names and multiplicities), the dotted descending line, and the class box on the end of the dotted line. In short, it is the whole lot – everything shown in the indicated area.

> An association class is an association that is also a class.

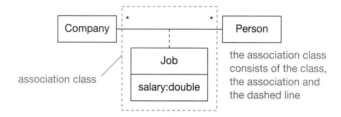

association class

the association class consists of the class, the association and the dashed line

**Figure 9.18**

In fact, an association class is an association that is *also* a class. Not only does it connect two classes like an association, it defines a set of features that belong to the association itself. Association classes can have attributes, operations, and other associations.

Instances of the association class are really *links* that have attributes and operations. The unique identity of these links is determined *exclusively* by the identities of the objects on either end. This factor constrains the semantics of the association class – you can only use it when there is a *single unique link* between two objects at any point in time. This is simply because each link, which is an instance of the association class, must have its own unique identity. In Figure 9.18, using the association class means that you constrain the model such that for a given Person object and a given Company object, there can only be *one* Job object. In other words, each Person can only have one Job with a given Company.

> An association class means that there can only be one link between any two objects at any point in time.

If, however, you have the situation where a given Person object can have more than one Job with a given Company object, then you can't use an association class – the semantics just don't match!

> A reified association allows more than one link between any two objects at a particular point in time.

But you still need somewhere to put the salary for each Person object, and so you reify (make real) the relationship by expressing it as a normal class. In Figure 9.19, Job is now just an ordinary class and you can see that a Person may have many Jobs where each Job is for exactly one Company.

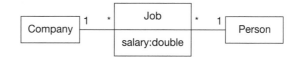

**Figure 9.19**

To be frank, many object modelers just don't understand the semantic difference between association classes and reified relationships, and the two are therefore often used interchangeably. However, the difference is really very simple – you can use association classes only when each link has a unique identity. Just remember that link identity is determined by the identities of the objects on the ends of the link.

## 9.4.6 Qualified associations

Qualified associations reduce an n-to-many association to an n-to-one association by specifying a unique object (or group of objects) from the target set. They are very useful modeling elements as they illustrate how you can look up, or navigate to, specific objects from a set.

Consider the model in Figure 9.20. A Club object is linked to a set of Member objects, and a Member object is likewise linked to a set of Club objects.

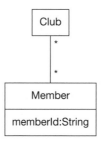

**Figure 9.20**

A qualified association selects a single member from the target set.

The following question arises – given a Club object that is linked to a set of Member objects, how could you navigate to one specific Member object? Clearly, you need some unique key that you can use to look up a particular Member object from the set. Many keys are possible (name, credit card number, social security number), but in the example above every Member object has a memberId attribute value that is unique to that object. This then, is the look-up key in this model.

You can show this look-up on the model by appending a qualifier to the Club end of the association. It is important to recognize that this qualifier belongs to the *association end* and *not* to the Club class. This qualifier specifies a unique key, and in doing so resolves the many-to-many relationship to a many-to-one relationship as shown in Figure 9.21.

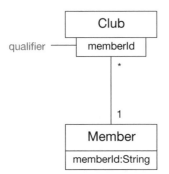

**Figure 9.21**

Qualified associations are a great way of showing how you select a specific object from the total set by using a unique key. Qualifiers *usually* refer to an attribute on the target class, but may be some other expression provided it is understandable.

## 9.5    What is a dependency?

*The UML Reference Manual* [Rumbaugh 1] states that, "A dependency is a relationship between two elements where a change to one element (the supplier) may affect or supply information needed by the other element (the client)". In other words, the client depends in some way on the supplier. We use dependencies to model relationships between classifiers where one classifier depends on the other in some way, but the relationship is not really an association.

For example, you may pass an object of one class as a parameter to a method of an object of a different class. There is clearly some sort of relationship between the classes of those objects, but it is not really an association. You can use the dependency relationship (specialized by certain predefined stereotypes) as a catch-all to model this kind of relationship. You have already seen one type of dependency, the «instantiate» relationship, but there are many more. We'll look at the common dependency stereotypes in the next sections.

UML 1.4 specifies four basic types of dependency.

> In a dependency relationship, the client depends in some way on the supplier.

**Table 9.2**

| Type | Semantics |
|------|-----------|
| Usage | The client uses some of the services made available by the supplier to implement its own behavior – this is the most commonly used type of dependency |
| Abstraction | This indicates a relationship between client and supplier, where the supplier is more abstract than the client |
| | What do we mean by "more abstract"? This could mean that the supplier is at a different point in development than the client (e.g. in the analysis model rather than the design model) |
| Permission | The supplier grants some sort of permission for the client to access its contents – this is a way for the supplier to control and limit access to its contents |
| Binding | This is quite an advanced type of dependency that we'll cover in Section 15.6. |
| | It is only relevant where the target language supports parameterized types (templates) – as such it is useful for C++ design, but not for Java, C#, Visual Basic, or Smalltalk |

Dependencies don't just occur between classes. They can commonly occur between:

● packages and packages;

● objects and classes.

They can also occur between an operation and a class, although it is quite rare to show this explicitly on a diagram. Some examples of different types of dependency are shown in Figure 9.22, and we discuss these in the remaining sections of this chapter.

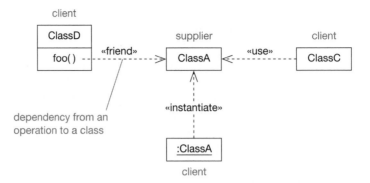

**Figure 9.22**

Most of the time, you just use an unadorned dotted arrow to indicate a dependency, and don't worry about what type of dependency it is. In fact, UML states that the type of the dependency is often clear without a stereotype just from context, and this is quite true. However, if you want or need to be more specific about the type of dependency, then UML defines a whole range of standard stereotypes that you can use.

## 9.5.1    Usage dependencies

All the usage dependencies are quite straightforward. The most common dependency stereotype is «use» which simply states that the client makes use of the supplier in some way.

### 9.5.1.1    «use»

The «use» dependency is the most common dependency between classes, and if you see just a dashed dependency arrow with no stereotype, then you can be pretty sure that «use» is intended.

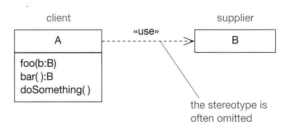

**Figure 9.23**

Figure 9.23 shows two classes, A and B, that have a «use» dependency between them. This dependency is generated by any of the following cases.

1 An operation of class A needs a parameter of class B.

2 An operation of class A returns a value of class B.

3 An operation of class A uses an object of class B somewhere in its implementation, but *not* as an attribute.

Cases 1 and 2 are straightforward, but case 3 is more interesting. You would have this case if one of the methods of class A created a transient object of class B. A Java code fragment for this case is shown in Figure 9.24 to illustrate the point.

```
Class A
{
    ...
    void doSomething()
        {
            B myB = new B();
            // Use myB in some way
            ...
        }
}
```

**Figure 9.24**

Although you can use a single «use» dependency as a catch-all for the three cases listed above, there are other more specific dependency stereotypes that you could apply.

You can model cases 1 and 2 more accurately by a «parameter» dependency, and case 3 by a «call» dependency. However, this is a level of detail that is rarely (if ever) required in a UML model and most modelers find it much clearer and easier to just put a single «use» dependency between the appropriate classes as shown above.

### 9.5.1.2 «call»
This dependency is between operations – the client operation invokes the supplier operation. This type of dependency tends not to be very widely used in UML modeling. It applies at a deeper level of detail than most modelers are prepared to go. Also, very few CASE tools currently support dependencies between operations.

### 9.5.1.3 «parameter»
This dependency is between an operation and a class. The supplier is a parameter or return value of an operation on the client. Again, this type of dependency tends not to be very widely used.

#### 9.5.1.4    «send»

The client sends the supplier (which must be a signal) to some unspecified target. We'll discuss signals in Section 13.10 but, for now, just think of them as special types of classes used to transfer data between the client and the target.

#### 9.5.1.5    «instantiate»

The client is an instance of the supplier.

### 9.5.2    Abstraction dependencies

Abstraction dependencies model dependencies between things that are at different levels of abstraction. An example might be a class in an analysis model, and the same class in the design model.

#### 9.5.2.1    «trace»

You often use a «trace» dependency to illustrate some general connection between elements where the supplier is at a different point in development to the client. The supplier could, for example, be an analysis view of a class, and the client a more detailed design view. Another example of «trace» might be from a functional requirement such as "The ATM shall allow the withdrawal of cash up to the credit limit of the card", to the use case that supports this requirement.

#### 9.5.2.2    «refine»

Whereas the «trace» dependency is a purely historical dependency that is often between two elements in different models, «refine» may be between elements in the same model. For example, you may have two versions of a class in a model, one of which is optimized for performance. As performance optimization is a type of refinement, you can model this as a «refine» dependency between the two classes, along with a note stating the nature of the refinement.

#### 9.5.2.3    «derive»

You use this stereotype when you want to show explicitly that a thing can be derived in some way from some other thing. For example, if you have a BankAccount class, and this class contains a list of Transactions where each Transaction contains a Quantity of money, you can always calculate the current balance on demand by summing Quantity over all the Transactions. There are three ways of showing that the balance of the account (a Quantity) can be derived. These are shown in Table 9.3.

**Table 9.3**

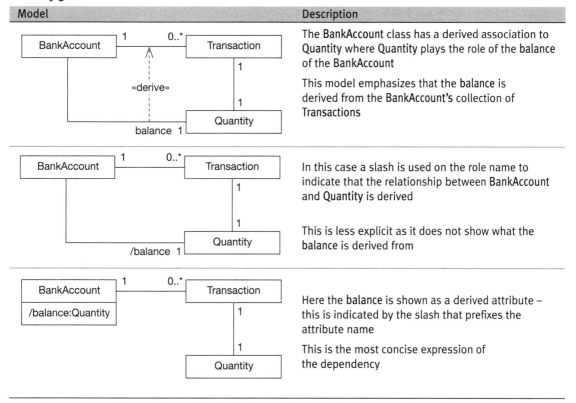

| Model | Description |
|---|---|
| | The BankAccount class has a derived association to Quantity where Quantity plays the role of the balance of the BankAccount |
| | This model emphasizes that the balance is derived from the BankAccount's collection of Transactions |
| | In this case a slash is used on the role name to indicate that the relationship between BankAccount and Quantity is derived |
| | This is less explicit as it does not show what the balance is derived from |
| | Here the balance is shown as a derived attribute – this is indicated by the slash that prefixes the attribute name |
| | This is the most concise expression of the dependency |

All of these ways of showing that balances can be derived are equivalent, although the first model in Table 9.3 is the most explicit.

## 9.5.3  Permission dependencies

Permission dependencies are about expressing the ability of one thing to access another thing.

### 9.5.3.1  «access»

This is a dependency between packages. Packages are used in UML to group things. The essential point here is that «access» allows one package to access all of the public contents of another package. However, packages each define a namespace and with «access» the namespaces remain separate. This means that items in the client package must use pathnames when they want to refer to items in the supplier package. See Chapter 11 for a more detailed discussion.

### 9.5.3.2    «import»

This is conceptually similar to «access» except that the namespace of the supplier is merged into the namespace of the client. This allows elements in the client to access elements in the supplier without having to qualify element names with the package name. However, it can sometimes give rise to namespace clashes when an element in the client has the same name as an element in the supplier. Clearly, in this case we must use pathnames to resolve the conflict. Chapter 11 provides a more detailed discussion.

### 9.5.3.3    «friend»

This type of dependency allows a *controlled* violation of encapsulation, but on the whole it should be avoided. The client element has access to the supplier element, whatever the *declared* visibility of the supplier. There is often a «friend» dependency between two very closely related classes where it is advantageous (probably for performance reasons) for the client class to access the private members of the supplier. Not all computer languages support «friend» dependencies – C++ allows «friend» between classes, but this feature has, perhaps wisely, been excluded from Java and C#.

## 9.6    What we have learned

In this chapter you have begun to look at relationships, which are the glue of UML models. You have learned the following.

- Relationships are semantic connections between things.
- Connections between objects are called links.
  - A link occurs when one object holds an object reference to another object.
  - Objects realize system behavior by collaborating together:
    - collaboration is when objects send each other messages across links;
    - when a message is received by an object, it executes the appropriate method.
  - Different OO languages implement links in different ways.
- Object diagrams show objects and their links at a particular point in time.
  - They are snapshots of an executing OO system at a particular point in time.
  - Objects may adopt roles with respect to each other – the role played by an object in a link defines the semantics of its part in the collaboration.
  - N-ary links may connect more than two objects – they are drawn as a diamond with a path to each object but are not widely used.

- Paths are lines connecting UML modeling elements:
  — orthogonal style – straight lines with right-angled bends;
  — oblique style – slanted lines;
  — be consistent and stick to one style or the other, unless mixing styles increases the readability of the diagram (it usually doesn't).

- Associations are semantic connections between classes.
  — If there is a link between two objects then there *must* be an association between the classes of those objects.
  — Links are instances of associations just as objects are instances of classes.
  — Associations may optionally have the following.
    – Association name:
      – may be prefixed or postfixed with a small black arrowhead to indicate the direction in which the name should be read;
      – should be a verb or verb phrase;
      – in CamelCase starting with a lowercase letter;
      – use either an association name or role names but *not* both.
    – Role names on one or both ends:
      – should be a noun or noun phrase describing the semantics of the role;
      – in CamelCase starting with a lowercase letter.
    – Navigability on one end:
      – shown by an arrowhead on the end of the relationship – if a relationship has no arrowhead, then it is bidirectional;
      – navigability indicates that you can traverse the relationship in the direction of the arrow;
      – you may also be able to traverse back the other way, but it will be computationally expensive to do so.
    – Multiplicity on one or both ends:
      – multiplicity indicates the number of objects that can be involved in the relationship at any point in time;
      – objects may come and go, but multiplicity constrains the number of objects at any point in time;
      – multiplicity is specified by a comma-separated list of intervals, e.g. 0..1, 3..5;
      – there is no default multiplicity – if multiplicity is not explicitly shown, then it is undecided.
  — An association between two classes is equivalent to one class having a pseudo-attribute that can hold a reference to an object of the other class:
    – you can often use associations and attributes interchangeably;
    – use association when you have an important class on the end of the association that you wish to emphasize;
    – use attributes when the class on the end of the relationship is unimportant (e.g. a library class such as String or Date).

— An association class is an association that is also a class:
  - it may have attributes, operations and relationships;
  - you can use an association class when there is exactly one unique link between any pair of objects at any point in time;
  - if a pair of objects may have many links to each other at a given point in time, then you reify the relationship by replacing it with a normal class.
— Qualified associations use a qualifier to select a unique object from the target set:
  - the qualifier must be a unique key into the target set;
  - qualified associations reduce the multiplicity of n-to-many relationships, to n-to-one;
  - they are a useful way of drawing attention to unique identifiers.

- Dependencies are relationships where a change to the supplier affects or supplies information to the client.
— The client depends on the supplier in some way.
— Dependencies are drawn as a dotted arrow from client to supplier.
— Usage dependencies:
  - «use» – the client uses the supplier as a parameter, return value or within its implementation – this is the catch-all;
  - «call» – the client operation invokes the supplier operation;
  - «parameter» – the supplier is a parameter or return value from one of the client's methods;
  - «send» – the client sends the supplier (which must be a signal) to the specified target;
  - «instantiate» – the client is an instance of the supplier.
— Abstraction dependencies:
  - «trace» – the client is an historical development of the supplier;
  - «refine» – the client is a version of the supplier;
  - «derive» – the client may be derived in some way from the supplier:
    - you may show derived relationships explicitly using a «derive» dependency;
    - you may show derived relationships by prefixing the role or relationship name with a slash;
    - you may show derived attributes by prefixing the attribute name with a slash;
— Permission dependencies:
  - «access» – a dependency between packages where the client package can access all of the public contents of the supplier package – the namespaces of the packages remain separate;

  − «import» – a dependency between packages where the client
    package can access all of the public contents of the supplier
    package – the namespaces of the packages are merged;
  − «friend» – a controlled violation of encapsulation where the client
    may access the private members of the supplier – this is not
    widely supported and should be avoided if possible.

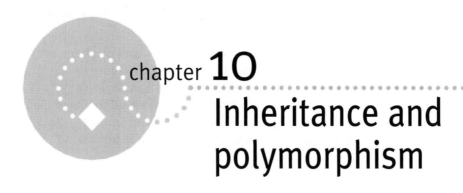

# chapter 10
# Inheritance and polymorphism

## 10.1 Chapter roadmap

In this chapter we focus on the key concepts of inheritance (Section 10.3) and polymorphism (Section 10.4). But before getting into these topics, it is important to understand the concept of generalization, which we discuss in Section 10.2.

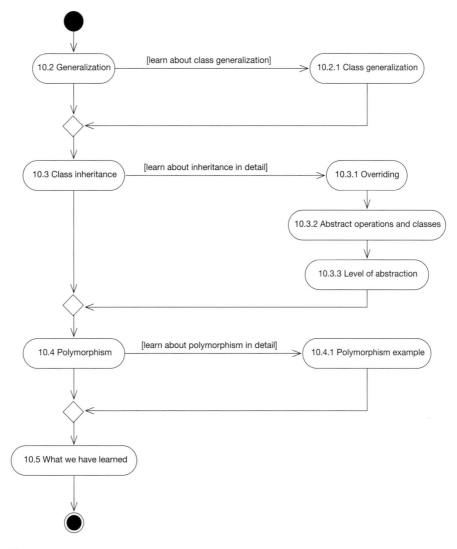

**Figure 10.1**

## 10.2  Generalization

Generalization is a
relationship between a
more general thing
and a more specific
thing.

Before we can discuss inheritance and polymorphism, we need to have a solid understanding of the idea of generalization. Generalization is a relationship between a more general element and a more specific element, where the more specific element is *entirely consistent* with the more general element, but contains more information.

The two elements obey the substitutability principle – we can use the more specific element *anywhere* the more general element is expected without breaking the system. Clearly this is a much stronger type of relationship than association, and indeed, generalization implies the very highest level of dependency (and therefore coupling) between two elements.

### 10.2.1    Class generalization

Conceptually, generalization is a very simple idea – you are already very familiar with the notion of general things such as a tree, and then more specific things such as an oak tree, which is a particular type of tree.

You have already seen generalization applied to use cases and actors, and now you will see how it is applied to classes. In fact, generalization applies to *all* classifiers and to some other modeling elements such as associations, states, events, and collaborations.

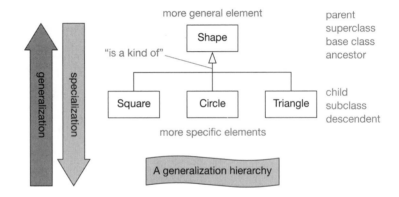

**Figure 10.2**

In Figure 10.2, we have a class called Shape – this is clearly a very general notion! From that, we derive children, subclasses, descendents (all these terms are in common use) that are more specific variants of the general idea of Shape. By the substitutability principle, we can use an instance of any of these subclasses *anywhere* an instance of the Shape superclass is expected.

As you will see when we look at the detailed attributes and operations of these classes, we could arrive at the above hierarchy in one of two ways – through either a process of specialization or a process of generalization. In specialization, we would first identify the general concept of Shape in analysis and then specialize this to specific types of shape. In generalization, we would identify the more specialized Square, Circle and Triangle in analysis, and then notice that they all have common features that we could factor out into a more general superclass.

> We create a generalization hierarchy by generalizing from more specialized things and specializing from more general things.

OO analysts tend to use both specialization and generalization hand-in-hand, although in our experience it is wise to train oneself to see the more general case as early in the analysis process as possible.

## 10.3 Class inheritance

When you arrange classes into a generalization hierarchy as shown in Figure 10.2, you implicitly have inheritance between the classes where the subclasses inherit all the features of their superclasses. To be more specific, subclasses inherit:

- attributes;
- operations;
- relationships;
- constraints.

> Subclasses inherit features from their superclass.

Subclasses can also add new features and override superclass operations. We'll look at all these aspects of inheritance in detail in the next few sections.

### 10.3.1 Overriding

In the example in Figure 10.3, the Shape subclasses Square and Circle inherit all of the attributes, operations, and constraints from the Shape superclass. This means that although you don't see these features in the subclasses, they are actually implicitly there. We say that Square and Circle are a type of Shape.

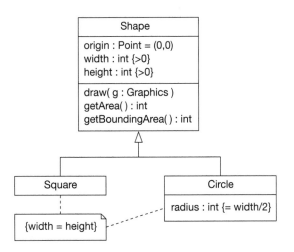

**Figure 10.3**

Notice that the operations draw() and getArea() defined in Shape can in no way be appropriate for the subclasses. You would expect a Square object, when sent the message draw(), to draw a square, and a Circle object, when sent the message draw(), to draw a circle. The default draw() operation that both subclasses have inherited from their parent clearly won't do – in fact, this operation may not draw anything at all as, after all, what should a Shape look like? The same arguments apply to getArea(). How do you calculate the area of a Shape?

These problems clearly point to the need for subclasses to be able to change superclass behavior. Square and Circle need to implement their own draw() and getArea() operations that override the default operations supplied by the parent and provide a more appropriate behavior.

Figure 10.4 shows this in action: the subclasses Square and Circle have provided their own draw() and getArea() operations that have the appropriate behaviors:

- Square::draw( g : Graphics ) – draws a square;
- Square::getArea() : int – calculates and returns the area of the square;
- Circle::draw( g : Graphics ) – draws a circle;
- Circle::getArea() : int – calculates and returns the area of the circle.

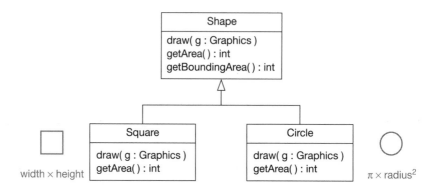

**Figure 10.4**

Subclasses override inherited operations by providing a new operation with the same signature.

To override a superclass operation, a subclass must provide an operation with *exactly* the same signature as the superclass operation it wishes to override. UML defines operation signature as the operation name, its return type, and the types of all of the parameters listed in order. The parameter names don't count, as they are just a convenient way of referring to a specific parameter within an operation body, and so are not really part of the signature.

This is all well and good, but it is important to know that different languages may define "operation signature" differently. For example, in C++ and Java, the operation return type is *not* part of the operation signature. So, if you override a superclass operation by a subclass operation that is identical apart from the return type, you will get a compiler or interpreter error in these languages.

## 10.3.2 Abstract operations and classes

Sometimes we would like to defer implementation of an operation to the subclasses. In our Shape example, the operation Shape::draw( g : Graphics ) is a case in point. We can't really provide any sensible implementation of this operation in the Shape class itself, as we just don't know how "shapes" should be drawn – the concept of "drawing a shape" is too abstract to have any concrete implementation.

> Abstract operations have no implementation.

You can specify that an operation lacks an implementation by making it an abstract operation. In UML you do this simply by writing the operation name in italics.

When you think about it, a class with one or more abstract operations is incomplete as there are some operations that don't have an implementation. This means that you can't instantiate such classes and they are therefore known as abstract classes. You write the class name in italics to show that it is abstract.

In the example in Figure 10.5, we have the abstract class *Shape* which has two abstract operations *Shape::draw( g : Graphics )* and *Shape::getArea() : int*. The implementations for these operations are provided by both the Square and the Circle subclasses. Although *Shape* is incomplete, and can't be instantiated, both of its subclasses provide the missing implementations, are complete and can be instantiated. Any class that can be instantiated is known as a concrete class.

> Abstract classes have one or more abstract operations, and they can't be instantiated.

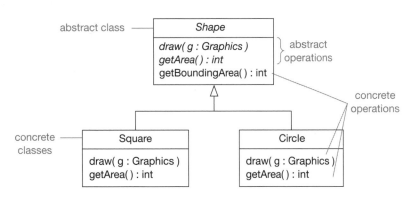

**Figure 10.5.**

The operation getBoundingArea() is a *concrete* operation of *Shape* because the bounding area of every kind of *Shape* is calculated in the exactly the same way – it is always the width of the shape multiplied by its height.

There are a couple of big advantages of using abstract classes and operations.

● You can define a set of abstract operations in the abstract superclass that must be implemented by all *Shape* subclasses. You can think of this as defining a "contract" that all concrete *Shape* subclasses *must* implement.

● You can write code to manipulate *Shapes* and then substitute Circle, Square and other *Shape* subclasses as appropriate. According to the substitutability principle, code written to manipulate *Shapes* should also work for all *Shape* subclasses.

We'll look at these advantages in greater depth when we discuss polymorphism in Section 10.4.

### 10.3.3   Level of abstraction

Before we get into polymorphism, it's a good idea to understand something about levels of abstraction. What's wrong with the model in Figure 10.6?

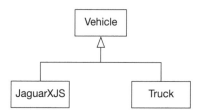

**Figure 10.6**

Things at the same level in a generalization hierarchy should be at the same level of abstraction.

The answer is "levels of abstraction". A generalization hierarchy defines a set of levels of abstraction from the most general at the top to the most specific at the bottom. You should always try to maintain a uniform level of abstraction at each level of the generalization hierarchy. In the example above, we have *not* achieved this. JaguarXJS is a *type* of car. Clearly this is a lower level of abstraction than Truck. You can fix the model quite easily by introducing a Car superclass between JaguarXJS and Vehicle.

## 10.4   Polymorphism

Polymorphism means "many forms". A polymorphic operation is one that has many implementations. You have already seen two polymorphic operations in the *Shape* example. The abstract operations *draw()* and *getArea()* in the *Shape* class have two different implementations – an implementation in the Square class and a different implementation in the Circle class. The operations have "many forms" and are therefore polymorphic.

Figure 10.7 illustrates polymorphism perfectly. We define an abstract *Shape* class with abstract operations *draw()* and *getArea()*.

Polymorphism means "many forms". Polymorphic operations have many implementations.

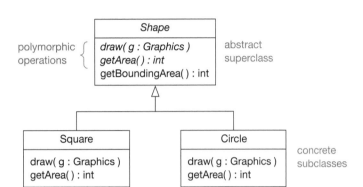

**Figure 10.7**

Square and Circle inherit from *Shape*, and provide implementations for the polymorphic operations *Shape::draw()* and *Shape::getArea()*. All concrete subclasses of *Shape must* provide concrete draw() and getArea() operations because they are abstract in the superclass. This means that for draw() and getArea() you can treat all subclasses of Shape in a similar way. A set of abstract operations is therefore a way to define a set of operations that *all* concrete subclasses *must* implement. This is known as a contract.

A concrete subclass *must* implement all the abstract operations that it inherits.

Clearly the implementation of draw() and getArea() will be different for Squares and Circles. The draw() operation will draw a square for objects of the Square class, and will draw a circle for objects of the Circle class. You can see that the getArea() operation will also have different implementations. It will return width*height for a square and $\pi*r^2$ for a circle. This is the essence of polymorphism – objects of different classes have operations with the *same* signature but *different* implementations.

Encapsulation, inheritance, and polymorphism are the "three pillars" of OO. Polymorphism allows you to design simpler systems that can more easily accommodate change because it allows you to treat different objects in the same way.

In fact, what makes polymorphism an essential aspect of OO is that it allows you to send objects of *different* classes the *same* message, and the objects respond appropriately. So if you send objects of the Square class the message draw() they will draw a square, and if you send objects of the Circle class the same message they will draw a circle. The objects seem to exhibit a kind of intelligence.

## 10.4.1 Polymorphism example

Here is an example of polymorphism in action. Suppose you have a Canvas class that maintains a collection of *Shapes*. Although this is a somewhat simplified picture, many graphics systems actually work in very much this way. The model for this simple graphics system is shown in Figure 10.8.

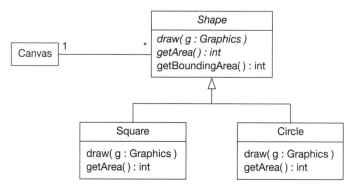

**Figure 10.8**

Now, you know that you can't create an instance of *Shape* (because it is abstract), but according to the substitutability principle, you can create instances of its concrete subclasses and substitute these anywhere a *Shape* is called for.

So, although Figure 10.8 shows that objects of type Canvas contain a collection of many *Shape* objects, the only objects that you can actually put in the collection are instances of concrete subclasses of *Shape* because *Shape* itself is abstract and can't be instantiated. In this case there are two concrete subclasses, Circle and Square, so the collection may contain Circle objects and/or Square objects.

In Figure 10.9 we have created an object model from the class diagram in Figure 10.8. This object model shows that a :Canvas object holds a collection of four *Shape* objects s1, s2, s3 and s4 where s1, s3 and s4 are objects of class Circle, and s2 is an object of class Square. What happens when the :Canvas object iterates over this collection, and sends each object in the collection the message draw()? Well, not surprisingly, each object does the right thing – Square objects draw squares, and Circle objects draw circles. It is the object's class that determines *what* the object draws – i.e. it is the object's class that determines the semantics of the set of operations that the object offers.

The key point here is that each object responds to a message by invoking the corresponding operation specified by its class. All objects of the same class will respond to the same message by invoking the same operation. This doesn't necessarily mean that all objects of the same class respond

With polymorphism, objects of different classes respond to the same message in different ways.

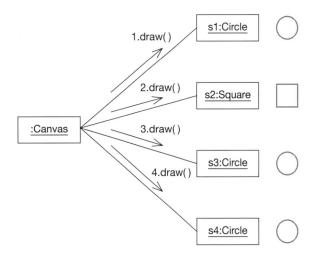

**Figure 10.9**

to the same message in exactly the same way. The results of an operation invocation often depend on the state of the object – the values of all its attributes and the state of all its relationships. For example, you might have three objects of class Square with different attribute values for width and height. When you send the message draw() to each of these objects in turn, they will each draw a square (i.e. the meaning, or semantics, of the operation remain the same) but each square will have a different size depending on the attribute values of width and height.

Here is another example. The business rules about making withdrawals and calculating interest are different depending on the type of bank account. For example, checking accounts tend to have an overdraft limit, and therefore may have a negative balance, while deposit accounts will not let the balance fall below zero. Similarly, interest is often calculated and accrued to the account differently. One simple way to model this is shown in Figure 10.10. An abstract class *Account* is defined and then concrete subclasses CheckingAccount and DepositAccount are provided. The abstract class defines abstract operations for *withdraw()* and *calculateInterest()* and these are implemented in different ways by each of the concrete subclasses.

Notice that we have also overridden the concrete deposit() operation by providing a new implementation in the ShareAccount class. Remember that to override a base class operation, all you need to do is to provide the subclass with an operation that has exactly the same signature. We have done this for ShareAccounts, because there happen to be business rules that make the process of depositing to a ShareAccount different to other types of *Account*. For example, there might be business rules that determine the minimum value of deposit that can be made. There are now two

Concrete operations may also be polymorphic – but this is bad style.

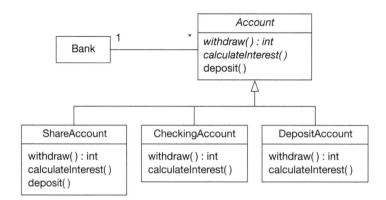

**Figure 10.10**

implementations of deposit() – one implementation in *Account* and another in ShareAccount. This means that deposit() is now a polymorphic operation. So even concrete operations like deposit() can be polymorphic!

However, overriding concrete operations is generally considered to be bad style. This is because, rather than just providing an implementation for an abstract superclass operation, we are now *ignoring* an existing implementation and providing our own. How do we know that it is safe to do this without first examining the specification of the superclass operation? Does it do something special that we don't know about? Abstract operations may always be safely overridden – that is what they are designed for. However, overriding concrete operations may have unexpected side effects and may be dangerous. Despite all this, overriding concrete superclass operations is still quite common. Often, the subclass operation just does something extra and then calls the superclass operation. In other words, it *adds* its own behavior to the superclass operation. This particular idiom is a legitimate way of reusing and extending the behavior of a concrete superclass operation as it is generally safe.

Some languages allow you to prevent subclasses from overriding a concrete superclass method. In Java, appending the keyword final to the operation signature explicitly prevents that operation from being overridden. In fact, in Java it is good style to define all operations as final except those you explicitly want to be polymorphic.

## 10.5    What we have learned

In this chapter we looked at class inheritance and polymorphism. You have learned the following.

- Generalization is a relationship between a more general thing and a more specific thing:
  — the more specific thing is consistent in every way with the more general thing;
  — the substitutability principle states that you can substitute the more specific thing anywhere the more general thing is expected;
  — generalization applies to all classifiers and some other modeling elements;
  — generalization hierarchies may be created by generalizing from specific things or by specializing from general things;
  — all things at the same level in a generalization hierarchy should be at the same level of abstraction.

- Class inheritance occurs in a generalization relationship between classes.
  — The subclass inherits the following features from its parents – attributes, operations, relationships, and constraints.
  — Subclasses may:
    – add new features;
    – override inherited operations:
      – the subclass provides a new operation with the same signature as the parent operation it wishes to override;
      – the operation signature consists of an operation name, types of all parameters in order, and return type.
  — Abstract operations are designed to have no implementation:
    – they serve as placeholders;
    – all concrete subclasses must implement all inherited abstract operations.
  — An abstract class has one or more abstract operations:
    – abstract classes can't be instantiated;
    – abstract classes define a contract as a set of abstract operations that concrete subclasses must implement.
  — Polymorphism means "many forms". It allows you to design systems to use with an abstract class and then substitute concrete subclasses at run-time – such systems are very flexible and easy to extend, just add more subclasses.
  — Polymorphic operations have more than one implementation:
    – different classes may implement the same polymorphic operation differently;
    – polymorphism allows instances of different classes to respond to the same message in different ways.

# chapter 11

# Analysis packages

## 11.1 Chapter roadmap

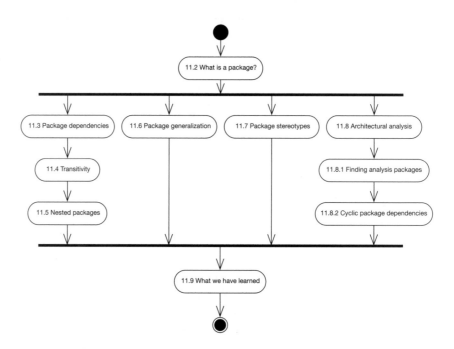

**Figure 11.1**

## 11.2 What is a package?

If we go back to the basic UML principles (Section 1.7), then we know that the set of UML building blocks consists of things, relationships, and diagrams. A package is the UML grouping thing – it is a container and owner for model elements. Each package has its own namespace within which all names must be unique.

In fact, a package is a general purpose mechanism for organizing elements and diagrams into groups. It can be used to:

- group semantically related elements;
- define a "semantic boundary" in the model;
- provide units of configuration management;
- in design, provide units for parallel working;
- provide an encapsulated namespace within which all names must be unique.

Packages let you create a navigable and well-structured model by allowing you to group things that have close semantic ties. You can create semantic boundaries in the model where different packages provide different aspects of the system functionality.

Every model element is owned by exactly one package and the ownership hierarchy forms a tree rooted in a top-level package. There is a special UML stereotype «topLevel» that can be used to mark this package. In UML CASE tools, if you don't explicitly place a modeling element in a package, then it goes into the top-level package by default. The package hierarchy also forms a namespace hierarchy where the top-level package is the root of the namespace.

Analysis packages may contain:

- use cases;
- analysis classes;
- use case realizations.

UML package syntax is quite straightforward. The package icon is a folder, and the package name may be shown on the tab or on the body of the folder. The syntax is summarized in Figure 11.2.

Elements inside a package may be given a visibility that indicates whether or not they are visible to clients of the package. The package visibilities are summarized in Table 11.1.

You can use the visibility of package elements to control the amount of coupling between packages. This can be done because the exported elements of a package act as the interface to, or the window into, the rest of the package. You must try to make this interface as small and simple as possible.

In order to ensure that a package has a small, simple interface, you need to minimize the number of public and protected package elements, and maximize the number of private package elements. This may be diffi-

*The package is the UML mechanism for grouping things.*

*Every model element is owned by one package. The packages form a hierarchy.*

*Visibility determines whether a package element is visible outside the package or not.*

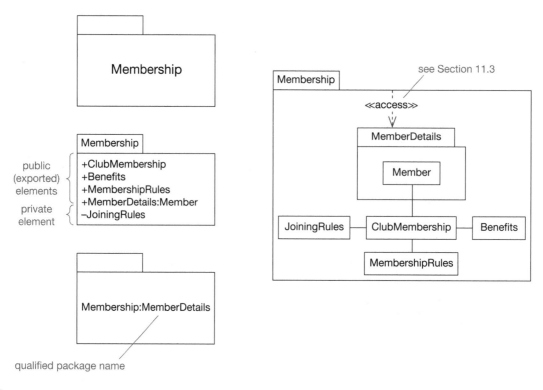

**Figure 11.2**

**Table 11.1**

| Symbol | Visibility | Semantics |
|--------|-----------|-----------|
| + | public | Elements with public visibility are visible to other packages |
| – | private | Elements with private visibility are completely hidden inside the package |
| # | protected | Elements with protected visibility are only visible to packages that are children of their package (see Section 11.5) |

cult to achieve in analysis, unless navigability is applied to the associations. Otherwise, there will be many bidirectional associations between classes, and so the classes involved in the association must either both be in the same package, or both be public. In design, relationships between classes become unidirectional, and so it is only the supplier class that needs to be public.

## 11.3    Package dependencies

A dependency relationship indicates that one package depends in some way on another.

Packages may be related to each other by a dependency. For example, looking back at Figure 11.2, any package that has a dependency relationship with the package Membership will be able to see the public elements of the package (ClubMembership, Benefits, etc.) but will not be able to see the private element JoiningRules. We say that the public elements are exported by the package.

There are four different types of package dependencies, each with different semantics. These are summarized in Table 11.2.

**Table 11.2**

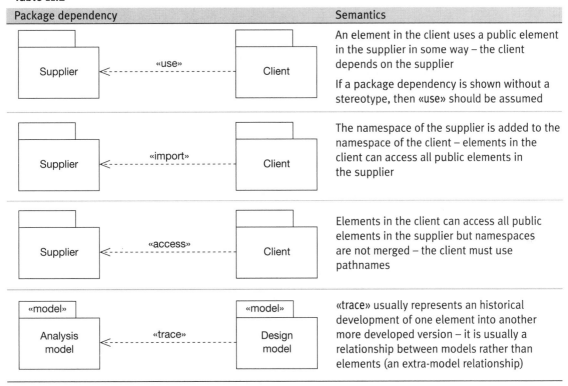

| Package dependency | Semantics |
|---|---|
| Supplier ←«use»── Client | An element in the client uses a public element in the supplier in some way – the client depends on the supplier<br><br>If a package dependency is shown without a stereotype, then «use» should be assumed |
| Supplier ←«import»── Client | The namespace of the supplier is added to the namespace of the client – elements in the client can access all public elements in the supplier |
| Supplier ←«access»── Client | Elements in the client can access all public elements in the supplier but namespaces are not merged – the client must use pathnames |
| «model» Analysis model ←«trace»── «model» Design model | «trace» usually represents an historical development of one element into another more developed version – it is usually a relationship between models rather than elements (an extra-model relationship) |

A package defines what is known as an encapsulated namespace. All this really means is that the package creates a boundary within which all the element names must be unique. It also means that when an element in one namespace needs to refer to an element in a different namespace, it has to specify both the name of the element it wants, *and* a way to navigate through nested namespaces to the namespace in which that element may be found. This is known as the pathname of the element. We discuss path-names in more detail when we look at nested packages in Section 11.5.

Namespaces give rise to an important semantic difference between the «import» and «access» dependencies. Both allow elements in a client package to access public elements in a supplier package, but they have different semantics with respect to the package namespaces.

For the «import» dependency, the supplier namespace is merged with that of the client. This means that when elements in the client package refer to elements in the supplier package, they can use the element name directly and don't have to qualify it with the package name. This is the most common type of package dependency, even though it can lead to namespace collisions where an element in the supplier has the same name as an element in the client.

On the other hand, the «access» dependency simply means that ele-ments in the client package can access public elements in the supplier package, but there is *no* merging of namespaces. Elements in the client package must *always* use pathnames to access elements in the supplier package. For example, if there is a public class A in the supplier package, then elements in the client package may access this class, but they must use a pathname that includes the package name – SupplierPackageName::A.

The «use» dependency is very similar in many ways to the «access» dependency. The essential difference is that «use» means that there are dependencies between *elements* in the packages, while «access» remains silent about any dependencies between package elements – it simply expresses a general dependency between the packages themselves. The dif-ference is subtle and doesn't make a great deal of difference from a modeling perspective. Most modelers prefer «use» or just a completely unre-fined dependency.

«trace» is the odd man out. Whereas the other package dependencies are between things in the same model, «trace» usually represents some historical development of one package into another. It therefore often shows relation-ships between *different* models. A complete UML model can be represented by a package with the stereotype «model», and in Table 11.2 we show the extra-model «trace» dependency between the analysis model and the design model. Clearly, such a diagram is a metamodel where we model the rela-tionships between models! As such, it is not used very often.

## 11.4    Transitivity

Transitivity is a term that applies to relationships. It means that if there is a rela-tionship between thing A and thing B and a relationship between thing B and thing C, then there is an implicit relationship between thing A and thing C.

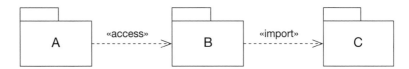

«access» and «import» are not transitive.

It is important to note, that the «access» and «import» package relationships are not transitive. There is an example in Figure 11.3 – package A accesses package B, and package B imports package C.

| A | «access» | B | «import» | C |

**Figure 11.3**

Lack of transitivity in «access» and «import» means that:

- elements in package A can see elements in package B;
- elements in package B can see elements in package C;
- elements in package A can't see elements in package C.

This lack of transitivity in «access» and «import» allows you to actively manage and control coupling and cohesion in the model. Nothing is accessed or imported unless it is *explicitly* accessed or imported – this is exactly as it should be.

## 11.5 Nested packages

Packages may be nested inside other packages to any depth. However, just two or three levels of nesting are generally enough. Much more than this, and the model may become difficult to understand and navigate.

UML gives two ways to show nesting. The first is very graphic, as it shows one package physically embedded in another. An example is shown in Figure 11.4.

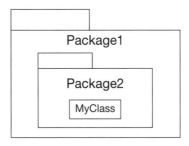

**Figure 11.4**

An alternative nesting syntax is shown in Figure 11.5. This is useful when there is a lot of nesting, or complex nesting, that might be confusing to show using embedding.

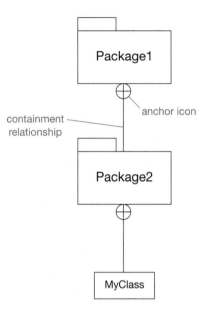

**Figure 11.5**

You can refer to nested packages or classes using a pathname. This tells you the name of the class or package, and where it is located in the nesting. It is very much the same idea as a pathname in a directory structure. In Figure 11.4 and Figure 11.5, the pathname for MyClass is Package1::Package2::MyClass.

Consider the example in Figure 11.6 – a class in package A is associated with a class from package B.

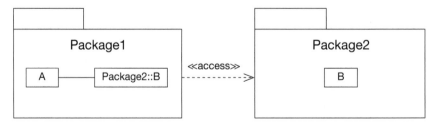

**Figure 11.6**

In Figure 11.6, Package1 is related to Package2 by an «access» dependency. This allows elements in Package1 to access public elements in Package2, but does *not* merge the namespaces of the two packages. Thus, if you need to refer to class B anywhere in Package1, you must use the pathname of B.

However, if Package1 and Package2 were related by an «import» dependency you would not need to use pathnames, as the Package2 namespace would be imported into the namespace of Package1.

A nested package can see all of the public elements in the outer package in which it is nested. The outer package can't see any of the elements of its nested packages *unless* it has an «access» or «import» dependency with those packages. This is actually very useful, as it allows you to hide implementation details inside nested packages.

In the example in Figure 11.7, there might be many classes inside the MemberDetails package, such as Name, Address, ElectronicAddress, etc., but these can all remain hidden from the view of the outer package provided that they are *private* elements in the nested package. The outer package has an «access» dependency with its nested MemberDetails package that allows it access to the public elements of that package. In this case, the MemberDetails package has a single public class called Member. The private elements of the MemberDetails package remain hidden and inaccessible.

> By default, nested packages can see the public elements of their outer package but not vice versa.

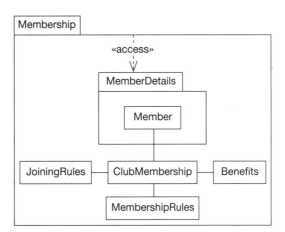

**Figure 11.7**

## 11.6  Package generalization

Package generalization is similar in many ways to class generalization. In package generalization, the more specialized child packages inherit the public and protected elements from their parent package. Child packages may add new elements, and may override elements in the parent package by providing an alternative implementation with the same name.

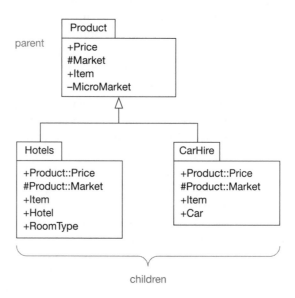

**Figure 11.8**

In the example in Figure 11.8, the Hotels and CarHire packages inherit all the public and protected members of their parent Product package. Both the Hotels and CarHire packages override the Item class inherited from their parent by providing an alternative class with the same name. Child packages may also add new elements and the Hotels package adds classes Hotel and RoomType, the CarHire package adds class Car.

Just like class inheritance, the substitutability principle must apply – anywhere we might use the Product package, we should be able to use either the Hotels or CarHire package.

> Child packages inherit elements from their parent. They may override parent elements. They may add new elements.

## 11.7  Package stereotypes

UML provides some standard stereotypes to tailor the semantics of packages for specific purposes – these are listed in Table 11.3.

The three most commonly used package stereotypes are «system», «subsystem», and «façade». Of the other two, «framework» tends not to be used very much, while «stub» may find some use in modeling distributed systems where on the client there is a stub or proxy to a package residing on the server.

**Table 11.3**

| Stereotype | Semantics |
| --- | --- |
| «system» | A package representing the entire system being modeled |
| «subsystem» | A package which is an independent part of the system being modeled |
| «façade» | A package that is only a view on some other package |
| «framework» | A package that contains patterns |
| «stub» | A package that serves as a proxy for the public contents of some other package |

## 11.8 Architectural analysis

In architectural analysis, all the analysis classes are organized into a set of cohesive analysis packages, and these are further organized into partitions and layers as illustrated in Figure 11.9. Each analysis package within a layer is a partition.

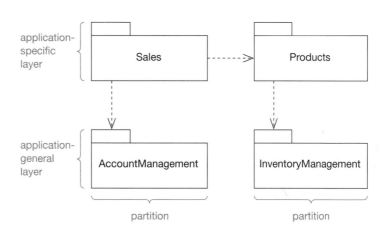

> Architectural analysis partitions related classes into analysis packages, and then layers the packages.

**Figure 11.9**

One of the goals in architectural analysis is to try to minimize the amount of coupling in the system. You can do this in three ways:

- minimize the dependencies between analysis packages;
- minimize the number of public and protected elements in each analysis package;
- maximize the number of private elements in each analysis package.

Reduction in coupling is one of the most important considerations in architectural analysis because systems that exhibit a high degree of coupling are

Always minimize
coupling.

typically complex and difficult to build and maintain. You should always try to keep coupling to the necessary minimum.

As the model deepens into a design model, so the number of layers will tend to increase. In analysis however, you can just arrange packages into application-specific and application-general layers. The application-specific layer contains functionality that is entirely specific to the particular application. The application-general layer contains functionality that is more generally useful. In Figure 11.9, AccountManagement and InventoryManagement might be reusable across several different applications, and so these packages naturally live in the application-general layer.

## 11.8.1   Finding analysis packages

Look for clusters of
classes that form a
cohesive unit.

Analysis packages are found by identifying groupings of model elements that have strong semantic connections. Analysis packages are often discovered over a period of time as the model develops and matures. It is imperative that the analysis packages reflect real, semantic groupings of elements, rather than just some idealized (but fictitious) view of the logical architecture.

Where do you begin looking for such groupings? The static model is the most useful source of packages. Look for:

- cohesive clusters of classes in the class diagrams;
- inheritance hierarchies.

You may also consider the use case model as a source of packages because it is important that you try to make packages as cohesive as possible from a business process perspective. However, it is very common for use cases to cut *across* analysis packages – one use case may be realized by classes from several different packages. Still, one or more use cases that support a particular business process or actor, or a set of related use cases, *may* indicate a potential package.

After a set of candidate packages has been identified, you should then attempt to minimize the public and protected members of the packages and the dependencies between the packages by:

- moving classes between packages;
- adding packages;
- removing packages.

The keys to good package structure are high cohesion *within* a package, and low coupling *between* packages. A package should contain a group of closely related classes. Classes are most closely related by inheritance (Chapter 10), next by composition (Chapter 16), then by aggregation (Chapter 16), and finally by dependencies (Chapter 9). Classes that are in inheritance or composition hierarchies are prime candidates for co-location in the same package. This will lead to high cohesion within the package and will probably lead to lower coupling with other packages.

As always, you should keep things simple when creating the analysis package model. It is more important to get the right set of packages than to make extensive use of features such as package generalization and dependency stereotypes. These can be added later if, and only if, they make the model more comprehensible. Part of keeping it simple is avoiding nested packages. The deeper something is buried in a nested package structure, the more obscured it becomes. We have seen models with very deeply nested packages where each package contained only one or two classes. These models were more like a standard top-down functional decomposition than an object model.

As a rule of thumb, expect to have between five and ten analysis classes per package. However, as with all rules of thumb, there will be exceptions and if breaking this rule makes the model clearer, then do so! Sometimes you need to introduce packages with just one or two classes because you need to break cyclic dependencies in the package model. In such circumstances, this is a perfectly reasonable thing to do.

## 11.8.2    Cyclic package dependencies

You should try to avoid cyclic dependencies in the analysis package model. When you think about it, if package A depends in some way on package B, and vice versa, there is a very strong argument for just merging the two packages and this is a perfectly valid way of removing cyclic dependencies. But a better approach, which very often works, is to try to factor the common elements out into a third package C. The dependency relationships are then recalculated to remove the cycle. This is shown in Figure 11.10.

Many CASE tools allow you to check the dependencies between packages automatically. The tool creates a list of access violations if an element in one package accesses an element in another package, but there is no visibility or dependency between the two packages.

In an analysis model, it can be impossible to create a package diagram that is free of access violations. This is because in analysis you often use completely unrefined (i.e. bidirectional) relationships between classes. Suppose we have a very simple model with one class in package A and another class in package B. If the class in package A has a bidirectional relationship with the class in package B, then package A depends on package B, but package B also depends on package A – we have a cyclic dependency between the two packages. The only ways to remove this violation are to

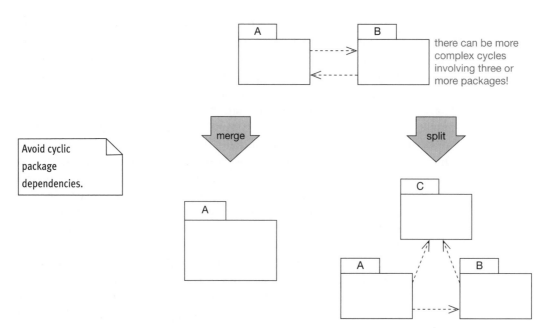

**Figure 11.10**

refine the relationship between A and B by making it unidirectional, or to put the two classes in the same package. Package dependencies thus provide an excellent argument for using navigability in analysis models! On the other hand, classes that truly have mutual dependencies (rather than dependencies that are just a feature of the incompleteness of the model) should normally live in the same package.

## 11.9   What we have learned

In this chapter we have looked at analysis packages. In particular, you have seen how you can maximize the cohesion within an analysis package and minimize the coupling between analysis packages. This helps to create more robust and maintainable systems. You have learned the following.

- The package is the UML mechanism for grouping things.
- Packages serve many purposes:
  — they group semantically related elements;
  — they create a "semantic boundary" in the model;
  — they provide units of configuration management;
  — in design, they provide units for parallel working;
  — they provide an encapsulated namespace in which all names must be unique – to access an element within the namespace you must specify both the element name and the namespace name.

- Every model element is owned by one package:
  — the packages form a hierarchy;
  — the root package may be stereotyped «topLevel»;
  — by default, model elements are placed in the «topLevel» package.

- Analysis packages may contain:
  — use cases;
  — analysis classes;
  — use case realizations.

- Package elements may have visibility:
  — visibility is used to control the coupling between packages;
  — there are three levels of visibility:
    – public (+) – elements are visible to other packages;
    – private (-) – elements are completely hidden;
    – protected (#) – elements are only visible to child packages.

- A dependency relationship between packages indicates that the client package depends in some way on the supplier package:
  — «use» – an element in the client package uses a public element in the supplier package;
  — «import» – elements in the client can access all public elements in the supplier, and the namespace of the supplier is added to the namespace of the client;
  — «access» – elements in the client can access all public elements in the supplier, but the package namespaces are not merged;
  — «trace» – the client is an historical development of the supplier; this usually applies to models rather than elements.

- Transitivity: if A has a relationship to B and B has a relationship to C, then A has a relationship to C.
  — «access» and «import» are not transitive.

- Nested packages:
  — the inner package can see all of the public members of its outer packages;
  — the outer package can't see any of the members of its inner packages, unless it has an explicit dependency to them (usually «access» or «import») – this allows you to hide implementation details in nested packages.

- Package generalization:
  — very similar to class generalization;
  — the child packages:
    – inherit elements from their parent package;
    – can add new elements;
    – can override parent elements.

- Package stereotypes:
  - «system» – a package representing the entire system being modeled;
  - «subsystem» – a package which is an independent part of the system being modeled;
  - «façade» – a package that is only a view on some other package;
  - «framework» – a package that contains patterns;
  - «stub» – a package that serves as a proxy for the public contents of some other package.

- Architectural analysis:
  - partitions cohesive sets of analysis classes into analysis packages;
  - layers analysis packages according to their semantics;
  - attempts to minimize coupling by:
    - minimizing package dependencies;
    - minimizing the number of public and protected elements in all packages;
    - maximizing the number of private elements in all packages.

- Finding analysis packages.
  - Examine analysis classes – look for:
    - cohesive clusters of closely related classes;
    - inheritance hierarchies;
    - classes are most closely related by (in order) inheritance, composition, aggregation, dependency.
  - Examine use cases:
    - clusters of use cases that support a particular business process or actor *may* have analysis classes that should be packaged together;
    - related use cases *may* have analysis classes that should be packaged together;
    - be careful – analysis packages often cut across use cases!
  - Refine the package model to maximize cohesion within packages and minimize dependencies between packages by:
    - moving classes between packages;
    - adding packages;
    - removing packages;
    - remove cyclic dependencies by merging packages or by splitting them to factor out coupled classes.

# chapter 12

# Use case realization

## 12.1 Chapter roadmap

This chapter has three main parts – general background about the UP activity "Analyze a use case" and collaborations and interactions (Sections 12.2 to 12.6), a detailed discussion of collaboration diagrams (Section 12.7), and a detailed discussion of sequence diagrams (Section 12.8).

Collaboration and sequence diagrams are just two views of the same underlying object interaction. We are, therefore, in danger of repeating material unnecessarily. Our approach is to give the most detailed discussion of interaction diagram semantics in the section on collaboration diagrams, and present a summarized form in the section on sequence diagrams. If you choose to read the section on sequence diagrams first, please remember that a more detailed discussion is available in the corresponding collaboration diagram sections.

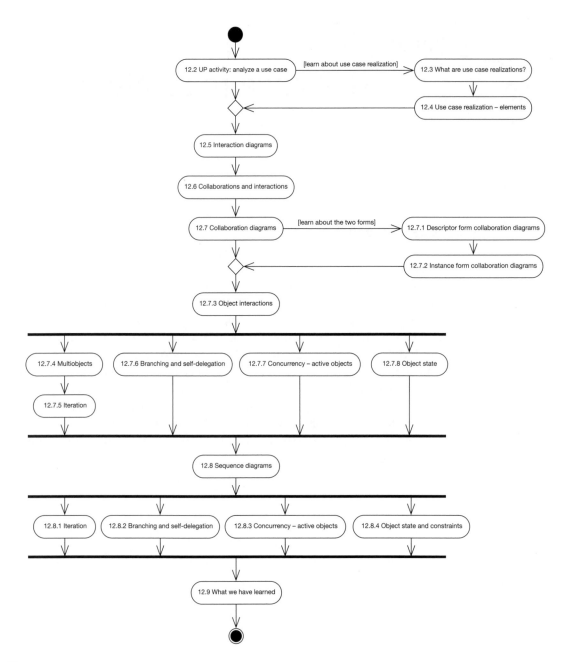

**Figure 12.1**

## 12.2    UP activity: analyze a use case

In previous chapters, you have seen how the analysis class artefact of the "Analyze a use case" activity is produced. The second artefact produced by this activity is the use case realization, as shown in Figure 12.2.

Analysis classes model the static structure of a system, and use case realizations show how instances of the analysis classes interact to realize the functionality of the system. This is part of the dynamic view of the system.

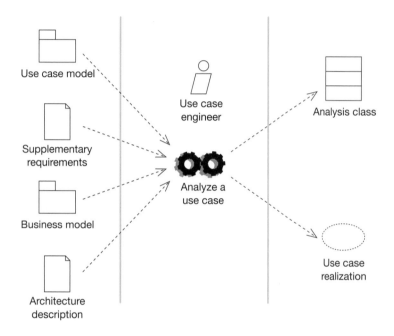

**Figure 12.2**    Adapted from Figure 8.25 [Jacobson 1] with permission from Addison-Wesley

## 12.3    What are use case realizations?

Use case realizations show how classes collaborate to realize system functionality.

The key to analysis, after finding the analysis classes, is finding the use case realizations. These consist of sets of classes that realize the behavior specified in a use case. For example, if you have a use case BorrowBook and have identified the analysis classes Book, Ticket, Borrower, and the actor Librarian, then you need to create a use case realization that demonstrates how these classes, and objects of these classes, interact to realize the behavior specified in BorrowBook. In this way, you turn a use case (which is a specification of functional requirements) into class diagrams and interaction diagrams (which are a high-level specification of a system).

Although UML provides a symbol for use case realizations, as shown in Figure 12.3, they are rarely modeled explicitly. This is simply because each use case has *exactly one* use case realization and so there is no extra information to be captured in creating a use case realization diagram. Instead, you just add the appropriate elements (see Table 12.1) to the CASE tool and let the use case realizations be an implicit part of the backplane of the model.

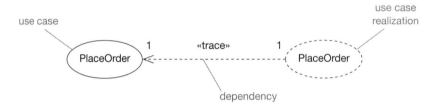

**Figure 12.3**

## 12.4    Use case realization – elements

Use case realizations consist of the elements shown in Table 12.1.

**Table 12.1**

| Element | Purpose |
| --- | --- |
| Analysis class diagrams | Show the analysis classes that interact to realize the use case |
| Interaction diagrams | Show collaborations and interactions between specific instances that realize the use case – they are "snapshots" of the running system |
| Special requirements | The process of use case realization may well uncover new requirements specific to the use case – these must be captured |
| Use case refinement | New information may be discovered during realization that means the original use case has to be updated |

Use case realization is fundamentally a process of refinement. You take a specification of one aspect of the system's behavior as captured in a use case and associated supplementary requirements, and then model how this may be realized by collaborations and interactions between instances of the analysis classes that you have identified. You go from a general specification of required behavior to a fairly detailed description of the interactions between classes and objects that will actually make this behavior real.

> Analysis class diagrams "tell a story" about one or more use cases.

Analysis class diagrams are a vital part of a use case realization. They should "tell a story" about the system – about how a set of classes are related such that instances of those classes can collaborate to realize the behavior specified in one (or more) use cases.

As well as analysis class diagrams, you can create diagrams that demonstrate explicitly how specific objects of those analysis classes collaborate together and interact to realize some, or all, of the use case behavior. These diagrams are known as interaction diagrams, and there are two types – collaboration diagrams and sequence diagrams. We'll look at both types in this chapter.

> Interaction diagrams show how objects interact to realize system behavior.

OO modeling is an iterative process, and so you should not be too surprised if you uncover new requirements, or if you need to modify existing use cases once you begin to model in more depth. This is all part of use case realization – you must keep existing documents up to date as you uncover more information about the system. As such, you must update any requirements documents, and refine the use case you are working on if need be.

## 12.5 Interaction diagrams

> Collaboration and sequence diagrams provide different views of the same underlying object interaction.

UML interaction diagrams model collaborations and interactions between objects that realize a use case, or part of a use case. In fact there is a common underlying UML model of object interactions that has two views.

- Collaboration diagrams – these emphasize the structural relationships between objects and are very useful in analysis, especially for creating a quick sketch of an object collaboration.

- Sequence diagrams – these emphasize the time-ordered sequence of message sends between objects. Users tend to be able to understand sequence diagrams better than collaboration diagrams, as they are much easier to read. Collaboration diagrams have a tendency to get cluttered very quickly.

The fact that collaboration and sequence diagrams are just two different representations of a single underlying UML model means that they are isomorphic. Because of this, most CASE tools can automatically convert between the two forms.

Both types of interaction diagrams come in two flavours.

- Descriptor form – this describes the collaborations and interactions between *roles* that instances of classifiers may play in the system.

- Instance form – this describes collaborations and interactions between *actual* instances of classifiers.

Remember, from Chapter 1, that UML has many different types of classifier and instance. Most of the time, when you are working with interaction diagrams, the classifier you use is a class and the instance is an object. However, it is always worth remembering that other types of classifier and instance may appear in these diagrams where appropriate. We'll see a specific example of this in Chapter 18.

## 12.6 Collaborations and interactions

Before we look at interaction diagrams and their role in use case realization, you need to be clear about the UML concepts of collaboration, interaction, and roles.

- A collaboration describes a static set of relationships between instances, and the roles that instances play in those relationships.

- An interaction describes the dynamic interaction between instances. It describes the messages that instances send to each other. Before instances can send each other messages, they *must* have a relationship to each other – so an interaction can *only* arise within the context of a collaboration.

- A role is one particular way in which something may behave or may be used. As well as instances and links, interaction diagrams may have classifier roles, which define ways in which instances of classifiers may be used, and association roles, which define ways in which instances of associations (links) may be used.

You can think of a collaboration as a set of instances and the relationships between them, and an interaction as one specific way that those instances may interact with each other by sending messages over the relationships. Roles define the way something may behave or be used in a specific collaboration.

A real-world example may be useful. One of the authors has a single long-standing collaboration with Zühlke Engineering. But this involves many different interactions with them – delivering training (role: trainer), doing consultancy (role: consultant), delivering course materials (role: author), etc.

## 12.7 Collaboration diagrams

Collaboration diagrams focus on the structural aspects of object interaction. They come in two different forms – the descriptor form, and the instance form. The descriptor form gives a very generic view of a collaboration by specifying the roles played by instances – these are known as classifier roles. It also

Collaboration diagrams emphasize the structural aspects of an object interaction.

specifies the relationships between those roles – these are known as association roles. The instance form collaboration diagram is much more concrete. It shows actual classifier instances (usually objects) and links between those instances. The two forms have slightly different capabilities in terms of the information that they can capture. These differences are summarized in Table 12.2.

**Table 12.2**

| Collaboration diagram contents | |
| --- | --- |
| Descriptor form | Instance form |
| Classifier roles (usually roles played by classes) | Instances (usually objects) |
| Association roles (roles played by associations) | Links |
| Messages | Messages |
| – | Iteration |
| – | Branching |

The key difference is that you can't sensibly show iteration or branching on the descriptor form collaboration diagram. This is because iteration and branching are predicated on the existence of instances, but the descriptor form has no instances, only roles.

The instance form of the collaboration diagram is the most useful and most widely used as it allows you to show specific object interactions. As it deals with actual instances, it is more concrete than the descriptor form and is easier to visualize in some ways.

### 12.7.1  Descriptor form collaboration diagrams

The descriptor form of the collaboration diagram shows roles that are to be played by unspecified instances of classifiers (usually classes), and unspecified instances of associations (links). It *doesn't* show specific instances or links. This can be quite useful if you want to model a collaboration in a very general way.

The easiest way to understand descriptor form collaboration diagrams is to take a simple example. Look at the class diagram shown in Figure 12.4.

In this diagram, the class Party represents the notion of a person or a business that has a name and address, but we've hidden the name attribute as it doesn't concern us here. In a real system, this general idea of Party is usually specialized to more specific things such as Person and Business – but we'll work at this level for now to keep it simple.

Classifier role – a role played by instances of the classifier.

The descriptor form collaboration diagram for this model is shown in Figure 12.5. This diagram shows classifier roles and association roles. A clas-

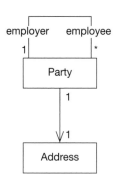

**Figure 12.4**

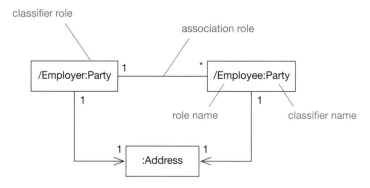

**Figure 12.5**

> **Association role – a role played by instances of the association.**

sifier role is a role that may be played by an instance of the classifier, and an association role indicates a role that may be played by an instance of the association (a link).

Although this diagram contains much the same information as the class diagram, it has allowed us to emphasize the different roles that are played by instances of the classes. As such, it is sometimes useful. Classifier roles are named as follows:

/RoleName:ClassifierName

The role name must *always* be prefixed by a slash, and the classifier name must *always* be prefixed by a colon. Both the role name and classifier name are optional but one of them *must* be present. You can leave out the classifier name if you just want to indicate that an instance plays a particular role, but don't want to specify its class at that point in time. Similarly, you can omit the role name when you want to show that a classifier plays a role in the collaboration, but don't want to name that role. You can see an example of this in Figure 12.5.

### 12.7.2   Instance form collaboration diagrams

The instance form collaboration diagram shows the collaboration between classifier instances. These instances are joined by links. Figure 12.6 shows the instance form of Figure 12.5.

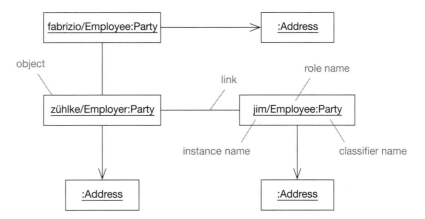

**Figure 12.6**

Instance form collaboration diagrams show specific instances collaborating at a particular point in time. They are like a snapshot of an executing OO system. Instances are named as follows:

instanceName/ClassifierRoleName:ClassifierName

The classifier role name is *always* prefixed by a slash, and the classifier name is *always* prefixed by a colon. All parts of this name are optional but at least one of the parts *must* be present. The classifier role name may correspond to a role name in a descriptor form collaboration diagram if an appropriate diagram exists.

### 12.7.3   Object interactions

Up to now, neither the descriptor form nor the instance form collaboration diagrams that we have seen show any interactions between the classifier roles or instances. They merely show the context in which interactions *may* occur. However, in order to use these diagrams effectively as part of a use case realization, you need to show how, specifically, objects in our system realize the behavior specified in the use case. You do this by adding interactions to the collaboration diagrams. Let's take as an example a simple course registration system. The use case we are going to realize is called AddCourse and its specification is given in Figure 12.7.

| Use case: AddCourse |
|---|
| **ID: UC8** |
| **Actors:**<br>Registrar |
| **Preconditions:**<br>The Registrar has logged on to the system. |
| **Flow of events:**<br>1.  The Registrar selects "add course".<br>2.  The system accepts the name of the new course.<br>3.  The system creates the new course. |
| **Postconditions:**<br>A new course has been added to the system. |

**Figure 12.7**

We have kept this use case specification as simple as possible so that we can focus on object interactions rather than use case modeling. Use cases are discussed in detail in Chapter 4.

From this use case, we can use the standard analysis techniques (described in Chapter 8) to obtain the classes shown in Table 12.3.

**Table 12.3**

| Element | Type | Semantics |
|---|---|---|
| Registrar | Actor | Is responsible for maintaining the course information in the course registration system |
| Course | Class | Contains details of a course |
| RegistrationManager | Class | Is responsible for maintaining a collection of Courses |

The RegistrationManager class was not mentioned explicitly in the use case specification for AddCourse. However, the responsibility of "maintaining collections of Courses" is implicit in AddCourse and so we introduce RegistrationManager to be the thing in the system that fulfils that responsibility.

The class diagram part of the use case realization would look like Figure 12.8.

**Figure 12.8**

An instance form collaboration diagram that realizes the behavior specified in AddCourse is given in Figure 12.9. In this collaboration diagram, we create two new Course objects, and so the use case actually executes *twice*.

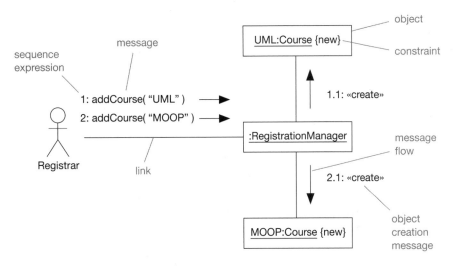

**Figure 12.9**

Figure 12.9 summarizes quite a lot of collaboration diagram syntax. You have already seen how objects and links are represented – objects are shown as boxes with the object name underlined, and links are shown as lines connecting the objects. Messages are shown as labeled arrows. These are placed near the appropriate association role or link. Message syntax is summarized here:

SequenceExpression returnValue := messageName( argument1, argument2, … )

The sequence expression indicates the order in which the message will be sent – it is usually a number. The return value is the name of a variable that holds any return value from the message – usually, this variable will be an attribute value of the object that sends the message.

The message name should start with a lowercase letter and be in CamelCase. The arguments are the parameter list for the message. The arrowhead indicates the type of communication that the message represents. The possibilities are summarized in Table 12.4.

When objects receive a message, they invoke an operation that has the same signature. So, for every message, there must be a corresponding operation in the class of the target object. UML allows the messages on interaction diagrams and the operations on classes to get out of step so that you can work on the model dynamically and flexibly, but by late analysis or design they *must* be brought into step.

**Table 12.4**

| Message flow | Semantics |
|---|---|
| ———————▶ | Procedure call – the sender waits until the receiver has finished |
| | This is the most common option |
| ———————▷ | Asynchronous communication – the sender carries on as soon as the message has been sent; it does not wait for the receiver |
| | This is often used when there is concurrency |
| ·····················▷ | Return from a procedure call – the return is always implicit in a procedure call, but it may be explicitly shown using this arrow |

When an object is performing an operation it is said to have focus of control. As the collaboration progresses over time, the focus of control moves between objects – this movement is the flow of control.

UML provides standard constraints that can be used to indicate creation and destruction of instances or links in an interaction. These are summarized in Table 12.5.

**Table 12.5**

| Constraint | Semantics |
|---|---|
| {new} | The instance or link is created in the interaction |
| {destroyed} | The instance or link is destroyed in the interaction |
| {transient} | The instance or link is created and then destroyed in the interaction – this is equivalent to using {new} and {destroyed} together, but it is clearer |

To demonstrate how collaboration diagrams work, and to show what information they can capture, Table 12.6 provides a walkthru of the example in Figure 12.9.

At first, these diagrams can be somewhat tricky to read as there is quite a lot going on. The key point is to realize that the message sends result in a function (i.e. an operation in analysis) being called on an object, and that the sequence numbering indicates the nesting of function calls within function calls. These are referred to as "nested flows of control".

As you work on collaboration diagrams, you begin to uncover more and more of the operations and attributes of the analysis classes. The analysis class diagrams should be updated with this information as part of the use case realization process.

**Table 12.6**

| Walkthru for Figure 12.9 | |
| --- | --- |
| 1: addCourse( "UML" ) | The message **addCourse** is sent to the object **:RegistrationManager** with the parameter "UML". The **:RegistrationManager** object invokes an operation called addCourse( ... ) with the parameter "UML" and focus of control passes to this operation. |
| 1.1: «create» | As the sequence number is 1.1, this tells us that we are still within the focus of control of the operation **addCourse**. The **:RegistrationManager** sends an anonymous message which is stereotyped «create». These «create» messages create new objects, and this particular message creates a new object, <u>UML:Course</u>. This object has the constraint **{new}** which means that it is created in this collaboration and did not exist previously. We will give this anonymous message a name, and possibly parameters, later in analysis or design but for now it is sufficient to show that we are creating a new <u>UML:Course</u> object. After object creation, there are no more messages sent within the focus of control of addCourse( ... ), and this flow returns. |
| 2: addCourse( "MOOP" ) | The message **addCourse**( ... ) is sent to the object **:RegistrationManager** with the parameter "MOOP". The **:RegistrationManager** invokes an operation called addCourse( ... ) with the parameter "MOOP". Focus of control passes to the operation addCourse( ... ). |
| 2.1: «create» | As the sequence number is 2.1, this tells us that we are still within the focus of control of addCourse( ... ). The **:RegistrationManager** sends an anonymous message which is stereotyped «create» which creates a new object, <u>MOOP:Course</u>. Again, the newly created object has the constraint **{new}** which means that it is created in this collaboration and did not exist previously. After object creation, the focus of control of addCourse( ... ) returns. |

## 12.7.4   Multiobjects

> Multiobjects represent sets of objects.

A multiobject represents a set of objects – it provides a way to represent a collection of objects in collaboration diagrams. Messages sent to the multiobject go to the set and *not* to any individual object.

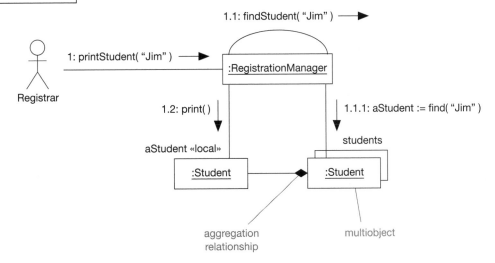

**Figure 12.10**

The example in Figure 12.10 is also from our simple course registration system. The use case that this collaboration diagram realizes is called PrintStudentDetails. In this example, our mission is to print out the details of a specific student uniquely identified by the name "Jim". We proceed as follows.

**Table 12.7**

| Walkthru for Figure 12.10 | |
| --- | --- |
| 1: printStudent( "Jim" ) | The Registrar actor sends the message printStudent( "Jim" ) to the :RegistrationManager object. The :RegistrationManager first has to find the required Student object from the set of students that it manages. |
| 1.1: findStudent( "Jim" ) | The :RegistrationManager sends itself the message findStudent( "Jim" ). This is known as self-delegation. |
| 1.1.1: find( "Jim" ) | The :RegistrationManager sends the message find("Jim") to the multiobject called students. This message *does not* go to any individual object in the multiobject set, but rather to the multiobject itself. An object reference to the required Student is returned in the local variable aStudent. |
| 1.2: print() | The :RegistrationManager object sends the message print() to the object referenced by the local variable aStudent. Notice how we have pulled the right object out of the multiobject set so that we can send a message to it. We use the stereotype «local» to indicate that this object reference is local to the printStudent() operation of the :RegistrationManager. We can tell this by looking at the sequence numbers – we are at 1.1, and so we are still within the focus of control of the :RegistrationManager's printStudent() operation. |

The aggregation relationship between the multiobject called students and the local object called aStudent, simply indicates that the object referenced by aStudent is actually part of the multiobject set.

Although UML tells us that a multiobject is a set of objects, it doesn't tell us what methods multiobjects support. This is because when you come to detailed design, each multiobject will be replaced by a specific instance of a particular collection class. However, in analysis you commonly assume that multiobjects may be sent the following messages:

If you prefix a message to a multiobject with *, then it is sent to each object in the multiobject set.

- find( uniqueIdentifier ) – returns a specific object given a unique identifier as a parameter;
- includes( anObject ) – returns true if the multiobject includes anObject;
- count() – returns the number of objects in the multiobject.

If a message sent to a multiobject is prefixed with the iteration specifier (*), then the message is sent to each element in the multiobject.

If you want to send a message to a specific instance in the multiobject set, then you have to do two things:

- find the instance you want in the set;
- send a message to that instance.

In order to show the message being sent to a specific instance, you need to show the instance *outside* the multiobject set, but still connected to it by an aggregation relationship as shown in Figure 12.10. We discuss the detailed semantics of aggregation relationships in Chapter 16 but, for now, just think of it as meaning "part of".

## 12.7.5  Iteration

Iteration allows you to repeat a message sent according to an iteration expression.

You show iteration by prefixing the sequence number with the iteration specifier (*) and an optional iteration expression. There is no formal UML syntax for the iteration expression, and any expression that is readable and makes sense will do. Some common iteration expressions are given in Table 12.8.

**Table 12.8**

| Iteration expression | Semantics |
| --- | --- |
| [i := 1..n] | Iterate n times |
| [i := 1..7] | Iterate 7 times |
| [while (some Boolean expression)] | Iterate while the Boolean expression is true |
| [until (some Boolean expression)] | Iterate until the Boolean expression is true |
| [for each (expression which evaluates to a collection of objects)] | Iterate over the contents of a collection of objects |

If there is an iteration specifier, but no iteration expression, then you iterate over the whole set.

The example in Figure 12.11 shows an iteration expression by which we iterate over the collection of courses, and print out each one in turn. Notice how you use the iteration counter (i) as a qualifier to select a specific object from the multiobject set. You then send the selected object the print message.

You can achieve exactly the same effect by removing the qualifier, and just sending the print message prefixed by the iteration specifier directly to the multiobject. However, in Figure 12.11 we have chosen to be very specific about how the iteration works, and about how we index into the multiobject. As such, it is more of a design model than an analysis model.

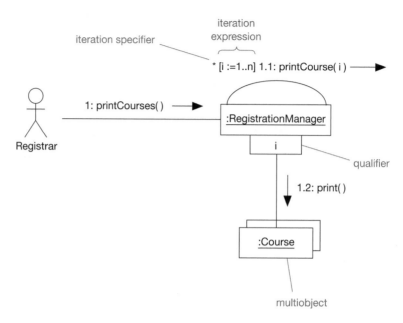

**Figure 12.11**

The iteration specifier (*) always indicates sequential processing of multi-object instances. However, sometimes you will want to indicate that some instances are processed at the same time in parallel. For this special case, you can use the iteration specifier followed by two slashes to indicate parallel processing (*//).

## 12.7.6 Branching and self-delegation

> Branching – the message is only sent if the condition is true.

You can model branching simply by adding conditions before the messages. A condition is a Boolean expression that evaluates to true or false. The message is only sent when the condition evaluates to true.

Figure 12.12 shows an example of branching in our course registration system. This collaboration diagram realizes the use case RegisterStudentForCourse. In this registration system, registration is a three-step process:

● find the right student record – we can't register students for courses unless they are in the system;

● find the right course;

● register the student with the course.

Self-delegation is when an object calls itself. There is an example in steps 1.1 and 1.2 of Figure 12.12. Self-delegation is very common in OO systems. Objects offer a set of public services (the public operations) that can be called

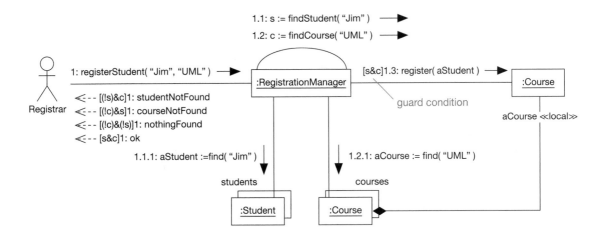

**Figure 12.12**

by client objects, but they also, generally, have a set of private "helper" operations that are specifically designed to be called by the object itself.

In Figure 12.12, we have made extensive use of conditions to show how they may be applied in collaboration diagrams. Conditions have no formal syntax, but are often expressions that involve temporary variables in the scope of the current focus of control, or attributes of the classes involved in the collaboration. In Figure 12.12, we record the success or failure of the findStudent(...) and findCourse(...) methods in two temporary variables s and c. We then use the values of these variables to make a branch at step 1.3, and finally to decide what we return to the Registrar. A complete walkthru for Figure 12.12 is given in Table 12.9.

It is quite difficult to show branching clearly on collaboration diagrams – the conditions seem to spread out all over the diagram and it can get complex quite quickly. As a general style guideline, only show very simple branching on these diagrams. It is much easier to show complex branches on sequence diagrams, which we'll look at shortly.

### 12.7.7 Concurrency – active objects

It is easy to model concurrency with collaboration diagrams. The basic principle is that each thread of control or concurrent process is modeled as an active object. This is an object that encapsulates its own thread of control.

Active objects execute concurrently and may each have focus of control simultaneously. Active objects are drawn just like a normal object but with a heavy border. The property keyword {active} may also be included in the object box if desired.

> Concurrency – each active object has its own thread of execution.

**Table 12.9**

| | Walkthru for Figure 12.12 |
|---|---|
| 1: registerStudent( "Jim", "UML" ) | The Registrar actor sends the message registerStudent( "Jim", "UML" ) to the :RegistrationManager object. |
| 1.1: findStudent( "Jim" ) | The :RegistrationManager sends itself the message findStudent( "Jim" ). The return value from this operation is stored in the variable s. It will be true if the search succeeded or false if it failed. |
| 1.1.1: find( "Jim" ) | The :RegistrationManager sends the message find( "Jim" ) to the multiobject called students. If the search succeeds, an object reference to the required Student is returned in the local variable aStudent. |
| 1.2: findCourse( "UML" ) | The :RegistrationManager sends itself the message findCourse( "UML" ). The return value from this operation is stored in the variable c. It will be true if the search succeeded or false if it failed. |
| 1.2.1: find( "UML" ) | The :RegistrationManager sends the message find( "UML" ) to the multiobject called courses. If the search succeeds, an object reference to the required Course is returned in the local variable aCourse. |
| [s&c]1.3: register( aStudent ) | The :RegistrationManager sends the message register( aStudent) to the Course object. This message is protected by a condition and will only be sent if both s and c are true. In other words, we only attempt to register the Student with the Course if both the Student and the Course objects have been found. |
| [s&c]1: ok | registerStudent(...) returns ok if the Student was successfully registered with the Course (s and c are both true). |
| [(!s)&c]1: studentNotFound | registerStudent(...) returns studentNotFound if the Student could not be found (s is false). |
| [(!c)&s]1: courseNotFound | registerStudent(...) returns courseNotFound if the Course could not be found (c is false). |
| [(!c)&(!s)]1: nothingFound | registerStudent(...) returns nothingFound if neither the Student nor the Course could be found (s and c are both false). |

Concurrency tends to be very important for embedded systems, such as the software that operates a photo-processing machine or an automated teller machine. So to investigate concurrency, we will consider a very simple embedded system – a security system. This security system monitors a set of sensors that can detect fire or intrusions. When a sensor is triggered, the system sounds an alarm. The use case model for the security system is shown in Figure 12.13.

The use case specifications for the system are given in Figure 12.14 – we don't consider the use case ActivateFireOnly as we are focusing on the concurrent aspects of the system in this section.

As well as the functional requirements expressed in the use cases, the system has two non-functional requirements of relevance to us.

- The security system shall be activated and deactivated using a key.

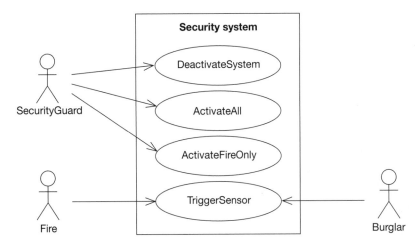

**Figure 12.13**

- The key switches between three modes – system deactivated, fire and security sensors activated, fire sensors only activated.

The classes are found through the following considerations. With embedded systems, the hardware that the system executes on can be an excellent source of classes. In fact, it is often the case that the best software architecture tends to be a close match with the physical hardware architecture. In this case, the alarm hardware consists of four components – the control box, the siren, the fire sensors, and the security sensors. Opening up the control box reveals that there is a controller card for each different type of sensor.

| Use case: DeactivateSystem |
|---|
| **ID: UC1** |
| **Actors:**<br>SecurityGuard |
| **Preconditions:**<br>The SecurityGuard has the activation key. |
| **Flow of events:**<br>1. The SecurityGuard uses the activation key to switch the system off.<br>2. The system stops monitoring security sensors and fire sensors. |
| **Postconditions:**<br>The security system is deactivated.<br>The security system is *not* monitoring the sensors. |

| Use case: ActivateAll |
|---|
| **ID: UC2** |
| **Actors:**<br>SecurityGuard |
| **Preconditions:**<br>The SecurityGuard has the activation key. |
| **Flow of events:**<br>1. The SecurityGuard uses the activation key to switch the system on.<br>2. The system begins monitoring security sensors and fire sensors.<br>3. The system pips the siren to indicate that it is armed. |
| **Postconditions:**<br>The security system is activated.<br>The security system is monitoring the sensors. |

| Use case: TriggerSensor |
|---|
| **ID: UC3** |
| **Actors:**<br>Fire<br>Burglar |
| **Preconditions:**<br>The security system is activated. |
| **Flow of events:**<br>1. If the Fire actor triggers a FireSensor<br>  1.1. The Siren sounds the fire alarm.<br>2. If the Burglar actor triggers a SecuritySensor<br>  2.1. The Siren sounds the security alarm. |
| **Postconditions:**<br>The Siren sounds. |

**Figure 12.14**

Given the use cases, and the information about the physical hardware, a class diagram can be derived for this system – it is shown in Figure 12.15.

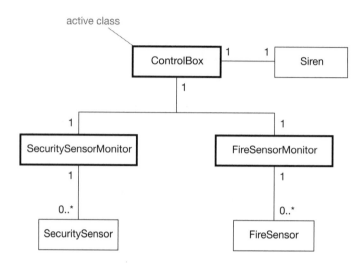

active class

Active classes have instances that are active objects.

**Figure 12.15**

Notice that the classes ControlBox, SecuritySensorMonitor, and FireSensorMonitor have heavy borders – this means that these classes are active classes. Active objects are instances of active classes. We need multi-threading in this case, as the security system must *continuously* monitor the fire and security sensors.

Now we have enough information to create some collaboration diagrams. The instance form collaboration diagram for the use case ActivateAll is shown in Figure 12.16.

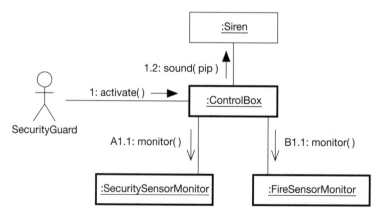

**Figure 12.16**

**Table 12.10**

| Walkthru for Figure 12.16 | |
|---|---|
| 1: activate() | When the SecurityGuard activates the system with the key, the activate() message is sent to the :ControlBox object which represents the main thread of control in the program. |
| A1.1: monitor()<br>B1.1: monitor() | :ControlBox then sends the message monitor() *asynchronously* to the :SecuritySensorMonitor and :FireSensorMonitor.<br>We have given each of these messages the *same* sequence number to indicate that the order in which the messages are sent doesn't matter – each monitor() message launches a new thread.<br>Thread **A** monitors the security sensors – we model this thread as the active object :SecuritySensorMonitor.<br>Thread **B** monitors the fire sensors – we model this thread as the active object :FireSensorMonitor. |
| 1.2: sound( pip ) | The system pips the siren to indicate that it is activated. |

Table 12.10 describes the walkthru for this collaboration diagram.

Next, let's look at the use case TriggerSensor. The collaboration diagram in Figure 12.17 shows a burglar triggering a security sensor positioned in the hall of the building.

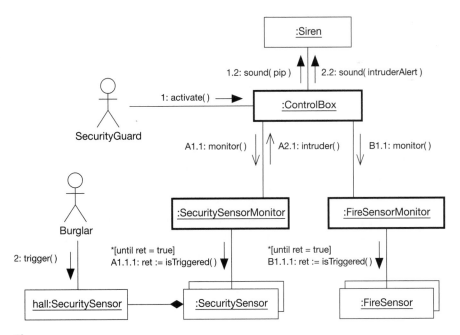

**Figure 12.17**

**Table 12.11**

| Walkthru for Figure 12.17 | |
|---|---|
| 1: activate() | When the SecurityGuard activates the whole system with the key, the activate() message is sent to the :ControlBox object which represents the main thread of control in the program. |
| A1.1: monitor() <br> B1.1: monitor() | :ControlBox then sends the message monitor() to the :SecuritySensorMonitor and :FireSensorMonitor. |
| 1.2: sound( pip ) | The system pips the siren to indicate that it is activated. |
| *[until ret = true] <br> A1.1.1: isTriggered() | This is an iteration – the iteration expression states that the message isTriggered() will be sent to each object in the multiobject set in turn, and that this will continue until isTriggered() returns true. <br> In other words, the :SecuritySensorMonitor continually polls each :SecuritySensor until one of them is triggered. |
| *[until ret = true] <br> B1.1.1: isTriggered() | This is an iteration – the iteration expression states that the message isTriggered() will  be sent to each object in the multiobject set in turn, and that this will continue until isTriggered() returns true. <br> In other words, the :FireSensorMonitor continually polls each :FireSensor until one of them is triggered. |
| 2: trigger() | The Burglar actor triggers the hall:SecuritySensor object. This causes ret to become false, and the iteration in step A1.1.1 to finish. |
| A2.1: intruder() | The :SecuritySensorMonitor sends the message intruder asynchronously to the :ControlBox. |
| 2.2: sound( intruderAlert ) | The :SecuritySensorMonitor sends the message sound (intruderAlert) to the :Siren which sounds the intruder alert. |

Table 12.11 follows the sequence of events from the beginning.

The example in Figure 12.17 illustrates a pattern which is quite characteristic of multi-threaded systems – there is often one central control object (:ControlBox in this case) that coordinates subsidiary threads which are modeled as active objects. The reason that this pattern is so common is that in concurrent systems, you need some way to start, stop, and synchronize the concurrent threads of execution in a controlled manner. Having a primary control object is a simple way to achieve this.

## 12.7.8   Object state

*The UML Reference Manual* [Rumbaugh 1] defines a state as "a condition or situation during the life of an object during which it satisfies some condition, performs some activity, or waits for some event". A state is a notable condition of an object that depends on the values of its attributes, its links to other objects, or what it happens to be doing.

In OO systems, the collaborating and interacting objects move through a sequence of states over time. Messages often cause an object to undergo transition from one state to another. For example, a BankAccount object may move between the states inCredit, overdrawn and empty as money is deposited and withdrawn from the account over time.

> We can show how object state changes as the object interaction progresses.

You can use instance form collaboration diagrams to show how objects undergo transition between states in response to messages. The object state can be shown in square brackets after the object name. There is no formal notation for object state, and any expression that makes sense can be used. If the class of the object has a statechart (see Chapter 19), then the state name *must* refer to one of the states modeled on that statechart.

In Figure 12.18 you can see that the anOrder:Order object changes state from unpaid to paid if, and only if, its balance attribute falls to exactly zero. If the balance should become greater than zero, this means that more money has been paid against the order than was owed. The object anOrder:Order

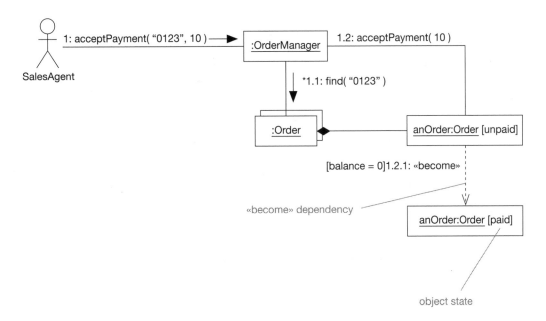

**Figure 12.18**

then changes state from unpaid to overpaid. This state transition may trigger another object interaction involving issuing a refund.

Step 1.2.1 in Figure 12.18 is a dependency. The «become» stereotype on the dependency indicates that this is an object interaction where the source object *becomes* the target object as the interaction progresses.

## 12.8 Sequence diagrams

> Sequence diagrams show object interactions arranged in a time sequence.

Sequence diagrams show object interactions arranged in a time sequence. They are isomorphic with collaboration diagrams and contain the same elements plus two others – object lifeline and focus of control. In collaboration diagrams, the nesting of the sequence numbers indicates focus of control, but in sequence diagrams we can show focus of control, also known as activation, more clearly and explicitly.

Sequence diagrams serve a slightly different purpose to collaboration diagrams in OO analysis. Collaboration diagrams are very good at showing the actual objects and their structural relationships (the collaboration), but they are weaker when it comes to showing the interactions between those objects as a time-ordered sequence of events. This is where sequence diagrams have a significant advantage. Sequence diagrams also come in descriptor and instance forms. However, it is the instance form that is most widely used, and that is what we will focus on here.

When modeling, you often start out by sketching a use case realization using a collaboration diagram as it is very easy to place objects on the diagram and connect them with links. However, when you need to focus on the actual *sequencing* of events, it is always much easier to use a sequence diagram. Fortunately, because the two diagrams are just different views on to the same underlying model, CASE tools can often convert one type of diagram automatically into the other. This makes it very easy to switch back and forth between the two views to obtain maximum modeling benefit from each.

To investigate sequence diagrams, we'll look at some use cases from our simple course registration system. Figure 12.19 shows the use case AddCourse that we discussed in Section 12.7.3.

Figure 12.20 shows a sequence diagram for the AddCourse use case.

Sequence diagrams have time running from top to bottom, and instances (or classifier roles) running from left to right. Instances are placed horizontally to minimize the number of crossing lines on the diagram, and are placed vertically according to when they are created.

Stretching beneath each instance is a dashed line that indicates the instance's lifeline. This represents the duration of the instance over time. To

| Use case: AddCourse |
|---|
| **ID: UC8** |
| **Actors:**<br>Registrar |
| **Preconditions:**<br>The Registrar has logged on to the system. |
| **Flow of events:**<br>1. The Registrar selects "add course".<br>2. The system accepts the name of the new course.<br>3. The system creates the new course. |
| **Postconditions:**<br>A new course has been added to the system. |

**Figure 12.19**

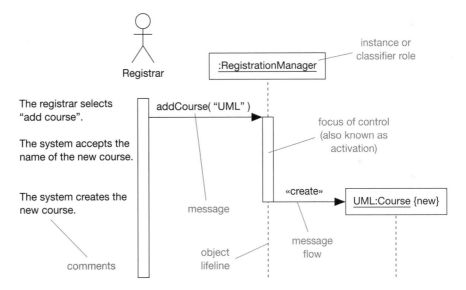

**Figure 12.20**

indicate instance destruction, you terminate the lifeline with a large cross as shown in Figure 12.21. If you don't know when the object is destroyed, or don't care, then you just terminate the lifeline normally.

You place long thin rectangles on the lifeline to indicate when a particular object gets the focus of control. In Figure 12.20 the Registrar actor starts with the focus of contol. It sends the message addCourse( "UML" ) to :RegistrationManager which invokes its addCourse(...) operation with the parameter "UML". During the execution of this operation, :RegistrationManager has

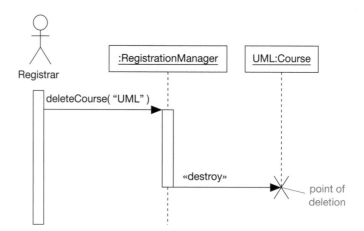

**Figure 12.21**

focus of control. However, notice that this focus of control is *nested* within the focus of control of the Registrar actor. This is quite normal – one object starts with focus of control and invokes an operation on another object nesting the focus of control. This object may then invoke an operation on another object nesting focus of control yet further, and so on.

Within the execution of the addCourse(...) operation, the :RegistrationManager creates a new object, the UML:Course object. You can show object creation by simply sending a message stereotyped «create» as in Figure 12.20, or you can send a specific, named object creation message which you may also stereotype «create». In C++, C#, or Java, object creation operations are special operations known as constructors – these have the same name as the class of the object, no return value, and zero or more parameters. So, in this example, if you were using Java, you could send the message «create» Course( "UML" ) which would invoke the Course class constructor. Not all OO languages have constructors however – in Smalltalk, for example, you would probably send the message «create» init: "UML".

We haven't bothered to show the operation returns in the examples above – we simply assume that the operation returns at the end of the focus of control. However, it is possible (and often desirable) to show the returns from operations explicitly, and you do this in the same way as we did in collaboration diagrams – with a dashed arrow going back from the supplier to the client. There's an example of this in Figure 12.24.

One very nice feature of sequence diagrams is that you can show a script for a diagram through comments added down the left-hand side. This makes the diagram much more accessible to non-technical stakeholders, such as users and business domain experts. The script may consist of actual steps from a use case (as in Figure 12.20), or just a textual summary of what is happening in the diagram.

## 12.8.1  Iteration

The iteration expression determines the number of times to repeat the contents of the box.

Iteration is shown on a sequence diagram by enclosing the set of messages to be repeated in a box, and placing the iteration expression below the box. We show an example of this in Figure 12.22.

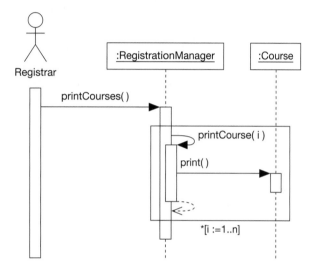

**Figure 12.22**

UML 1.4 does not currently support multiobject sets on sequence diagrams. This makes it difficult to show iteration over the contents of a multiobject set clearly. Figure 12.22 is actually the sequence diagram version of the collaboration diagram shown in Figure 12.23.

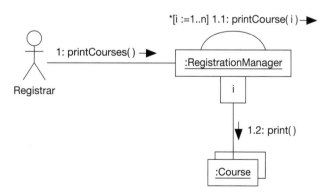

**Figure 12.23**

While the sequence diagram version is quite clear and understandable, notice how we have been able to be much more specific about the mechanism of the iteration in the collaboration diagram by using multiobjects and qualifiers. Neither feature is available in the sequence diagram form.

## 12.8.2 Branching and self-delegation

Sequence diagrams are very good at showing branching.

Sequence diagrams show branching much more clearly than collaboration diagrams. This is because sequence diagrams are concerned with the time-ordered sequence of events, whereas collaboration diagrams are more concerned with instances and relationships.

Figure 12.24 is the sequence diagram version of the collaboration diagram in Figure 12.12. It shows how you can model branching, self-delegation, and nested focus of control.

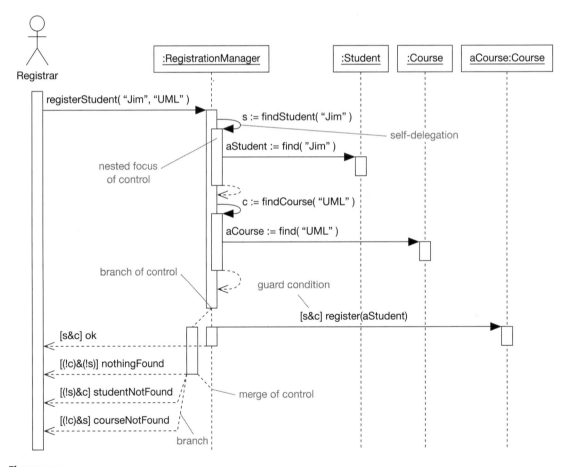

**Figure 12.24**

You can model branching by splitting the focus of control for an object into two or more, and protecting the *first* message in each with a condition. If you don't protect the first message in each branch, then you get concurrency rather than branching.

## 12.8.3 Concurrency – active objects

You model concurrency using active objects (as we did with collaboration diagrams), but you need some way to show parallel execution of the threads. You do this by creating a fork in the focus of control. You can see in Figure 12.25 (the sequence diagram version of the collaboration diagram in Figure 12.17) that when either of the two threads finishes, you come back to the same point in the original :ControlBox focus of control and then send the message activate(...) to the :Siren.

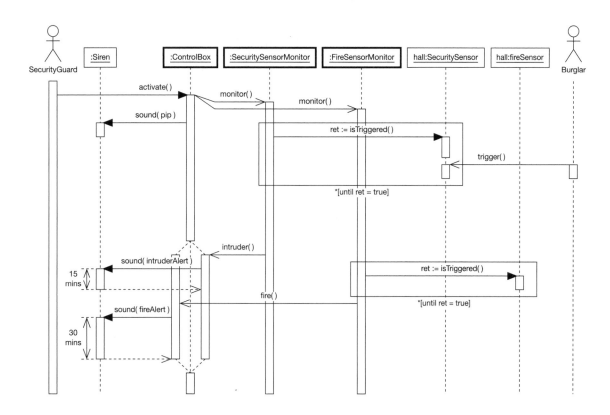

**Figure 12.25**

### 12.8.4 Object state and constraints

You can use sequence diagrams to show how an object changes state over time. You do this by placing the object state on the lifeline at the appropriate point. This allows you to see very clearly which events give rise to state changes. An example of this is shown in Figure 12.26. The message acceptPayment(...) causes a state transition on the :Order object from state unpaid to paid. Similarly, the message deliver() sent from the :DeliveryManager object to the :Order object causes a state transition in :Order from state paid to delivered.

> You can show how an object changes state over time.

Figure 12.26 also shows how you can label specific points on the time axis and then express timing constraints. Actually, it is a very flexible syntax and you can put whatever constraints you like down the left-hand axis of a sequence diagram, not just timing constraints. Reading Figure 12.26, the timing constraint says that there must be 28 days or less between time A and time B. Time A marks the point at which the :Order object undergoes transition into the state paid, and time B marks the point at which the :Order object undergoes transition into the state delivered. The sequence diagram therefore tells you that in the order processing part of this system, there must be no more than 28 days from payment until delivery of an order.

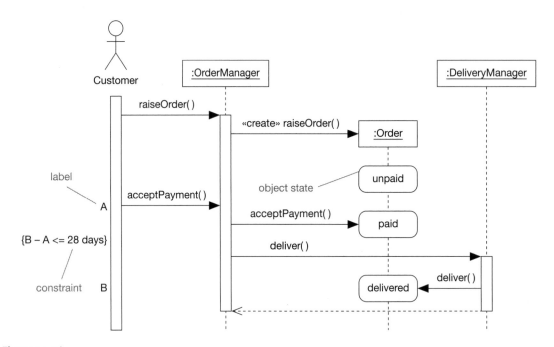

**Figure 12.26**

## 12.9    What we have learned

Use case realization is an essential part of the analysis process. It allows you to test your theories against reality by explicitly demonstrating how objects of your classes can interact to deliver the specified system behavior. Interaction diagrams show how classes and objects realize requirements as specified in use cases.

You have learned the following.

● The UP activity "Analyze a use case" is where you create use case realizations – this activity creates part of the dynamic view of the system.

● Use case realizations show how instances of analysis classes interact to realize the functional requirements specified by a use case.
  — Each use case realization realizes exactly one use case.
  — Use case realizations consist of:
    – analysis class diagrams – these should "tell a story" about one (or more) use cases;
    – interaction diagrams – these demonstrate how objects interact to realize the use case behavior;
    – special requirements – you always uncover new requirements during use case realization and you need to record these;
    – use case refinement – you may need to change a use case as you begin to realize it.

● Interaction diagrams may be in descriptor form or instance form.
  — Descriptor form interaction diagrams show:
    – classifier roles – a role that will be played by the classifier instances;
    – association roles – a role played by an association;
    – messages and message flow.
  — Instance form interaction diagrams show:
    – classifier instances (objects);
    – links;
    – you can show instance and link creation and destruction:
      – {new} – the instance or link is created in the interaction;
      – {destroyed} – the instance or link is destroyed in the interaction;
      – {transient} – the instance or link is created and destroyed in the interaction;
    – messages and message flow;

- you can show message flow with an arrow – there are three types of flow:
  - procedure call – the sender waits for the procedure to finish;
  - asynchronous communication – the sender doesn't wait for the call to finish;
  - return from procedure call – return is always implicit, so you may choose not to show this;
- iteration;
- branching.

● There are two isomorphic types of interaction diagram:
— collaboration diagrams;
— sequence diagrams.

● Collaboration diagrams emphasize the collaboration between objects.
— A collaboration describes a static set of relationships between instances, and the roles played by instances in those relationships.
— Collaboration diagrams may show:
  - multiobjects – these represent a set of objects:
    - qualifiers allow you to select a specific object from a multiobject by using a unique identifier;
    - you can assume that multiobjects have at least the following implicit methods:
      ● find(uniqueIdentifier) – returns a specific object given a unique identifier as a parameter;
      ● includes( anObject ) – returns true if the multiobject includes anObject;
      ● count() – returns the number of objects in the multiobject;
  - iteration:
    - if a message sent to the multiobject is prefixed with an iteration specifier, then it is sent to each object in the set:
      ● * – sequential processing of multiobject instances;
      ● *// – parallel processing of multiobject instances;
    - after the iteration specifier you may put an iteration expression that determines the number of iterations:
      ● nothing – iterate over the whole set;
      ● [i := 1..n];
      ● [while (some Boolean expression)];
      ● [until (some Boolean expression)];
      ● [for each (expression that evaluates to a collection of objects)];

- branching – protect a message sent with a Boolean condition – only send the message if the condition is true;
- concurrency – each active object has its own thread of control:
  - active objects are instances of active classes;
  - show active objects and classes with a heavy border or include the property {active} in the box;
  - name each thread e.g. A and B – append thread name to sequence number e.g. A1.1 and B1.1.
- show object state in square brackets after the class name:
  - this gives us an object in state – an object that happens to be in a specific state;
  - use the «become» dependency between two objects in state to show how an object changes its state over time.

- Sequence diagrams emphasize the interaction between instances.

  — An interaction describes the time-ordered sequence of message sends between instances.
  — Instances or classifier roles run across the top of the sequence diagram; time runs down the sequence diagram.
  — You can show everything you can show on a collaboration diagram:
    - except multiobjects and qualifiers;
    - plus a script – possibly the text of a use case listed down the left-hand side of the diagram;
    - plus an object lifeline – a vertical dotted line that shows how long the object lives:
      - you can show the point of creation of an object by sending a «create» message to an object icon;
      - you can show the point of destruction of an object by showing a «destroy» message sent to a large X on the object's lifeline;
    - plus focus of control – a box on the lifeline that indicates when the object is active.
  — Iteration:
    - draw a box around the sequence of message sends that is to be repeated;
    - place an iteration expression below the box.
  — Branching – the object lifeline splits into alternative branches:
    - protect each branch with a condition on the first message in each branch;
    - all conditions must be mutually exclusive – if not, you get concurrency, not branching.

— Concurrency:
  – use active objects;
  – create forks and joins in the focus of control.
— Object state can be shown using state icons at the appropriate place on the object lifeline.
— You can show conditions anywhere on the sequence diagram, but you usually keep them down the left-hand side.

# chapter 13

# Activity diagrams

## 13.1 Chapter roadmap

If activity diagrams are new to you, then you need to progress though each section in this chapter in turn. If you already know something about activity diagrams you may be able to skip most of this chapter, although you might still find Sections 13.9 (Object flows) and 13.10 (Signals) interesting.

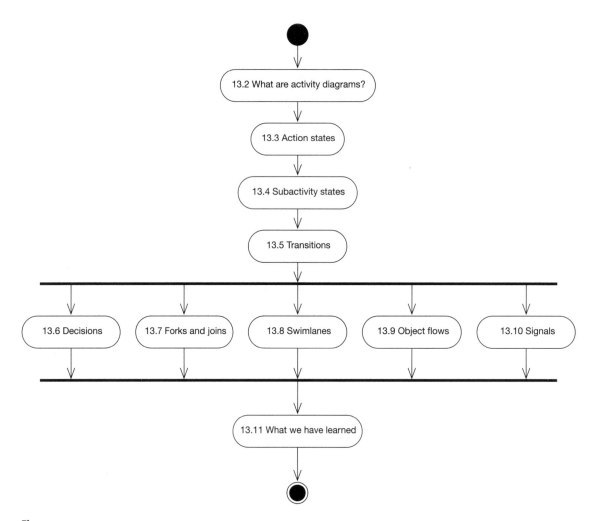

**Figure 13.1**

## 13.2   What are activity diagrams?

Activity diagrams
are OO flowcharts.

Activity diagrams are "OO flowcharts". They allow you to model a process as a collection of activities and transitions between those activities. Activity diagrams are really just special cases of statecharts (see Chapter 19) where every state has an entry action that specifies some process or function that occurs when the state is entered.

An activity diagram can be attached to *any* modeling element for the purpose of modeling the behavior of that element. Activity diagrams are typically attached to:

- use cases;
- classes;
- interfaces;
- components;
- nodes;
- collaborations;
- operations and methods.

You can also very profitably use activity diagrams to model business processes and workflows.

Although a common use of activity diagrams is to flowchart operations, it is worth considering that the actual source code for an operation may be its best and most concise representation! So judge each case on its merits.

The essence of a good activity diagram is that it is focused on communicating one specific aspect of a system's dynamic behavior. As such, it must be at the correct level of abstraction to communicate that message to its target audience. It is very important that the diagram contains the minimum necessary amount of information to communicate the point. It is easy to adorn activity diagrams with object states and objects flows, etc., but you must always ask if those adornments clarify or obscure.

## 13.3   Action states

Activity diagrams contain action states and subactivity states. Action states are the finest granularity building block of activity diagrams, and represent actions – tasks that can't be broken down into subtasks.

Action states are represented as boxes with rounded ends. This is illustrated in Figure 13.2.

The action expression indicates the entry action of the state. This is the piece of work that the action state will perform when it is entered. It may be written in pseudo-code or plain English. If written in English, then it should be a verb or verb phrase, as action states always *do* something. Actions are:

An action state represents an atomic piece of work.

**Figure 13.2**

- atomic – can't be broken down into smaller pieces;
- uninterruptible – once the piece of work starts it always progresses to the finish;
- instantaneous – the work of an action state is generally considered to take an insignificant amount of time.

According to the UML specification (version 1.4), an action state is just a simplified version of a more general element called a state. In fact, the action state is a shorthand notation for a state that has one entry action and at least one outgoing transition. Action states and states have different visual syntax – action states are drawn as rectangles with rounded ends, whereas states are drawn as rectangles with rounded corners ("round-tangles"). We look at states in detail in Chapter 19.

Every activity diagram begins with the start state and ends with the stop state.

UML gives action states their own visual syntax and simplified semantics because, as you will see later, states have very rich and complex syntax and semantics that would be overkill for the purposes of activity diagrams.

Each activity diagram has two special states – the start state and the stop state. The start state marks the beginning of the workflow, and the stop state marks the end – their symbols are shown in Figure 13.3.

start state          stop state

**Figure 13.3**

## 13.4   Subactivity states

Subactivity states are non-atomic – they can be broken down into other subactivity and action states. They may be interrupted, and may take a finite amount of time. They have a special syntax shown in Figure 13.4.

Subactivity states contain a nested activity graph.

Each subactivity state invokes an entire activity graph that is nested within it. As we've already said, this nested activity graph may contain both action states and other subactivity states. In many UML CASE tools, clicking or double clicking on a subactivity state will open the activity diagram of its nested activity graph.

You tend to use subactivity states when you are modeling complex business processes as a workflow. Each workflow element can be modeled as a

**Figure 13.4**

subactivity state that can be broken down into finer granularity subactivity states, and ultimately to action states.

## 13.5 Transitions

Whenever an action or subactivity state finishes its work, there is a transition out of the state into the next state. This is known as an automatic transition. We'll see in Section 19.6, when we look at UML statecharts, that an automatic transition is really just a state transition that is *not* triggered by any specific event, i.e. it just happens automatically when the state finishes its work.

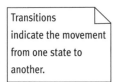

Transitions indicate the movement from one state to another.

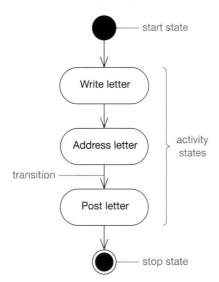

**Figure 13.5**

In the example activity diagram shown in Figure 13.5, we begin (as we must) with the start state and then automatically transition into the first action state Write letter. Once the action specified by this state finishes, we automatically transition to the next action state. This continues until we reach the stop state.

## 13.6   Decisions

A decision specifies alternative paths based on some Boolean guard expression. The UML syntax for a decision (Figure 13.6) is a diamond shape, just like in a normal flowchart. The same symbol is also used for a merge, when the two alternative paths reunite.

There can only be one input path to a decision, but there may be many output paths. Each path out of the decision is protected by a guard expression. The path can be taken if, and only if, the guard expression evaluates to true. The keyword else specifies the path that is taken if none of the guard expressions are true. Guard expressions must be carefully formulated to be mutually exclusive – otherwise the activity diagram would be non-deterministic!

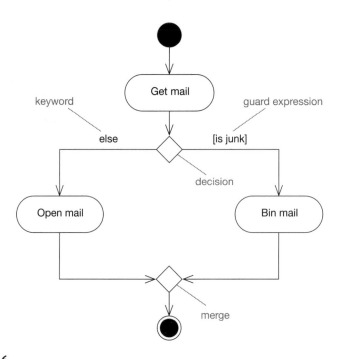

Decisions allow you to model decision points.

**Figure 13.6**

In the example in Figure 13.6, we transition from the start state to the Get mail action state. When this state finishes its work, we transition to the branch. This branch has two possible output transitions. If the mail is junk mail then [is junk] evaluates to true, so the right-hand transition fires and we go into the state Bin mail, and thence to the stop state. Otherwise, the left-hand branch fires and we go into the state Open mail, and thence to the stop state.

## 13.7   Forks and joins

Forks split a
path into two or more
concurrent flows.

Joins synchronize
two or more
concurrent flows.

Activity diagrams are very good for modeling concurrent flows of work. You can split a path into two or more concurrent flows using a fork, and then synchronize these concurrent flows using a join.

Forks have exactly one incoming transition and two or more outgoing transitions. Joins have two or more incoming transitions and exactly one outgoing transition. The outgoing transition only fires when *all* the incoming transitions have fired, i.e. when the concurrent flows of work have all finished.

As we only transition out of the join to the next state when all of the incoming transitions to the join have occurred, a join is a point in the activity diagram where concurrent flows synchronize. These concurrent flows may represent concurrent workflows, concurrent business processes, concurrent system processes, concurrent threads each executing in its own address space, or concurrent threads of work within the same process each sharing the same address space.

Figure 13.7 shows a very simple model of concurrent workflows. This activity diagram shows (at a very high level) the business process of bring-

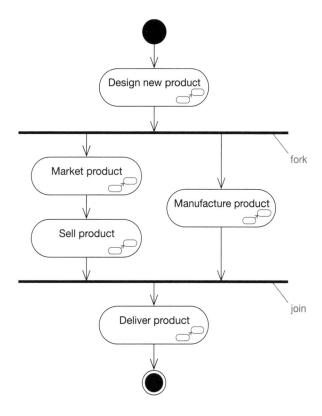

**Figure 13.7**

ing a new product to market. Each state on this high-level diagram is a sub-activity state which itself contains an activity graph.

We begin at the start state, and then transition to the subactivity state Design new product. When the product has been designed, we automatically transition into the fork. This spawns two concurrent workflows, a marketing workflow and a manufacturing workflow. In the marketing workflow, we enter the state Market product where we perform the marketing campaign for the product. We then enter the state Sell product where we take orders for a product. Concurrently, in the manufacturing workflow, we are in the state Manufacture product. When both the marketing and manufacturing workflows have completed, we transition out of the join into the Deliver product state. This model tells us that while we can do marketing and selling for a product, we can't actually deliver a product until it has been manufactured.

## 13.8  Swimlanes

UML does not give any detailed semantics for swimlanes. You can therefore use them to partition activity diagrams in any way you like! Swimlanes are commonly used to represent:

Swimlanes allow us to partition activity diagrams.

- use cases;
- classes;
- components;
- organizational units (in business modeling);
- roles (in workflow modeling).

However, these are not the only possibilities. For example, in design models for distributed systems, you can even use swimlanes to model the distribution of processes across physical machines.

There is often a connection between swimlanes and concurrent flows of control. In the example in Figure 13.8, the swimlanes represent organizational units within the business – the marketing department, the manufacturing department, and the delivery department. The activity diagram shows that the marketing department can get on with its various activities while the manufacturing department is manufacturing the product. However, the delivery department is dependent on the other two departments finishing their work. It is very common that separate departments or business units perform concurrent lines of work and then have to come into synchronization at some point. Activity diagrams with swimlanes are an excellent way of modeling this.

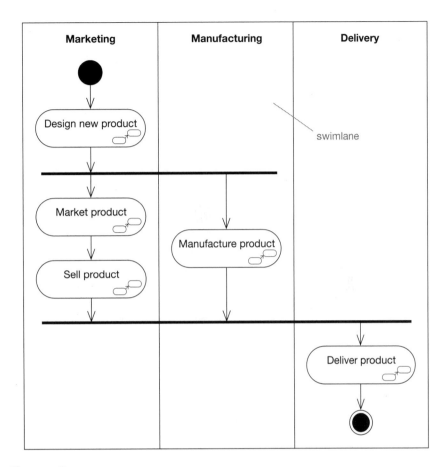

**Figure 13.8**

## 13.9 Object flows

An object flow shows how objects are input to, output from, and changed by states.

Activities may input and output objects and can modify object state. You can show this on an activity diagram as an object flow. Given that activities may work with many objects in an OO system, you should only show the important objects on an object flow. In Figure 13.9, there are two important objects – the :ProductSpec object which is output from the Design new product subactivity state and input to the Manufacture product subactivity state; and the :Order object which allows capture of payment and delivery details, and which provides an audit trail for the selling process.

You can show the object's state, as it migrates across activities, by writing the name of the state in square brackets below the object's name. This

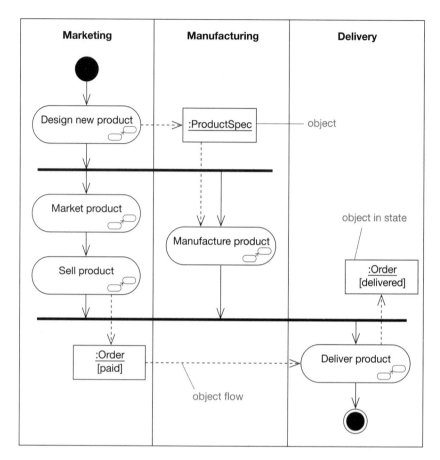

**Figure 13.9**

name of the state must refer to a state on the statechart for the object's class (we discuss statecharts in Chapters 19 and 20).

Another way of showing object state changes is to show actual attribute values. In fact, this is the only way of showing object state changes if the object's class doesn't have a statechart. You can show attribute values in a compartment below the object's name.

## 13.10  Signals

A signal is a way of representing a package of information that is communicated asynchronously between two objects. A signal event occurs when an object receives a signal.

An event is something that happens. When an event is received by an object it may trigger a state transition in it. With the sole exception of the signal event, you don't normally show events on activity diagrams, only on statecharts. We discuss events in more detail in Section 19.7.

A signal send is modeled on an activity diagram as a convex pentagon labeled with the name of the signal that is sent. The signal send has one input transition and one output transition. There is no action associated with this state, all it does is send the signal. You can draw a dashed arrow from the signal send to the object that receives the signal.

In the example in Figure 13.10, the signal called Order is sent to the :MailOrderCompany external object.

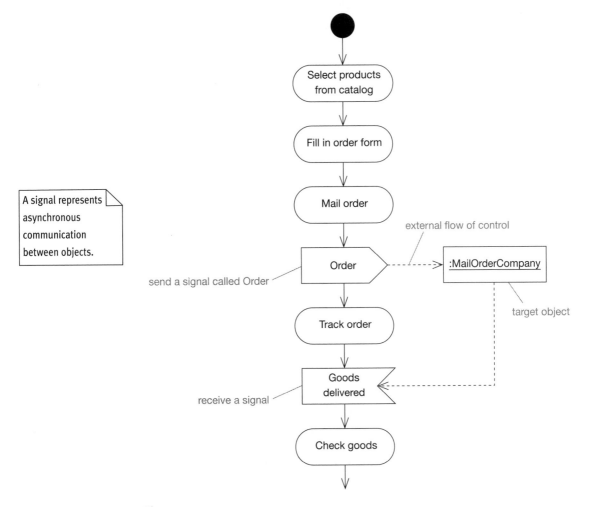

**Figure 13.10**

A signal receipt is modeled with a concave pentagon labeled with the name of the signal that is received. The signal receipt is just a state with no actions – it merely receives the signal. In Figure 13.10 we wait in the signal receipt for a signal called Goods delivered, which is passed back to us from the :MailOrderCompany object.

Signals are classifiers, so you can model them as stereotyped classes. The purpose of a signal is to provide asynchronous communication of *information* between objects and so, unlike ordinary classes, they *only* have attributes and the single implicit operation send(targetSet) which allows them to be sent to a set of target objects. As this operation is implicit, it is never actually shown on signal diagrams – it is just assumed that it is there for every signal. The signal attributes specify the information content of the signal.

The example in Figure 13.11 shows a generalization hierarchy of raw GUI events modeled as signals.

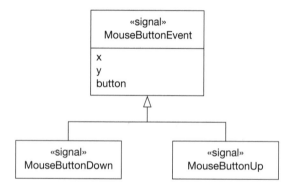

**Figure 13.11**

Because signals only have attributes and no interesting operations, they are somewhat like normal data types and can only model data being passed between objects. This means that they are not really that useful for modeling distributed OO systems. However, they are still useful for modeling data passed between an OO system and a non-OO system.

## 13.11　What we have learned

In this chapter, you have seen that you can use activity diagrams to model many different kinds of processes. You have learned the following.

- Activity diagrams are OO flowcharts:
  - you use them to model all types of process;
  - you can attach activity diagrams to *any* modeling element to capture its behavior;
  - a good activity diagram communicates one specific aspect of a system's behavior.

- Action states are a simplified form of a state that has a single entry action. They are:
  - atomic;
  - uninterruptible;
  - instantaneous.

- The start state marks the beginning of the activity diagram.

- The stop state marks the end of the activity diagram.

- Subactivity states contain a complete activity graph. They are:
  - non-atomic;
  - interruptible;
  - may take a finite amount of time.

- Transitions indicate the movement from one state to another – automatic transitions occur as soon as a state has finished its work.

- Decisions allow you to model decision points:
  - the main flow splits into two or more alternative paths;
  - each path is protected by a Boolean guard expression;
  - all guard expressions must be mutually exclusive;
  - the keyword else indicates the path taken if none of the guard expressions evaluates to true.

- Forks split a path into two or more concurrent flows – a fork has a single input transition and two or more output transitions.

- Joins synchronize two or more concurrent flows:
  - a join has one output transition and two or more input transitions;
  - the output transition only occurs when all of the input transitions have occurred.

- Swimlanes allow you to partition activity diagrams. You can choose your own semantics for swimlanes. They may represent:
  - organizational divisions;
  - use cases;
  - classes;
  - processes;
  - etc.

- Object flows show how objects are input to, output from and changed by action or subactivity states.
- A signal is a type of event.
  — A signal is a way of representing a package of information that is communicated asynchronously between two objects.
  — A signal event occurs when an object receives a signal.
  — Signals are modeled as classes with the standard stereotype «signal»:
    – they only have attributes;
    – they have an implicit send(targetSet) method – this allows the signal to be sent to a set of target objects.
  — A signal send is a special state that sends a signal.
  — A signal receive is a special state that receives a signal – the automatic transition out of the signal receive only occurs when the signal has been received.

part **4**

# Design

# Chapter 14
# The design workflow

## 14.1 Chapter roadmap

This chapter is about the UP design workflow. One of the main issues we consider is how the analysis model evolves into the design model, and whether or not you need to maintain the analysis and design models separately – we discuss this important topic in Section 14.3.1. The rest of the chapter is about the design workflow detail and artefacts.

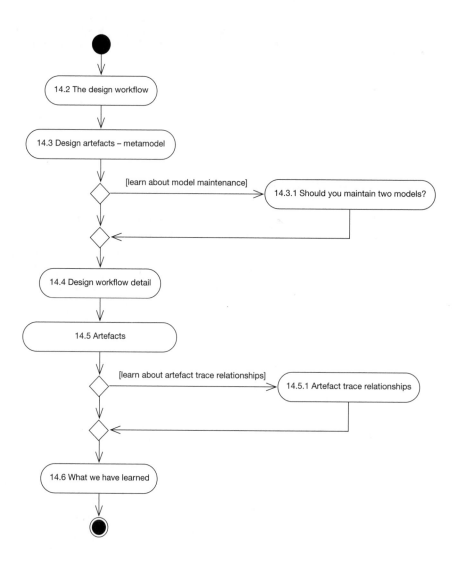

**Figure 14.1**

## 14.2   The design workflow

Most design work is done as you move from the Elaboration to the Construction phase.

The design workflow is the primary modeling activity during the last part of the Elaboration phase and the first half of the Construction phase. As you can see from Figure 14.2, the main focus of the early iterations is requirements and analysis, and as the analysis activity becomes more and more complete, the modeling focus shifts to design. To a great extent, analysis and design can occur in parallel. However, as you will see, it is important to distinguish clearly between the artefacts of these two workflows – the analysis model and the design model.

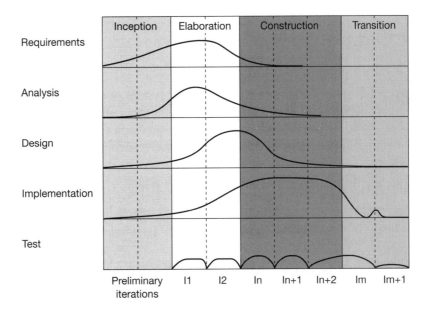

**Figure 14.2**   Adapted from Figure 1.5 [Jacobson 1] with permission from Addison-Wesley

Rather than have a team of analysts and a separate team of designers, UP recommends that one team is responsible for taking an artefact (such as a use case) from requirements through analysis and design, and ultimately to implementation. Instead of organizing the team around specific activities, UP organizes the team around deliverables and milestones. UP provides a "goal" focus rather than a "task" focus.

In analysis, the focus was on creating a logical model of the system that captured the functionality that the system must provide in order to satisfy the user requirements. The purpose in design is to specify fully how this functionality will be implemented. One way of looking at this is to consider the problem domain on one hand, and the solution domain on other. Requirements come from the problem domain, and you can think of analysis as being the exploration of this domain from the point of view of the system stakeholders. Design involves merging in technical solutions from the solution domain (class libraries, persistence mechanisms, etc.) to provide a model of the system (the design model) that can actually be implemented.

In design, OO designers decide on strategic design issues such as object persistence and distribution, and create a design model accordingly. The project manager and architect should also create policies to deal with any tactical design issues.

## 14.3   Design artefacts – metamodel

A subsystem is a part of the physical system.

Figure 14.3 shows the metamodel for the design model. The design model contains exactly one design system that contains many design subsystems (we only show five such subsystems here). In design, you use the term "subsystem" rather than "package" to indicate that you have progressed from the purely conceptual view of analysis to a physical model of the system.

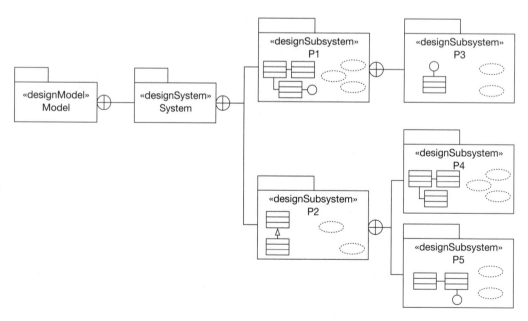

**Figure 14.3**

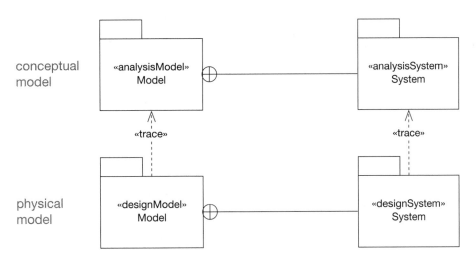

**Figure 14.4**

Although you may have identified several key interfaces in analysis, when you come to design you put much more emphasis on interfaces. This is because it is ultimately the interfaces between design subsystems that hold your system together. Interfaces, therefore, have a strong architectural role in design, and you will spend quite a lot of time looking for, and modeling, key interfaces.

There is a simple «trace» relationship between the analysis and design models – the design model is based on the analysis model, and can be considered to be just a refinement and elaboration thereof (this is shown in Figure 14.4). Similarly, there is a simple, one-to-one «trace» relationship between the analysis system and the design system.

The relationship between analysis packages and design packages is a bit more complex. Often, one analysis package will «trace» to one design subsystem, but this isn't always the case. You might have good architectural and technical reasons for breaking down a single analysis package into more than one design subsystem. For example, if you are doing component-based development, you often let one design subsystem represent a single coarse-grained component. In this case, depending on the desired granularity of the components, you may find that one analysis package actually resolves to several design subsystems.

## 14.3.1   Should you maintain two models?

In an ideal world, you would have a single model of your system, and your CASE tool would be able to give either an analysis view of that model, or a design view. However, this is a more difficult requirement than it at first appears, and there is no UML CASE tool currently on the market that does an entirely convincing job of providing analysis and design views of the same underlying model. It seems that we are left with four strategies – these are described in Table 14.1.

**Table 14.1**

| | Strategy | Consequences |
|---|---|---|
| 1 | Take the analysis model and refine it into a design model | You have a single design model, but you have lost the analysis view |
| 2 | Take the analysis model, refine it into a design model and use a CASE tool to recover an "analysis view" | You have a single design model, but the analysis view recovered by the CASE tool might not be satisfactory |
| 3 | Freeze the analysis model at some point in the Elaboration phase – refine a copy of the analysis model into a design model | You have two models, but they are out of step |
| 4 | Maintain two separate models – an analysis model and a design model | You have two models – they are in step, but there is a maintenance burden |

There is no best strategy – it depends on your project. However, the fundamental question you need to ask is, "Do we need to preserve an analysis view of the system?" Analysis views give you the "big picture" of your system. An analysis view may only have between 1% and 10% of the classes that are in the detailed design view and they are therefore much more understandable. They are invaluable for:

> Keep an analysis model for large, complex or strategic systems.

- introducing new people to the project;
- understanding the system months or years after delivery;
- understanding how the system satisfies user requirements and providing traceability;
- planning maintenance and enhancements;
- understanding the logical architecture of the system;
- outsourcing the construction of the system.

If you need to do any of the above, then you definitely need to preserve an analysis view. Typically, you should preserve an analysis view for any system that is large, complex or strategic, or that has a long projected lifetime. This means that you need to choose between strategies 3 and 4. Always think very carefully about allowing the analysis and design models to get out of step. Is this really acceptable to your project?

If your system is small (say less than 200 design classes) then the design model itself is small enough to be understandable, so a separate analysis model may not be needed. Also, if the system is not strategic, or has a short projected lifespan, then separate analysis and design models may be overkill. Your choice is then between strategies 1 and 2, and the deciding factor will be the capabilities of your UML CASE tool. Some CASE tools maintain a single underlying model, and allow filtering and information hiding to try to recover an "analysis" view from the design model. This is a reasonable halfway house for many medium-sized systems, but it is probably still not good enough for very large systems.

Finally, a word of caution – it is wise to remember that many systems long outlive their projected life span!

## 14.4   Design workflow detail

The UP workflow for design is shown in Figure 14.5. The main participants in design are the architect, the use case engineer, and the component engineer. In most OO projects, one or more dedicated individuals perform the architect role, but it is often the same individual who will act as use case engineer and component engineer at different points in time.

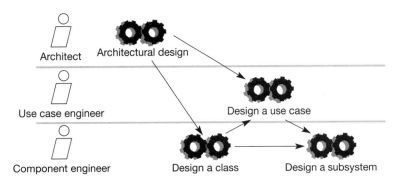

**Figure 14.5**   Reproduced from Figure 9.16 [Jacobson 1] with permission from Addison-Wesley

One of the UP goals is that individuals take ownership and responsibility for part of the system right through from analysis to implementation. Thus, the individual or team responsible for creating a particular piece of OO analysis will often refine this into a design and, perhaps with some extra programming expertise mixed into the team, into code. The advantage of this approach is that it prevents "passing the buck" between analysts, designers, and programmers – this can be common in OO projects.

## 14.5   Artefacts

You can think of the design model as being an elaboration of the analysis model where you have added detail and specific technical solutions. The design model contains the same sorts of things as the analysis model, but all the artefacts are more fully formed and must now include implementation details. For example, an analysis class may be little more than a sketch with few attributes and only key operations. A design class, however, must be fully specified – all attributes and operations (including return types and parameter lists) must be complete.

Design models are made up of:

- design subsystems;
- design classes;
- interfaces;
- use case realizations – design;
- a deployment diagram.

One of the key artefacts that you produce in design are interfaces. You will see in Chapter 17 that these allow you to decouple your system into subsystems that can be developed in parallel.

In design, you also produce a first-cut deployment diagram that shows how your software system is distributed over physical computational nodes. Clearly, this is an important and strategic diagram. However, as most of the work on the deployment diagram occurs in implementation, we defer discussion of them until Chapter 23.

### 14.5.1   Artefact trace relationships

An analysis class may be resolved into one or more interfaces or design classes. This is because analysis classes are a high-level conceptual view of the classes in the system. When we get down to physical modeling (design), these conceptual classes may well need to be implemented as one or more physical design classes and/or interfaces, as shown in Figure 14.6.

The "use case realization – analysis" has a simple one-to-one «trace» relationship with "use case realization – design". In design, the use case realization simply has more detail.

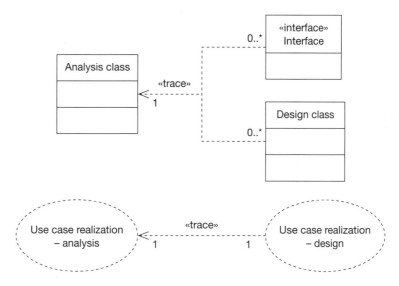

**Figure 14.6**

## 14.6  What we have learned

The design workflow is about determining how the functionality specified in the analysis model will be implemented. You have learned the following.

- The design workflow is the primary modeling activity in the last part of the Elaboration phase and the first part of the Construction phase.
  — Analysis and design can occur in parallel to some extent.
  — One team should take an artefact through analysis into design.
  — OO designers should focus on strategic design issues such as distributed component architectures – policies and standards should be introduced to deal with tactical design issues.

- The design model contains:
  — exactly one design system;
  — design subsystems;
  — use case realizations – design;
  — interfaces;
  — design classes;
  — a deployment diagram (first-cut).

- There are trace relationships between:
  — the design model and analysis model;
  — the design system and analysis system;
  — one or more design subsystems and an analysis package.

● Maintain separate analysis and design models if the system is:
  — large;
  — complex;
  — strategic;
  — subject to frequent change;
  — expected to be long-lived;
  — outsourced.

# chapter 15

# Design classes

## 15.1 Chapter roadmap

This chapter is about design classes. These are the building blocks of the design model, and it is vital for the OO designer to understand how to model these classes effectively.

We describe the anatomy of a design class and then, in Section 15.4, move on to a consideration of what makes a well-formed design class. We discuss the requirements of completeness and sufficiency, primitiveness, high cohesion, low coupling, and the applicability of aggregation versus inheritance.

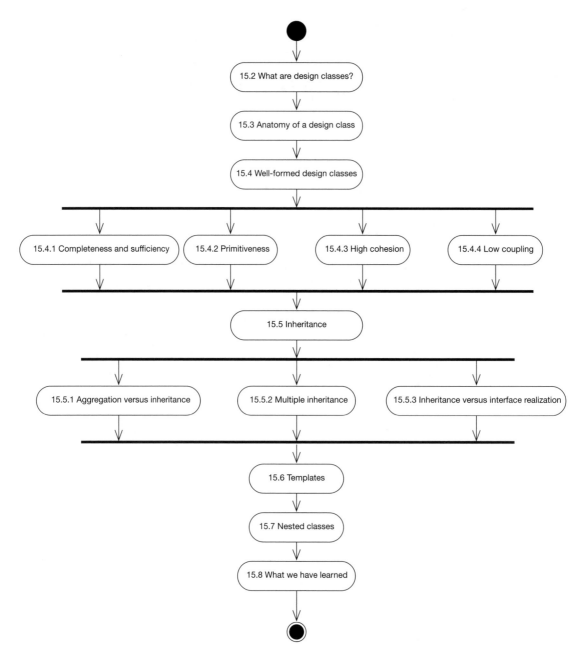

**Figure 15.1**

## 15.2   What are design classes?

Design classes are classes whose specifications have been completed to such a degree that they can be implemented.

In analysis, the source of classes is the problem domain. This is the set of requirements that describes the problem you are trying to solve. You have seen that use cases, supplementary requirements specifications, glossaries, and any other pertinent information may be used as a source of analysis classes.

Design classes come from two places.

> Design classes come from the problem domain and the solution domain.

● The problem domain via a refinement of analysis classes – this refinement involves adding implementation details. As you do this, you often find that you need to break a very high-level analysis class into two or more detailed design classes. There is a «trace» relationship between an analysis class and the one or more design classes that describe its implementation.

● The solution domain – the solution domain is the realm of utility class libraries and reusable components such as Time, Date, String, collections, etc. Middleware such as communications middleware, databases (both relational and object), and component frameworks such as DCOM, CORBA or Enterprise JavaBeans, live here as well. The solution domain also contains GUI frameworks. This domain provides the technical tools that allow you to implement a system.

Analysis is about modeling *what* the system should do. Design is about modeling *how* that behavior may be implemented.

Why may an analysis class refine into one or more design classes or interfaces? Well, an analysis class is specified at a very high level of abstraction. You don't bother with the complete set of attributes, and the set of operations is only really a sketch that captures the key services offered by the class. When you move this class into design, you must fully specify all of the operations and attributes, so it is quite common to find that the class has become too large. If this happens, you should break it down into two or more smaller classes. Remember that you should always be trying to design classes that are small, self-contained, cohesive units that do one or two things really well. You must avoid, at all costs, the large "Swiss Army Knife" type of class that tries to be all things to all men.

## 15.3    Anatomy of a design class

In analysis, you are just trying to capture the required behavior of the system without worrying at all about how this behavior is going to be implemented. In design, you have to specify exactly how the class will fulfill its responsibilities. To do this, you must do the following:

- complete the set of attributes and fully specify them including name, type, visibility and (optionally) a default value;
- turn the operations specified in the analysis class into a complete set of one or more methods.

This process of refinement is illustrated with a very simple example in Figure 15.2.

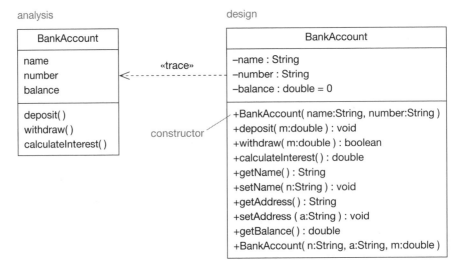

**Figure 15.2**

As you saw in Chapter 9, an operation is a high-level logical specification of a piece of functionality offered by a class. A method, on the other hand, is a fully specified function that can be implemented as source code. Therefore, one high-level operation may actually resolve into one or more implementable methods.

To illustrate this, consider the following example. In an airline check-in system, you may specify in analysis a high-level operation called checkIn(). However, as you'll know if you have ever waited in line to check in to a flight, check-in is actually a fairly complex business process that involves collecting and verifying a certain amount of information from the passenger, taking baggage, and allocating a seat on a plane. It is reasonable, therefore, to suppose that the high-level checkIn() analysis operation will break down into a cascade of lower-level methods when you do the detailed design of the process. It might be that you still maintain a high-level checkIn() method, but in design this method will call a cascade of "helper" methods and methods of other classes, to discharge its responsibility. It may also be that the check-in process is sufficiently complex to require some new helper classes.

## 15.4   Well-formed design classes

> Always assess a design class from the point of view of the users of that class.

When creating a design class, it is important to always look at the class from the point of view of its potential clients. How will they see the class – is it too complex? Are any bits missing? Is it highly coupled to other classes or not? Does it do what they might expect from its name? These are important considerations and may be summarized in the following four minimal characteristics that a design class must have to be considered well-formed:

- complete and sufficient;
- primitive;
- high cohesion;
- low coupling.

> Public methods of a class define a contract.

The design model will be passed to programmers to produce actual source code, or code may be generated directly from the model itself if the CASE tool supports this. Design classes, therefore, need to be completely specified and part of this specification process is deciding if the classes are "well-formed" or not.

### 15.4.1   Completeness and sufficiency

The public methods of a class define a contract between the class and clients of the class. Just like a business contract, it is important that this contract is clear, well-defined, and acceptable to all parties.

Completeness is about giving the clients of a class what they might expect. Clients will make assumptions from the class name about the set of methods that it should make available. To take a real-world example – if you buy a new car, then you can reasonably expect it to have wheels! It is the same with classes – when you name a class and describe its semantics, clients of the class will take this information and infer what methods should be available. For example, a BankAccount class that provides a withdraw(...) method will also be expected to have a deposit(...) method. Again, if you design a class such as a ProductCatalog, then any client could reasonably expect this class to allow them to add, remove and find Products in the catalog. These semantics are clearly implied just by the class name. Completeness is about making sure that the classes satisfy all reasonable client expectations.

Sufficiency, on the other hand, is making sure that all methods of the class are entirely focused on realizing the intent behind the class. A class should never surprise a client. It should contain exactly the expected set of methods and no more. For example, a typical beginner's mistake is to take a simple, sufficient class like BankAccount and then add methods to process credit cards, or manage insurance policies, etc. Sufficiency is about keeping the design class as simple and focused as possible.

> A complete and sufficient class gives users of the class the contract they expect – no more and no less.

The golden rule for completeness and sufficiency is that a class should do what the users of the class expect – no more and no less.

## 15.4.2   Primitiveness

Methods should be designed to offer a single primitive, atomic service. A class should *not* offer multiple ways of doing the same thing as this is confusing to clients of the class and can lead to maintenance burdens and consistency problems.

> Primitiveness – services should be simple, atomic, and unique.

For example, if a BankAccount class has a primitive method for making a single deposit, it should not have a more complex method that makes two or more deposits. This is because you can achieve the same effect by repeated application of the primitive method. Your aim is that classes should always make available the simplest and smallest possible set of methods.

Although primitiveness is a fine rule, there are occasions when it may need to be relaxed. A common reason to relax the primitiveness constraint is to improve performance. For example, if there was a sufficient performance increase on making bank deposits in a batch, rather than individually, then you might relax the primitiveness constraint in order to let a BankAccount class have a more complex deposit(...) method that handled several transactions at once. However, your starting point in design should *always* be the most primitive possible set of methods. You should only add complexity by relaxing primitiveness if there is a genuine and proven case for doing so.

## 15.4.3   High cohesion

Each class should model a single abstract concept and should have a set of methods that support the intent of the class – this is cohesion. If a class needs to have many different responsibilities, then "helper" classes should implement some of these. The main class then delegates responsibilities to its helpers.

Cohesion is one of the most desirable features of a class. Cohesive classes are generally easy to understand, reuse, and maintain. A cohesive class has a small set of responsibilities that are all intimately related. Every method, attribute, and association of the class is specifically designed to implement this small, focused set of responsibilities.

> Each class should capture a single, well-defined abstraction using the minimal set of features.

**Figure 15.3**

We came across the perplexing model in Figure 15.3 in a selling system. There is a HotelBean class, a CarBean class, and a HotelCarBean class (the "beans" are Enterprise JavaBeans (EJBs)). The HotelBean was responsible for selling room stays in hotels, the CarBean for selling car hire, and the HotelCarBean for selling a package of car hire with a hotel stay. Clearly this model is wrong from several perspectives.

- The classes are badly named – HotelStay and CarHire would be much better names.
- The suffix "Bean" is unnecessary as it just refers to a specific implementation detail.
- The HotelCarBean class has very poor cohesion – it has two primary responsibilities (selling hotel stays and selling car hire) which are already carried out by two other classes.

From a cohesion perspective, HotelBean and CarBean are quite plausible (provided they were renamed), but HotelCarBean is just absurd.

## 15.4.4 Low coupling

A particular class should be associated with *just enough* other classes to allow it to realize its responsibilities and we should only associate classes if there is a genuine semantic link between them – this is low coupling.

> A class should be associated with the minimum number of other classes to allow it to fulfill its responsibilities.

One of the common mistakes of the novice OO designer is to connect everything in the model to everything else on a more or less ad hoc basis. In fact, coupling is your worst enemy in object modeling, and you must be really proactive about trying to limit the relationships between classes in order to minimize coupling as much as you can.

A highly coupled object model is the equivalent of "spaghetti code" in the non-OO world, and will lead to a system that is incomprehensible and unmaintainable. Highly coupled OO systems often result from projects in which there is no formal modeling activity, where the system is simply allowed to evolve in an ad hoc manner over time.

Novice designers must be careful not to make connections between classes just because one class has a code fragment that another class could use. This is the worst sort of reuse, as you sacrifice the architectural integrity of the system for a small saving in development time. In fact, all associations between classes need to be thought about very carefully. Many of the associations in the design model will come directly from the analysis model, but there are a whole set of associations that are introduced by implementation constraints, or by the desire to reuse code. These are the associations that need to be examined most carefully.

Of course, some coupling is good and is desirable. High coupling within a package is generally OK as this indicates high cohesion within the package. You only compromise the architecture when coupling is *between* packages, and you must actively seek to reduce this sort of coupling.

## 15.5    Inheritance

When you get to design, you have to consider inheritance much more than in analysis. In analysis, you would *only* use inheritance if there was a clear and unambiguous "is a" relationship between analysis classes. In design, however, you may also choose to use inheritance to reuse code. This is a different strategy, as you are really using inheritance to ease the implementation of a child class rather than to express a business relationship between a parent and child.

We will look at some strategies for using inheritance effectively in design in the next few sections.

### 15.5.1    Aggregation versus inheritance

Inheritance is a very powerful technique – it is the mechanism that generates polymorphism in strongly typed languages such as Java, C#, and C++. However, novice OO designers and programmers often abuse it. You should realize that inheritance has certain undesirable characteristics.

> Inheritance is the strongest form of coupling between two classes. It is an inflexible relationship.

- It is the strongest form of coupling possible between two or more classes.
- Encapsulation is weak within a class hierarchy. Changes in the base class ripple down to change the subclasses. This leads to what is known as the "fragile base class" problem, where changes to base classes have a large impact on other classes in the system.

● It is a very inflexible type of relationship. In all commonly used OO languages, inheritance relationships are fixed at run-time. You can modify
both aggregation and composition hierarchies at run-time by creating and
destroying relationships, but inheritance hierarchies remain fixed. This
means that it is the most inflexible type of relationship between classes.

The example in Figure 15.4 is a typical beginner's solution to the problem of
modeling roles in an organization. At first glance, it looks quite plausible, but it
has problems. Consider this case – the object john is of type Programmer, and you
wish to promote it to be of type Manager. How can you do this? You have seen
that you can't change john's class at run-time, and so the only way you can
achieve the promotion is to create a new Manager object (called john:Manager),
copy all of the relevant data from the john:Programmer object across, and then
delete the john:Programmer object to maintain consistency in the application.
This is clearly complex, and not at all how the real world works.

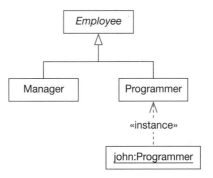

**Figure 15.4**

In fact, there is a fundamental semantic error in the model in Figure 15.4. Is
an employee *just* their job, or is it rather that an employee *has* a job? This
question leads us to the solution to the problem shown in Figure 15.5.

Using aggregation you get the correct semantics – an Employee *has* a
Job. With this more flexible model, Employees can also have more than one
Job if required.

We have achieved a much more flexible and semantically correct model
by replacing inheritance with aggregation as the mechanism for assigning
jobs to employees. There is an important general principle here – subclasses
should always represent "is kind of", rather than "is role played by". When
we think about the business semantics of companies, employees, and jobs,
it is clear that a job is a *role played* by an employee and does not really indicate a *kind of* employee. As such, inheritance is definitely the wrong choice
for modeling this sort of business relationship. On the other hand, there are
many *kinds of* jobs in a company. This indicates that an inheritance hierarchy of jobs (rooted in the abstract base class *Job*) is probably a good model.

> Subclasses should
> always represent a
> "special kind of"
> rather than a "role
> played by".

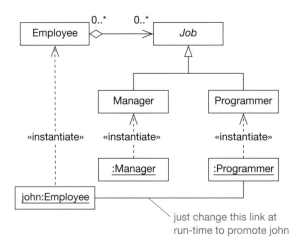

**Figure 15.5**

## 15.5.2    Multiple inheritance

Multiple
inheritance allows a
class to have more
than one parent.

Sometimes you may want to inherit implementation from more than one parent. This is multiple inheritance and it is not supported by all OO languages. For example, Java and C# only allow single inheritance. In practice, this lack of support for multiple inheritance is not a problem, as it can always be replaced by single inheritance and delegation. Even though multiple inheritance sometimes offers the most elegant solution to a design problem, it can *only* be used if the target implementation language supports it.

The important points about multiple inheritance are the following.

Parents must be
semantically disjoint.

● All the parent classes involved must be semantically disjoint. If there is any overlap in semantics between the base classes, then there is the possibility of unforeseen interactions between them. This could lead to strange behavior in the subclass. We say that the base classes must all be orthogonal (at right angles to each other).

● The "is kind of" and substitutability principles must apply between the subclass and all of its superclasses.

● Typically, the superclasses should have no parent in common. Otherwise, you have a cycle in the inheritance hierarchy and there may be multiple paths whereby the same features could be inherited from the more abstract classes. Languages that support multiple inheritance (such as C++) have specific, language-dependent ways of resolving cycles in the inheritance hierarchy.

One common idiom for using multiple inheritance effectively is the "mixin" class. These are classes that are not really stand-alone classes, but

Mixin classes are designed to be "mixed in" using multiple inheritance. This is a safe and powerful idiom.

rather are designed specifically to be "mixed in" with other classes using inheritance. In Figure 15.6, the Dialer class is a simple mixin. All it does is dial a phone number, and thus is not too useful on its own. However, it does provide a cohesive package of useful behavior that can be widely reused by other classes via multiple inheritance. This mixin is an example of a general utility class that could become part of a reuse library.

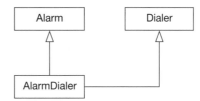

**Figure 15.6**

### 15.5.3 Inheritance versus interface realization

With inheritance you get two things:

- interface – the public methods of the base classes;
- implementation – the attributes, associations, protected and private methods of the base classes.

With interface realization (see Chapter 17) you get exactly one thing:

- an interface – a set of public operations that have no implementation.

Inheritance and interface realization have something in common as both mechanisms allow you to define a contract (a set of methods) that subclasses must implement. However, the two techniques have very different semantics and usage.

You only need to use inheritance when you are concerned about inheriting some implementation details (methods, attributes, associations) from a superclass. This is a kind of reuse, and in fact in the early days of OO it was often considered to be the primary mechanism for reuse. However, the world has moved on since then and designers have recognized the sometimes unacceptable constraints that inheritance imposes and have moved away from its usage to some extent.

Interface realization is useful whenever you want to define a contract but are not concerned about inheriting implementation details. While interface realization gives you no actual reuse of code, it does give a very clean mechanism for defining contracts and ensuring that classes conform to those contracts. Because nothing is really inherited in interface realization, it is more flexible and robust in some ways than inheritance.

## 15.6 Templates

Up to now, when we have defined a design class, we have had to explicitly specify the types of the attributes, the return types of all methods, and the types of all method parameters. This is fine and works well in most of the cases but it can sometimes limit the ability to reuse code.

In the example in Figure 15.7 we have defined three classes that are all bounded arrays. One is a bounded array of int, the next is a bounded array of double, and the last is a bounded array of String. When you examine these classes, you see that they are identical except for the type that is stored in the array. Yet, despite this similarity, we have had to define three separate classes.

| BoundedIntArray |
| --- |
| size : int<br>elements[ ] : int |
| addElement( e:int ) : void<br>getElement( i:int ) : int |

| BoundedDoubleArray |
| --- |
| size : int<br>elements[ ] : double |
| addElement( e:double ) : void<br>getElement( i:int ) : double |

| BoundedStringArray |
| --- |
| size : int<br>elements[ ] : String |
| addElement( e:String ) : void<br>getElement( i:int ) : String |

**Figure 15.7**

Templates allow you to parameterize a type. What this means is that instead of specifying the actual types of attributes, method return values, and method parameters, you can define a class in terms of placeholders or parameters. These may be replaced by actual values to create new classes. In Figure 15.8, we have defined the class BoundedArray in terms of the parameters T (which is by default a classifier) and size, which is an int.

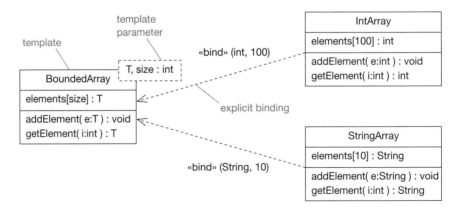

**Figure 15.8**

By binding specific values to these formal parameters you can create new classes – this is known as template instantiation. Notice that when you instantiate a template, you get a class, and this class may then be instantiated to get objects.

A template may be instantiated by using a dependency relationship stereotyped with «bind» – this is known as explicit binding. If you remember, we mentioned «bind» when we discussed dependencies in Section 9.5 but deferred its discussion until now. To instantiate a template, you also have to specify the actual values that will be bound to the template parameters, and you list these in brackets after the «bind» stereotype. When you instantiate the template, these values are substituted for the template parameters, and this gives a new class.

This is clearly a powerful mechanism for reuse – you can define a class very generally as a template, and then create many customized versions of this class by binding the template parameters to appropriate actual values.

In Figure 15.8, we actually use binding in two ways. First, we bind a classifier to the parameter T. When a template parameter has no type, then it defaults to a classifier. Second, we bind an actual integer value to the parameter size. This allows us to specify the bound for the bounded array as a template parameter.

The template parameter names are local to a particular template. This means that if two templates have a parameter called T, it is a different T in each case.

There is a variation on template syntax known as implicit binding. Here you don't use an explicit «bind» dependency to show template instantiation, but rather you bind implicitly by using a special syntax on the instantiated classes. To instantiate a template implicitly, you simply list the actual values in angle brackets after the template class name as shown in Figure 15.9. The disadvantage of this approach is that you can't give the instantiated class its own name.

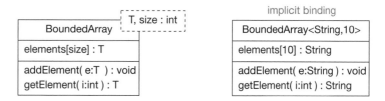

**Figure 15.9**

Our feeling is that it is better style to use explicit binding so that the template instantiation classes can each have their own descriptive name.

While templates are a very powerful feature, at the moment C++ is the only commonly used OO language that supports them (see Table 15.1). Clearly, they can only be used in design when the implementation language supports them.

**Table 15.1**

| Language | Template support |
|----------|------------------|
| Java | No |
| C++ | Yes |
| Smalltalk | No |
| Python | No |
| Visual Basic | No |
| C# | No |

## 15.7   Nested classes

Some languages, such as Java, allow you to place a class definition inside another class definition. This creates what is known as a nested class. In Java, this is also known as an inner class.

A nested class is declared within the namespace of its outer class, and is *only* accessible by that class or by objects of that class. Only the outer class or its objects can create and use instances of the nested class.

Nested classes can be used in Java event handling. The example in Figure 15.10 shows a simple window class called HelloFrame. It inherits basic window behavior from its parent Frame class. HelloFrame has a nested class called MouseMonitor that inherits the ability to handle mouse events from its parent MouseAdapter class.

Each HelloFrame instance uses a MouseMonitor instance to process its mouse events. To achieve this, the HelloFrame instance must:

● create an instance of MouseMonitor;

● set this MouseMonitor to be its mouse event listener.

This approach makes quite a lot of sense, as the mouse handling code becomes completely encapsulated in the nested MouseMonitor class.

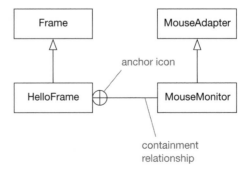

**Figure 15.10**

## 15.8  What we have learned

Design classes are the building blocks of the design model. You have learned the following.

- Design classes are classes the specifications of which have been completed to such a degree that they can be implemented.
- Design classes come from two sources:
  - the problem domain:
    - a refinement of analysis classes;
    - one analysis class may become zero, one or more design classes;
  - the solution domain:
    - utility class libraries;
    - middleware;
    - GUI libraries;
    - reusable components;
    - implementation-specific details.

- Design classes have complete specifications:
  - complete set of attributes including:
    - name;
    - type;
    - default value when appropriate;
    - visibility.
  - methods:
    - name;
    - names and types of all parameters;
    - optional parameter values if appropriate;
    - return type;
    - visibility.

- Well-formed design classes exhibit certain characteristics:
  - the public methods of the class define a contract with the clients of the class;
  - completeness – the class does no less than its clients may reasonably expect;
  - sufficiency – the class does no more than its clients may reasonably expect;
  - primitiveness – services should be simple, atomic, and unique;

- — high cohesion:
  - each class should embody a single, well-defined abstract concept;
  - all the methods should support the intent of the class;
- — low coupling:
  - a class should be coupled to just enough other classes to fulfill its responsibilities;
  - only couple two classes when there is a true semantic relationship between them;
  - never couple classes just to reuse some code.
- — Always assess a design class from the point of view of the clients of that class.

- Inheritance.
  - — Only use inheritance when there is a clear "is a" relationship between two classes or to reuse code (but be careful not to introduce coupling).
  - — Disadvantages:
    - it is the strongest possible coupling between two classes;
    - encapsulation is weak within an inheritance hierarchy, leading to the "fragile base class" problem – changes in the base class ripple down the hierarchy;
    - very inflexible in most languages – the relationship is decided at compile time and fixed at run-time.
  - — Subclasses should always represent "is kind of" rather than "is role played by" – always use aggregation to represent "is role played by".

- Multiple inheritance allows a class to have more than one parent.
  - — Of all the common OO languages only C++ has multiple inheritance.
  - — Design guidelines:
    - the multiple parent classes must all be semantically disjoint;
    - there must be an "is kind of" relationship between a class and all of its parents;
    - the substitutability principle must apply to the class and its parents;
    - the parents should themselves have no parent in common;
    - use mixins – a mixin is a simple class designed to be mixed in with others in multiple inheritance; this is a safe and powerful idiom.

- Inheritance versus interface realization.
  - — Inheritance:
    - you get interface – the public methods;
    - you get implementation – the attributes, associations, protected and private members.

- — Interface realization – you only get interface.
- — Use inheritance when you want to inherit some implementation.
- — Use interface realization when you want to define a contract.

● Templates.
  - — Of all the commonly used OO languages, only C++ supports templates.
  - — Templates allow you to "parameterize" a type – you create a template by defining a type in terms of formal parameters and you instantiate the template by binding specific values for the parameters.
    - – Explicit binding uses a dependency stereotyped «bind»:
      - – you show the actual values on the relationship;
      - – you can name each template instantiation.
    - – Implicit binding:
      - – you specify the actual values on the class inside angle brackets (< >);
      - – you can't name the template instantiations – names are constructed from the template name and the argument list.

● Nested classes:
  - — you define a class inside another class;
  - — the nested class exists in the namespace of the outer class – only the outer class can create and use instances of the nested class;
  - — nested classes are known as inner classes in Java, and are used extensively for event handling in GUI classes.

# chapter 16

# Refining analysis relationships

## 16.1 Chapter roadmap

This chapter presents techniques for refining analysis relationships into design relationships. The first part of the chapter discusses converting analysis relationships into one of the whole-part relationships – aggregation (Section 16.4) or composition (Section 16.5).

The second part discusses how to deal with multiplicities in analysis associations. We provide specific techniques for refining analysis associations where the multiplicity is one-to-one (Section 16.7), many-to-one (Section 16.8), one-to-many (Section 16.9), and many-to-many (Section 16.11.1). We also cover bidirectional associations (Section 16.11.2) and association classes (Section 16.11.3).

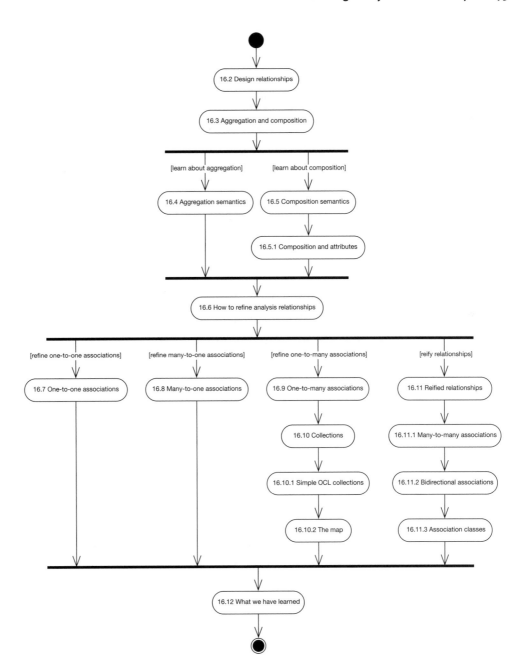

**Figure 16.1**

## 16.2    Design relationships

Analysis associations must be refined to design relationships that are directly implementable in the target OO language.

When you move to design, you have to refine the relationships between analysis classes into relationships between design classes. Many of the relationships captured in analysis are not directly implementable as they stand, and they must be made so. For example, there is no commonly used OO programming language that directly supports bidirectional associations, association classes, or many-to-many associations. To create a design model, you have to specify *how* these associations are going to be realized.

Refining analysis associations to design associations involves several procedures:

● refining associations to aggregation or composition relationships where appropriate;

● implementing association classes;

● implementing one-to-many associations;

● implementing many-to-many associations;

● implementing bidirectional associations.

All design associations *must* have:

● navigability;

● multiplicity on both ends.

All design associations *should* have a role name on at least the target end.

## 16.3    Aggregation and composition

In design, you may refine an association relationship into an aggregation relationship or a stronger form of aggregation known as the composition aggregation relationship. We normally refer to composition aggregation simply as composition.

You can get a very good idea about the semantic differences between the two types of aggregation by thinking about some real-world examples.

● Aggregation – this is a loose relationship between objects – an example might be a computer and its peripherals.

● Composition – this is a very strong type of relationship between objects – it is like a tree and its leaves.

If you consider these examples, illustrated in Figure 16.2, then you can see that a computer is only weakly related to its peripherals. These peripherals may come and go, may be shared between computers, and are not in any meaningful sense "owned" by any particular computer – this is aggregation. On the other hand, a tree is very intimately related to its leaves. Leaves are owned by exactly one tree, they can't be shared between trees, and when the tree dies the leaves go with it – this is composition.

Aggregation                              Composition

Some objects are weakly          Some objects are strongly
related, like a computer and     related, like a tree and
its peripherals                  its leaves

**Figure 16.2**

It will be very useful to keep these simple analogies in mind as you study the detailed semantics of aggregation and composition in the rest of this chapter.

## 16.4 Aggregation semantics

Aggregation is a type of whole–part relationship where the aggregate is made up of many parts. In a whole–part relationship, one object (the whole) uses the services of another object (the part). As such, the whole tends to be the dominant and controlling side of the relationship, whereas the part just tends to service requests from the whole and is therefore more passive. Indeed, if you only have navigability from the whole to the part, then the part doesn't even know that it is part of a whole.

In the particular aggregation example in Figure 16.3, you can see that:

- a Computer may be attached to 0 or more Printers;
- at any *one point in time* a Printer is connected to 0 or 1 Computer;
- *over time*, many Computers may use a given Printer;
- the Printer may exist even if there are no attached Computers;
- the Printer is, in a very real sense, independent of the Computer.

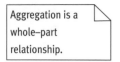

Aggregation is a
whole–part
relationship.

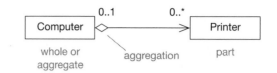

Figure 16.3

We can summarize aggregation semantics as follows:

- the aggregate can sometimes exist independently of the parts, sometimes not;
- the parts can exist independently of the aggregate;
- the aggregate is in some sense incomplete if some of the parts are missing;
- it is possible to have shared ownership of the parts by several aggregates.

Aggregation is transitive. If you consider Figure 16.4, this means that if C is part of B and B is part of A, then C is also part of A.

Aggregation is
transitive. If C is part
of B, and B is part of
A, then C is part of A.

Figure 16.4

Aggregation is asymmetric. This means that an object can never, either directly or indirectly, be part of itself. In the aggregation example in Figure 16.5, you can see that Product objects may be composed of other Product objects – this is fine provided they are all *different* objects.

Aggregation is
asymmetric. An
object can never be
part of itself.

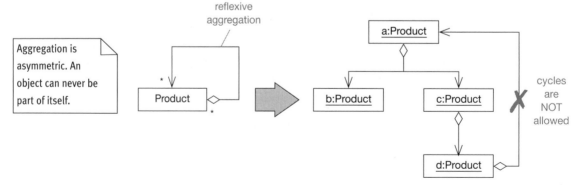

Figure 16.5

Considering Figure 16.5 further, sometimes you might need to model the case where object d has a link to object a as shown. This would occur when object d needed to *call back* and use some of the services of the aggregate object a. But how would you model this on the class diagram? The reflexive aggregation relationship on the Product class won't do as the asymmetry constraint on aggregation precludes object a being, either directly or indirectly, a part of itself. You therefore need to introduce a reflexive, unrefined *association* between class Product and itself to handle the link between objects d and a as shown in Figure 16.6.

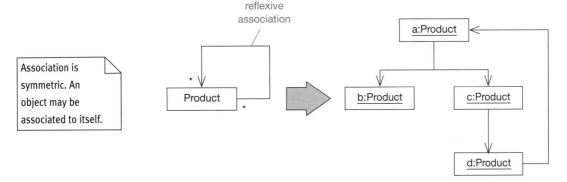

**Figure 16.6**

The example in Figure 16.7 shows another typical example of aggregation. You can model a home computer (the whole) as a set of parts. These parts are quite loosely related to the whole as they are interchangeable with other computers, and so you can use aggregation semantics in your model. The

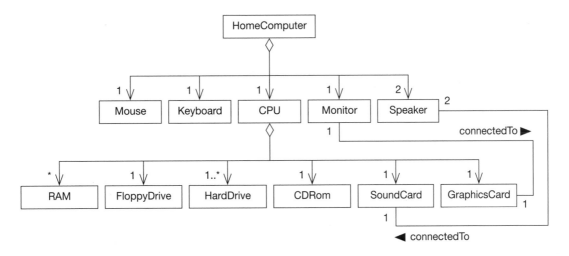

**Figure 16.7**

model says that a home computer can be thought of as an aggregate of the following parts – a Mouse, a Keyboard, a CPU, a Monitor and two Speakers. The CPU can itself be modeled as an aggregate of various hardware components such as RAM, HardDrives, etc.

## 16.5 Composition semantics

Composition is a stronger form of aggregation and has similar (but more constrained) semantics. Like aggregation, it is a whole-part relationship and is both transitive and asymmetric.

The key difference between aggregation and composition is that in composition the parts have no independent life outside of the whole. Furthermore, in composition each part belongs to one and only one whole, whereas in aggregation a part may be shared between wholes.

> Composition is a strong form of aggregation.

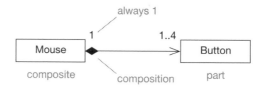

**Figure 16.8**

In the example in Figure 16.8, Button objects have no independent existence apart from their owning Mouse object. If you destroy the Mouse object, you destroy its Button objects as they are an integral part of it. Each Button object can belong to exactly one Mouse object. This is just like leaves and trees – the life of the leaf is determined by the life of the tree, and a leaf can only belong to exactly one tree.

We can summarize composition semantics as follows:

> The composite has sole ownership and responsibility for its parts.

- the parts belong to exactly one composite at a time;
- the composite has sole responsibility for the disposition of all its parts – this means responsibility for their creation and destruction;
- the composite may also release parts, provided responsibility for them is assumed by another object;
- if the composite is destroyed, it must either destroy all its parts, or give responsibility for them over to some other object.

Because the composite has sole responsibility for the lifecycle and disposition of its parts, when you create a composite, the composite object will create its parts. Similarly, when you destroy a composite, the composite must destroy all of its parts *or* arrange for them to be adopted by another composite.

Another difference between aggregation and composition is that although you may have reflexive aggregation hierarchies *and* networks, you can only have reflexive composition hierarchies. This is because in composition, a part object can only be part of *one* composite at any point in time.

UML provides an alternative "nested" composition syntax which, in some ways, illustrates more graphically the nature of composition. There is no semantic difference between the two types of composition syntax and both styles are shown in Figure 16.9. The tree form of composition syntax is more widely used because it can be clearer and easier to draw.

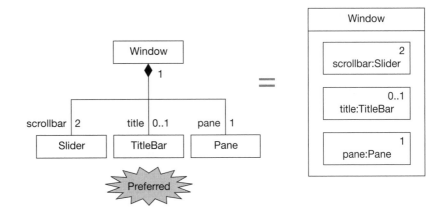

**Figure 16.9**

## 16.5.1 Composition and attributes

A part in a composite is equivalent to an attribute.

When you think about composition semantics, you should see that they are very similar to the semantics of attributes. Both have lifecycles that are controlled by their owners, and both have no independent existence outside of their owners. In fact, attributes are exactly equivalent to a composition relationship between the composite class and the class of the attribute. Why, then, do we need two ways to express the same thing? There are two reasons.

● Attributes may be primitive data types. Some hybrid OO languages like C++ and Java have primitive types such as int and double that are not classes. Now, you could model these as classes stereotyped «primitive», but to be frank this would just clutter the model. These primitive types should *always* be modeled as attributes.

- There are certain utility classes like Time, Date and String that are used pervasively. If you were to model every usage of one of these classes by a composition relationship to the class itself, then pretty soon your models would be entirely obscured. It is much better to model classes like these as attributes.

The bottom line is that if you have a primitive type or a utility class, or even a class that is just not very interesting or useful to show explicitly on the model, you should consider using an attribute rather than a composition relationship. There is no hard and fast rule here, but the key guiding points to keep in mind are always the clarity, usefulness, and readability of the model.

## 16.6    How to refine analysis relationships

Analysis associations should be refined into one of the aggregation relationships wherever possible.

In analysis, you use simple associations without really considering the semantics of the relationship (or how the relationship is finally to be implemented) in any great detail. In design, however, you should always try to be as specific as possible, and so you refine associations into one of the aggregation relationships wherever you can. In fact, the only case where you *must* use an association in design is where there would otherwise be a cycle in the aggregation graph (see Section 16.4). This is quite rare, and so most analysis associations end up as either aggregation or composition.

Having decided to use aggregation or composition, you should proceed as follows:

- add multiplicities and role names to the association if they are absent;
- decide which side of the association is the whole, and which is the part;
- look at the multiplicity of the whole side – if it is exactly 1, then you *may* be able to use composition; otherwise, you *must* use aggregation;
- add navigability *from* the whole *to* the part – design associations *must* be unidirectional.

This gets you to the stage where you have refined the association into either an aggregation or a composition.

If the multiplicities on either the whole or the part end are greater than 1, then you have to decide how you will implement this. This is the next step in the refinement.

## 16.7    One-to-one associations

Whenever you see a one-to-one association, this almost always becomes composition. In fact, a one-to-one association implies such a strong relationship between two classes, that it is often worth seeing if they could be merged into a single class without breaking any of the design rules for design classes (see Section 15.4). Assuming that they can't be merged, you refine a one-to-one relationship as shown in Figure 16.10.

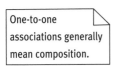

One-to-one associations generally mean composition.

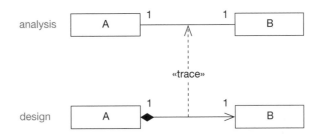

**Figure 16.10**

You may also consider making B an attribute of A if B is not a particularly important class.

## 16.8    Many-to-one associations

A many-to-one association is where there is a multiplicity of many on the whole side, and a multiplicity of exactly 1 on the part side.

Because there are many on the whole side, you know immediately that you *can't* use composition as the part is shared between many wholes. But you *may* be able to use aggregation. You should check at this point for cycles in the aggregation graph (see Section 16.4) – provided there are none, you can refine the analysis association as shown in Figure 16.11.

Many-to-one associations mean aggregation provided there is no cycle in the aggregation graph.

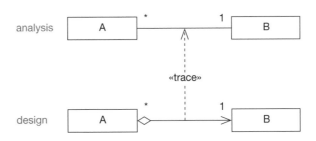

**Figure 16.11**

## 16.9    One-to-many associations

In one-to-many associations, there is a *collection* of objects on the part side of the relationship. In order to implement such a relationship you have to use either native support for collections provided by the implementation language, or a collection class.

Most OO languages provide minimal built-in support for collections of objects. In fact, most languages only offer arrays. An array is an indexed collection of object references that is normally bounded to some maximum size. The advantage of built-in arrays is that they tend to be very fast. However, this speed is offset by their inflexibility compared to other types of collection.

Collection classes are typically much more powerful and flexible than native collections. They offer a whole range of different semantics, of which array semantics is just one possibility. We will look at designing with collection classes in the rest of this chapter.

## 16.10    Collections

> Collection classes are classes whose instances hold collections of objects.

A collection class is a class whose instances specialize in managing collections of other objects. Most languages have standard libraries of collection classes (and other utilities) available.

One of the keys to excellent OO design and implementation is having a mastery of collection classes. All collection classes have methods for:

- adding objects to the collection;
- removing objects from the collection;
- retrieving a reference to an object in the collection;
- traversing the collection, i.e. stepping through the collection from the first object to the last.

There are many different types of collection and each is specialized to handle collections of objects in a particular way. Choosing the right collection for the job in hand is an important aspect of OO design and implementation and we'll look at this in the next section.

As an example of using collections, Figure 16.12 shows a one-to-many association in analysis being implemented by a collection class called Vector. This class comes from the Java standard library java.util. The relationship from the whole (A) to the Vector is usually a composition as the Vector typically is just a part of the implementation of the whole, and has no life outside of this. However, the relationship between the Vector and the parts

(B) may be an aggregation or a composition. If A is responsible for creating and destroying the parts, then you may use composition. Otherwise, you must use aggregation.

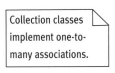

Collection classes implement one-to-many associations.

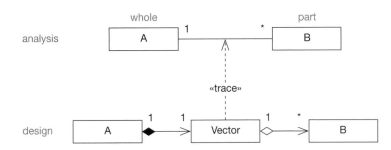

**Figure 16.12**

In terms of modeling with collections, there are three fundamental strategies.

- Model the collection class explicitly – this is the case shown in Figure 16.12. It has the advantage of being very explicit, but also the big disadvantage of adding a lot of clutter to the design model. If you replace every one-to-many association in the model with a collection class, then the model rapidly becomes bloated. Choice of a collection class is usually a tactical implementation decision and can be left to the developers. We should *only* replace one-to-many associations with specific collection classes when the choice of collection is strategic.

- Tell the CASE tool how each specific one-to-many association is to be implemented. Many CASE tools allow a specific collection class to be assigned to each one-to-many association. This is usually accomplished by adding tagged values to the association to specify the code generation properties for that relationship. This approach is shown in Figure 16.13, where we have added the property {Vector} to the appropriate end of the relationship. Notice that we only use the name part of the tagged value – the value part is redundant in this case.

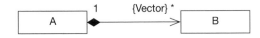

**Figure 16.13**

Don't "over model" when using collections.

- Specify the semantics of the collection, but don't specify any implementation class. It is important not to "over model" when using collections. As we've said, the actual type of collection used is often a tactical, rather than a strategic, issue and it can be left to the programmer to make a reasonable assumption at implementation time. This approach usually precludes automatic code generation, however.

UML provides two standard properties {ordered} and {unordered} that you can apply to relationship ends to tell you if the collection of objects is maintained in a strict order or if the ordering is random. For example, assuming you need an ordered collection of B, you can express Figure 16.13 as shown in Figure 16.14.

**Figure 16.14**

As well as {ordered} and {unordered}, you can use one or more of your own non-standard properties to indicate the required semantics of the collection. Some useful examples are given in Table 16.1.

**Table 16.1**

| Property | Semantics |
| --- | --- |
| {sorted} | The collection is sorted according to some key – the key may be specified in the property, e.g. {sorted by name} |
| {indexed} | Each element in the set is accessible via a numeric index |
| {set} | Duplicates are not allowed in the collection |
| {lifo} | "Last in, first out" – a stack where the last element placed on the stack is the first element that can be taken off it |
| {queue} | A queue where the first element placed on the queue is the first element that can be taken off it |

Because these are non-standard properties, make sure you document them somewhere on the model.

## 16.10.1   Simple OCL collections

The Object Constraint Language (OCL) is a formal language for expressing constraints – it is part of the UML 1.4 specification. It is not that widely used (and so we don't cover it in any detail in this book) but it does offer a completely generic set of collection classes that provide useful examples of the types of collection that are commonly available in OO implementation languages.

The OCL collections are Set, Bag and Sequence. You might choose to use OCL collections in the late stages of analysis, or in the early stages of design when you need to specify some collection semantics but don't yet want to introduce implementation language dependencies.

The semantics of OCL collections are shown in Table 16.2.

**Table 16.2**

| Collection | Duplicate objects allowed | Indexed | Ordered |
|------------|---------------------------|---------|---------|
| Set | No | No | No |
| Bag | Yes | No | No |
| Sequence | Yes | Yes | Yes |

- Set behaves just like a mathematical set – duplicate objects are not allowed. There is no indexing of the elements in the set, and the elements are maintained in a random order.

- Bag is less constrained than Set in that it can accept duplicates. Otherwise, the semantics are the same.

- Sequence also accepts duplicate objects, but is indexed and ordered. This means that the objects stored in Sequence have an index just like in an array, and the objects always maintain their relative positions in the collection.

## 16.10.2 The map

> Maps are optimized to quickly return a value given a key.

Another very useful type of collection class is the map, also sometimes known as the dictionary. These classes act a bit like a database table with just two columns – the key and the value. Given a key, maps are designed so that you can *rapidly* find the associated value. Whenever you need to store collections of objects that need to be accessed according to the value of a unique key, or when you need to build fast access indexes into other collections, a map is a good choice.

Unfortunately, maps are not part of OCL and so if you want to use a map you are really forced to specify a language-dependent implementation.

Maps usually work by maintaining a set of nodes where each node points to two objects – the key object and the value object. They are optimized to find a value object very quickly when given a specific key object.

Figure 16.15 shows a simplified representation of a Java HashMap. Finding a value (given a particular key) is very fast, as the collection is indexed using a hash table.

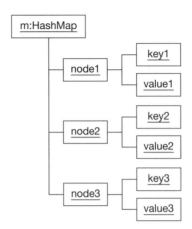

**Figure 16.15**

## 16.11  Reified relationships

Some types of relationship are pure analysis artefacts and are not themselves directly supported by any of the commonly used OO languages. The process of taking these analysis relationships and implementing them is known as reification (to make concrete, or real). You need to reify the following analysis relationships:

- many-to-many associations;
- bidirectional associations;
- association classes.

### 16.11.1  Many-to-many associations

Many-to-many associations are not directly supported in any of the commonly used OO languages (although some object databases do support them directly) so they must be reified into normal classes, aggregations, compositions, and dependencies. In analysis, you could be quite vague about issues such as ownership and navigation, but there is no room for such vagueness in design. As such, you first have to decide which side of the many-to-many association is the whole and then use aggregation or composition as appropriate.

In the example in Figure 16.16, based on the requirements of the system, we have decided that Resource is the whole. This is because the system is mainly about managing the lines of work associated with Resources, i.e. it is resource-centric. However, if the system were task-centric, then we would make Task the whole, reversing the relationships shown in Figure 16.16.

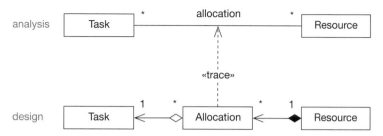

**Figure 16.16**

We've also chosen to give Resource responsibility for the lifecycle of its Allocation objects, and so have used a composition relationship.

If the system tries to present *both* points of view, then we might say it is allocation-centric, and so we would introduce a new object (AllocationManager perhaps), which maintains a list of Allocation objects where each object points to both a Resource and a Task object.

### 16.11.2　Bidirectional associations

Often you need to model the circumstance where an object a of class A uses the services of an object b of class B, and object b needs to call back and use the services of object a. An example of this might be a GUI Window control owning one or more Button objects where each of these Button objects needs to call back and use the services of their owning Window.

In analysis, this is straightforward – you model it as a single bidirectional association. In design, however, none of the commonly used OO languages support true bidirectional associations, and so you must reify this bidirectional association into two unidirectional associations or dependencies, as illustrated in Figure 16.17.

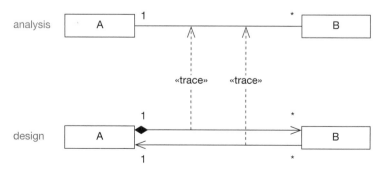

**Figure 16.17**

When you are modeling callbacks, you need to be aware of the asymmetry constraint on aggregation and composition – an object must *never* directly or indirectly be a part of itself. This means that if class A has an aggregation or composition relationship to class B, you have to model the callback relationship from B back to A as an unrefined association. If instead you used an aggregation relationship from B back to A, then object <u>b</u> would be part (by composition or aggregation) of object <u>a</u>, and object <u>a</u> would be part (by aggregation) of object <u>b</u>. This cycle of ownership clearly breaks the aggregation asymmetry constraint.

Bidirectional associations also exist where the whole passes a reference to itself as a parameter to one of the part's methods, or where the part instantiates the whole in one of its methods. In these cases, you should use a dependency relationship instead of an association.

### 16.11.3   Association classes

Association classes are pure analysis artefacts that are not directly implementable in any commonly used OO programming language. Thus, they have no direct analog in design and you need to remove them from your design model.

You reify the association class into a normal class and use a combination of association, aggregation, composition, or even dependency to capture the

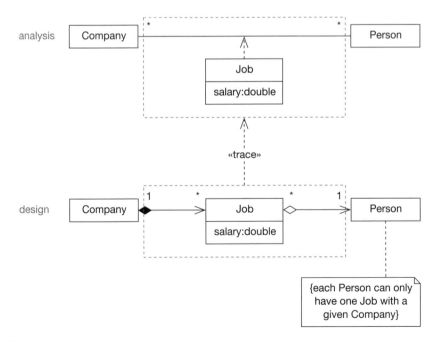

**Figure 16.18**

association class semantics. This may involve adding constraints to the model. You decide which side of the association is the whole and use composition, aggregation, and navigability accordingly. An example is shown in Figure 16.18.

Notice that when you reify an association class, you lose the association class semantics. These semantics state that the objects on each end of the association class must form a unique pair (see Section 9.4.5). However, as shown in Figure 16.18, you can easily restore these semantics by adding a note containing the appropriate constraint.

## 16.12  What we have learned

In this chapter you have seen how relationships in analysis are converted to implementable design relationships. You have learned the following.

- Refining analysis associations to design associations involves:
  — refining associations into aggregation or composition aggregation where appropriate;
  — implementing association classes;
  — implementing one-to-many associations;
  — implementing many-to-many associations;
  — implementing bidirectional associations;
  — adding navigability;
  — adding multiplicity to both ends of the association;
  — adding a role name at both ends of the association, or at least on the target end of the association.

- Aggregation and composition.
  — These are whole–part types of relationship where objects of one class act as the whole or aggregate, and objects of the other class act as the parts:
    – the whole uses the services of the parts; the parts service the requests of the whole;
    – the whole is the dominant, controlling side of the relationship; the part tends to be more passive.
  — These relationships are transitive – if C is part of B and B is part of A, then C is part of A.
  — These relationships are asymmetric:
    – a whole can never directly or indirectly be a part of itself;
    – there must never be a cycle in the aggregation graph.

- — There are two types of aggregation relationship:
  - – aggregation;
  - – composition aggregation – usually referred to simply as composition.

- Aggregation.
  - — Aggregation semantics:
    - – the aggregate can sometimes exist independently of the parts, sometimes not;
    - – the parts can exist independently of the aggregate;
    - – the aggregate is in some way incomplete if some of the parts are missing;
    - – it is possible to have shared ownership of the parts by several aggregates;
    - – aggregation hierarchies and aggregation networks are possible;
    - – the whole always knows about the parts, but if the relationship is one-way from the whole to the part, then the parts don't know about the whole.
  - — Aggregation is like a computer and its peripherals:
    - – a computer is only weakly related to its peripherals;
    - – peripherals may come and go;
    - – peripherals may be shared between computers;
    - – peripherals are not in any meaningful sense "owned" by any particular computer.

- Composition.
  - — This is a strong form of aggregation:
    - – the parts belong to exactly one composite at a time;
    - – the composite has sole responsibility for the disposition of all its parts – this means responsibility for their creation and destruction;
    - – the composite may also release parts, provided responsibility for them is assumed by another object;
    - – if the composite is destroyed, it must destroy all its parts or give responsibility for them over to some other object;
    - – each part belongs to exactly one composite so you can only have composition hierarchies – composition networks are impossible.
  - — Composition is like a tree and its leaves:
    - – leaves are owned by exactly one tree;
    - – leaves can't be shared between trees;
    - – when the tree dies, its leaves go with it.

— A part in a composite is equivalent to an attribute:
- use explicit composition when the parts are important and interesting;
- use attributes when the parts are neither important nor interesting.

● Refining analysis associations.
— Analysis associations should be refined into one of the aggregation relationships wherever possible. If this would create a cycle in the aggregation graph, then it is impossible, and you must use an association or a dependency.
— Procedure for refining associations to aggregation relationships:
- add multiplicities and role names;
- decide which side of the relationship is the whole, and which is the part;
- look at the multiplicity of the whole side:
  - if it is 1, then you may be able to use composition – check that the association has composition semantics, then apply composition;
  - if it is not 1, then you *must* use aggregation;
- add navigability from the whole to the part.

● Different types of association.
— One-to-one association – this almost always becomes composition. However, you may also choose to use an attribute instead or to merge the two classes.
— Many-to-one association – use aggregation as there are many on the whole side, so you can't use composition.
— One-to-many association:
- there is a collection of objects on the part side;
- use an in-built array (most OO languages directly support arrays) – they are generally quite inflexible but are usually fast;
- use a collection class – they are more flexible than in-built arrays and are faster than arrays where searching the collection is required (otherwise slower).
— Collections:
- These are classes specialized so that their instances can manage a collection of other objects.
- All collection classes have methods for:
  - adding objects to the collection;
  - removing objects from the collection;
  - retrieving a reference to an object in the collection;
  - traversing the collection – stepping through the collection from the first object to the last.

- Modeling with collections – options:
  - model the collection class explicitly;
  - tell the CASE tool which collection to use by adding a property to the relationship – e.g. {Vector};
  - tell the programmer what collection semantics are required by adding a property to the relationship:
    - {ordered} – the collection is maintained in a strict order (this is a standard UML property);
    - {unordered} – the collection is not maintained in a strict order (this is a standard UML property);
    - {sorted} – the collection is sorted according to some key;
    - {indexed} – each element in the collection has a numeric index, like in an array;
    - {set} – duplicate elements are not allowed;
    - {lifo} – last in, first out stack;
    - {queue} – first in, first out queue.
  - Don't "over model" – the choice of a specific collection class is often a tactical issue that can be left to the programmer at implementation time.
- OCL collections:
  - Set – duplicates not allowed, not indexed, not ordered;
  - Bag – duplicates allowed, not indexed, not ordered;
  - Sequence – duplicates allowed, indexed, ordered.
- The map:
  - also known as the dictionary;
  - given a key, the corresponding value may be found very quickly;
  - acts like a database table with two columns, the key and the value;
  - keys must be unique.
— Reified relationships.
  - Some relationships are pure analysis artefacts and must be made implementable by the process of reification.
  - Many-to-many associations:
    - decide which side is the whole and which is the part;
    - replace the relationship with a class – this reduces the many-to-many association to two one-to-many associations.
  - Bidirectional associations – replace with a unidirectional aggregation or composition from whole to part, and a unidirectional association or dependency from part to whole.

- Association classes:
  - decide which side is the whole and which is the part;
  - replace with a class (usually with the same name as the association class);
  - add a constraint in a note to indicate that objects on each end of the reified relationship must form a unique pair.

# chapter 17

# Interfaces and subsystems

## 17.1 Chapter roadmap

This chapter has two main threads – interfaces and design subsystems. We discuss these two topics together because, as you will see in Sections 17.6.1 and 17.6.2, using interfaces combined with design subsystems allows the creation of flexible system architectures.

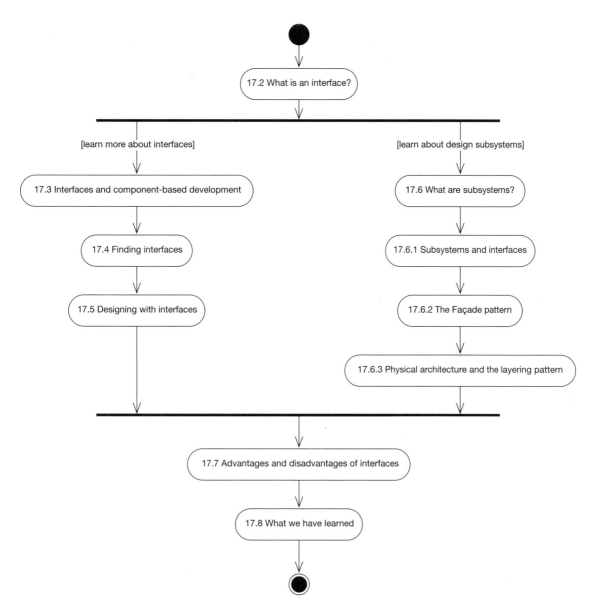

**Figure 17.1**

## 17.2    What is an interface?

An interface specifies a named set of operations. The key idea behind interfaces is to separate the *specification* of functionality (the interface) from its *implementation* by a classifier such as a class or subsystem. The interface defines a contract that is implemented by the classifier.

Interfaces separate the specification of functionality from its implementation.

This classifier may itself be physically packaged in a subsystem or component (we discuss components in Chapter 22). If the interface is public in this subsystem or component, then the subsystem or component also realizes the interface. Anything that realizes an interface agrees to abide by the contract that it defines. This contract consists of the set of specifications for all the operations that comprise the interface.

Interfaces can have a profound effect on the way you design. Up to now, we have been designing by connecting specific classes together – we might call this "designing to an implementation". However, it is more flexible to "design to a contract" where you connect to an interface, and this interface may then be realized by any number of classes. The Java standard libraries bear testament to the flexibility and power of this approach. We often say that an interface defines a *service* offered by a class, subsystem or component. Modern software architectures are often service based.

Interfaces define a contract.

Interfaces become architecturally very important in design, as they provide the "plugs and sockets" that allow you to connect your design subsystems together without connecting specific classes in those subsystems. Each operation in an interface *must* have:

- the complete operation signature (name, types of all parameters, and return type);
- the semantics of the operation – this can be recorded as text or pseudocode;
- optionally, a stereotype, and sets of constraints and tagged values.

Interfaces may *not* have:

- attributes;
- operation implementations;
- relationships navigable *from* the interface *to* anything else.

It is important to remember that an interface defines operation signatures and semantics, stereotypes, constraints and tagged values but *nothing* else. It never specifies or implies any kind of implementation – that is left entirely to the classes, subsystems, or components that implement the interface.

An interface is a bit like an abstract class with no attributes and a set of operations that are all abstract. However, what makes interfaces sufficiently different to warrant a separate notation is that they have the extra constraint that there must be no associations *from* the interface *to* anything else.

It is worth noting that Java interfaces are a little bit different from the UML definition. This is because Java interfaces can contain constant values – values that never change. The names of the days of the week, and months of the year are typical examples of constant values. Allowing constant values to be embedded in an interface has no real impact on design with interfaces, and it does give Java programmers a convenient packaging mechanism for their constants!

Although Java is the first commonly used language to explicitly introduce a language construct for interfaces, it is quite possible to program using interfaces in other languages. For example, in C++ you would simply define an abstract class with a set of abstract operations and no associations to anything else.

UML interface syntax is shown in Figure 17.2 and there are two variants – the "class" style notation (on which you may show the operations) and the concise "lollipop" style notation (on which you can't show the operations).

> If the implementation language doesn't directly support interfaces, just use abstract classes.

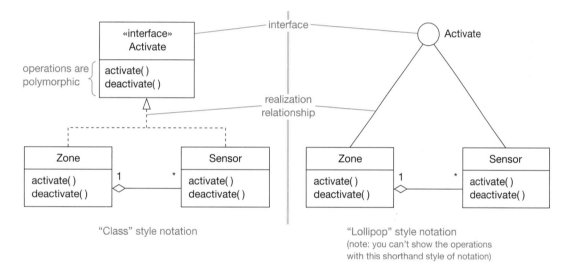

"Class" style notation

"Lollipop" style notation
(note: you can't show the operations with this shorthand style of notation)

**Figure 17.2**

The realization relationship shows the relationship between a specification (in this case an interface) and the things that realize the specification (in this case the classes Zone and Sensor). We'll see later that it is not just classes that can realize an interface – packages and components can as well.

Notice that in the "class" style notation, the realization relationship is drawn as a dotted line with an unfilled arrowhead, while in the "lollipop" style notation it becomes a single solid line with no arrowhead. The idea here is that the "lollipop" notation is kept as concise as possible. You would use the "class" notation when you want to show the operations, and the "lollipop" notation when you don't. However, they both mean exactly the same thing.

Looking at Figure 17.2, which is taken from a burglar alarm system, you can see that the interface Activate specifies an activate/deactivate service. This is obviously a very useful service for such a system! We have shown that the interface is realized by two classes – a Zone class and a Sensor class. Burglar alarm systems normally have many Zones, each of which may be independently activated and deactivated. Within those Zones are Sensors, and these can also be activated and deactivated. It clearly makes sense from a system perspective to activate and deactivate Zones and Sensors in exactly the same way. The best way to ensure this is to define an interface for the activate/deactivate service – Activate. Once you have done this, then everything in the system that needs an activate/deactivate service will simply realize this interface.

Interfaces are typically named just like classes. However, in Visual Basic and C# there is a common standard to prefix each interface name with uppercase I, for example IActivate.

## 17.3 Interfaces and component-based development

> Component-based development is about constructing software from plug-in parts.

Interfaces are the key to component-based development (CBD). This is about constructing software from plug-in parts. If you want to create flexible component-based software where you can plug in new implementations at will, then you must design with interfaces. Because an interface only specifies the contract, it allows for *any number* of specific implementations, provided each abides by the contract.

In Figure 17.3, you can see how interfaces allow you to connect things together without introducing coupling to specific classes.

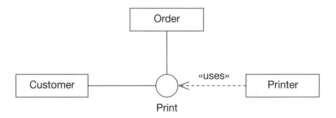

**Figure 17.3**

In this example, the Printer class knows how to print anything that implements the Print interface. This interface defines a single abstract polymorphic method called print( g : Graphics ), which we can't show in the diagram as we are using the concise "lollipop" notation. This method *must* be implemented by *all* classes that implement Print. Notice that the Printer class remains completely decoupled and independent of the actual classes that implement Print – it only knows about the Print interface.

You can use interfaces very effectively with subsystems as shown in Figure 17.4. In this example, the GUI subsystem *only* knows about the CustomerManager and AccountManager interfaces. It does not know anything about the subsystem itself. You could, in principle, replace the BusinessLogic subsystem with another subsystem entirely, or even with several subsystems, provided these all implemented the necessary set of interfaces. Using interfaces in this way can provide much architectural flexibility.

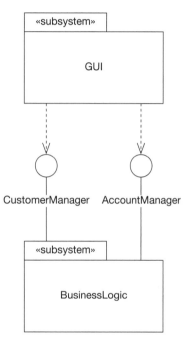

Interfaces allow you to connect components together in a flexible way.

**Figure 17.4**

The example in Figure 17.5 is based on a real security system in an office. Each floor of the building is a separate Zone, which comprises a number of subsidiary Zones, as well as passive infrared and other security sensors. Each Zone has a card reader that activates or deactivates ID cards for that Zone. A card activated for an aggregate Zone would also be valid for all of its part Zones.

In our model of this system, each Zone is made up of a collection that can contain any object that realizes the Activate interface. This makes it very easy to plug in new devices such as smoke alarms and ID card readers.

Notice that the aggregation relationship from Zone to Activate is unidirectional. This is necessary because although other things can have associations

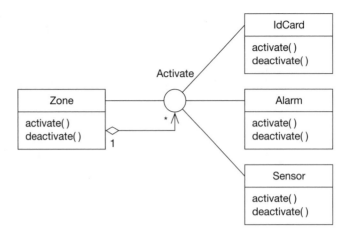

**Figure 17.5**

*to* an interface, an interface itself can't have an association *to* anything else. Also, notice how aggregation asymmetry prevents a given Zone object from being a part of itself.

Java makes extensive use of interfaces throughout its standard libraries. A particularly good example is the set of Java collection classes (Figure 17.6). Although there are only six interfaces defined, there are actually ten different implementations, all of which have different characteristics. By designing to an interface, the Java designer can leave the actual realization of the interface to implementation time, and let the Java programmer choose the most appropriate solution.

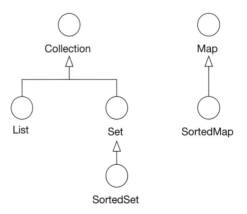

**Figure 17.6**

## 17.4    Finding interfaces

When you have designed a system or part of a system, it is worth examining the model to try to find some interfaces. This is quite easy to do.

- Challenge each association – look at each one and ask the question, "Should this association really be to a particular class of objects, or should it be more flexible than this?" If you decide that the association really needs to be more flexible than it would be if it were tied to a particular class, then consider using an interface.

- Challenge each message send – look at each one and ask the question, "Should this message send really be to objects of just one class, or should it be more flexible than this?" If it should be more general (i.e. if you can think of cases where the same message could be sent to objects of other classes) then consider using an interface.

- Factor out groups of operations that might be reusable elsewhere. For example, if many classes in your system need to be able to print themselves to some output device, think of designing a Print interface.

- Factor out sets of operations that repeat in more than one class.

- Look for classes that play the same role in the system – the role may indicate a possible interface.

- Look for possibilities for future expansion. Sometimes, with just a little forethought, you can design systems that can be expanded easily in the future. The key question is, "In the future, will other classes need to be added to the system?" If the answer is yes, try to define one or more interfaces that will define the protocol for adding these new classes.

## 17.5    Designing with interfaces

When designing a system, it is always helpful if things behave as uniformly as possible. Using interfaces, you can design common sets of operations that might be realized by many classes. A good example of this is a system we were working on to provide a common interface to several legacy systems. The problem was that each system had a different communications protocol. We were able to hide this complexity behind a single interface consisting of the methods open(), read(), write(), and close().

Here's another example. If you consider a system that models an organization (a human resources system for example), there are many classes of things that have a name and address – for example, Person, OrganizationalUnit, Job. All of these classes can play the common role of addressableUnit. It clearly makes sense that all of these classes should have the same interface for handling name and address details. You might therefore define a NameAndAddress interface that they could all realize. There are other solutions to this problem using inheritance, but the interface solution is more flexible.

It is worth remembering that classes may have reflexive associations (to themselves) and that there may be roles that are internal to the class. These are also good candidates for interfaces.

A very powerful use of interfaces is to provide the ability to plug things in to systems. One of the ways to make systems flexible and resilient to change is to design the system such that extensions can be plugged in easily. Interfaces are the key to this. If you can design systems around interfaces, then associations and message sends are no longer tied to objects of a particular class but instead are tied to a specific interface. This makes it much easier to add new classes to a system, as the interfaces define the protocols that the new classes must support in order to plug in seamlessly.

A good example of a software module that would be useful to plug in at will is a plug-in algorithm. We were working on a system some time ago that did a big and complex calculation on a large data set. The users also wanted to experiment with the calculation algorithm to try to find the optimum strategy. However, the system had not been written taking this into account, and every small change to the algorithm took several man-days as the existing code had to be changed and the system rebuilt. We worked with one of the designers to refactor the system to use an interface to pluggable algorithms. After this work, new algorithms could be tried out in a matter of hours. In fact, we could even switch algorithms while the system was still running.

## 17.6 What are subsystems?

A subsystem is a package stereotyped «subsystem». You use subsystems in both design and implementation. These are known as design subsystems and implementation subsystems. We will usually just use the term "subsystem" in this book as it is always clear from the context which type of subsystem we are talking about at any point.

Design subsystems contain:

- design classes and interfaces;
- use case realizations;
- other subsystems;
- specification elements such as use cases.

Subsystems are used to:

- separate design concerns;
- represent large-grained components;
- wrap legacy systems.

In fact, design subsystems are how you begin to "componentize" your model. You break the analysis packages into one or more design subsystems and also introduce new design subsystems that only contain artefacts from the solution domain, such as database access classes or communications classes.

As in analysis, you get dependencies between subsystems when an element in one subsystem depends in some way on an element in another.

There are several ways to draw subsystems, as Figure 17.7 illustrates. You can use the stereotype name in guillemots (the most common way), or you can use the fork icon. The stereotype name or fork can be placed in the tab, the stereotype name can be placed in the body of the package just above the subsystem name, or the fork can be placed in the top right corner of the main rectangle.

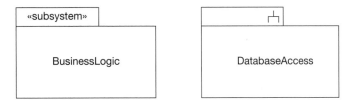

**Figure 17.7**

The subsystem icon can be divided into one or more of the following compartments:

- operations;
- realization elements;
- specification elements.

All of the compartments are optional, and in fact you can just leave the icon empty, or include everything in a single, unlabeled compartment. An example is shown in Figure 17.8 where we have used three compartments.

The top left-hand compartment is the Operations compartment, which is never labeled. This compartment contains the operations that the subsystem makes available. Each of these operations is realized by a public method of a public class in the subsystem. In this example, you can see that the three subsystem operations are realized by the class RegistrationManager. You can deduce from this that the RegistrationManager class must be public within the subsystem and must have three public methods – addCourse(...), removeCourse(...) and findCourse(...) – which realize the three subsystem operations.

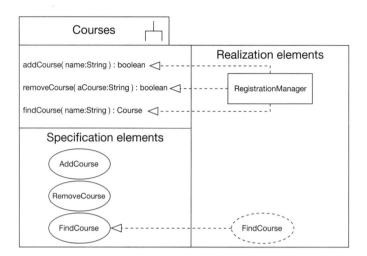

**Figure 17.8**

The Specification elements compartment is for elements such as use cases and interfaces that specify some aspect of the system. The Realization elements compartment is for elements that realize system behavior. As shown in Figure 17.8, you can show explicit realization relationships between elements in this compartment and elements in the other two compartments.

## 17.6.1　Subsystems and interfaces

Use interfaces to hide the implementation details of subsystems.

It would be useful for subsystems to act as "black boxes" where the classes inside the subsystem are completely hidden from the rest of the classes in the system. You can do this by introducing interfaces and making these interfaces public in the subsystem. Most of the other classes in the subsystem can then be made private.

Note that using interfaces is substantially different from just listing subsystem operations. When you use subsystem operations, you must have public classes to realize those operations. This exposes some classes outside the subsystem.

Whenever a public class within a subsystem realizes an interface, we say that the subsystem realizes the interface. You can show the interface attached directly to the subsystem, as in Figure 17.9.

Using interfaces in this way, you can think of a subsystem as a type of component as it provides a set of services by realizing one or more interfaces.

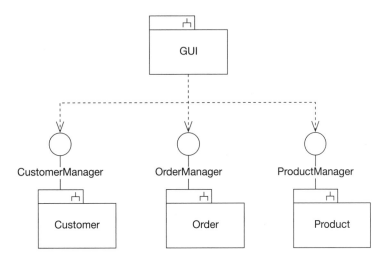

**Figure 17.9**

## 17.6.2    The Façade pattern

> The Façade pattern hides a complex implementation behind a simple interface.

Hiding complex subsystems behind a well-defined, simple interface is known as the Façade pattern. This is documented in [Gamma 1]. This book is a treasure trove of powerful, reusable design patterns that may be used in many different contexts in design models. Gamma has this to say about the Façade pattern, "Structuring a system into subsystems helps reduce complexity. A common design goal is to minimize the communication and dependencies between subsystems. One way to achieve this goal is to introduce a façade object that provides a single, simplified interface to the more general facilities of a subsystem."

The Façade pattern allows information hiding and separation of concerns – you can hide the complex details of the internal workings of a subsystem behind a simple interface. This reduces the complexity of the system and allows you to control and manage coupling between the subsystems.

Interfaces used as a façade can be used to create "seams" in a system. You do this as follows:

- identify cohesive parts of the system;
- package these into a «subsystem»;
- define an interface to that subsystem.

### 17.6.3 Physical architecture and the layering pattern

The layering pattern organizes subsystems into semantically cohesive layers.

The collection of design subsystems and interfaces constitutes the physical architecture of a model. However, in order for this architecture to be easy to understand and maintain, you still need to organize the collection of subsystems and interfaces in some coherent way. You can do this by applying an architectural pattern known as layering.

The layering pattern arranges design subsystems and interfaces into layers where the subsystems in each layer are semantically cohesive. The essence of creating a robust layered architecture is to manage the coupling between subsystems by:

- introducing new interfaces where needed;
- repackaging classes into new subsystems in such a way as to reduce the coupling between subsystems.

Dependencies between layers must be managed very carefully as these dependencies determine the coupling between layers. Ideally, you want the layers to be as decoupled as possible, so try to ensure that:

- dependencies go one way;
- all dependencies are mediated by interfaces.

There are many ways of producing layered architectures, and you can have as many layers as make sense. However, the basic pattern is a split into presentation, business logic, and utility layers. As shown in Figure 17.10, it is also quite common to further subdivide the business logic layer. In this case we have two layers – domain and services. The domain layer contains subsystems specific to this particular application, and the services layer contains subsystems that may be reusable in other applications.

Wherever possible, it is best to design to an interface. In Figure 17.10, you can see that the subsystems we have designed ourselves are all connected via interfaces. However, the Java packages are just connected with dependencies, although each one makes available several interfaces. The reason for this is that, while showing your own interfaces is interesting and useful, showing the interfaces made available by standard Java libraries doesn't seem to serve any useful purpose. Notice also that the java.util package, which contains generic components like Strings, is used everywhere and so it is marked with the {global} keyword. This means that the entire public contents of the package are visible everywhere.

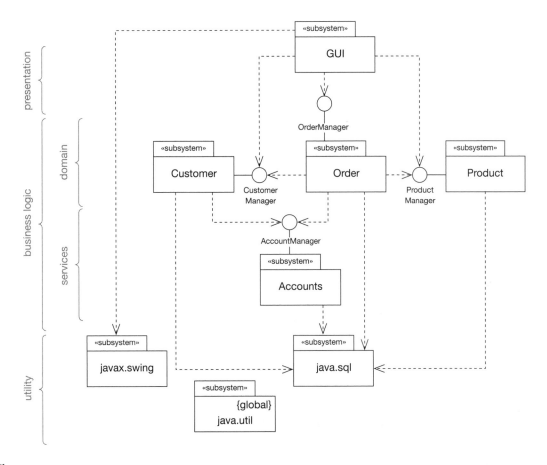

**Figure 17.10**

## 17.7  Advantages and disadvantages of interfaces

When you design with classes, you are constraining the design to specific implementations. But when you design with interfaces, you are instead designing to contracts that may be realized by many different implementations. Designing to contracts frees the model (and ultimately the system) from implementation dependencies and therefore increases its flexibility and extensibility.

Designing with interfaces allows you to reduce the number of dependencies between classes, subsystems, and components and hence begins to give control over the amount of coupling in a model. In a real sense, coupling is the worst enemy of the object developer, as highly coupled

Designing to a
contract is more
flexible than designing
to an implementation.

systems are hard to understand, maintain, and evolve. Appropriate use of interfaces can help to reduce coupling and to separate the model into cohesive subsystems.

However, there are drawbacks in using interfaces. Generally speaking, whenever you make something more flexible you make it more complex. When you design with interfaces, you are looking for a trade-off between flexibility and complexity. In principle, you could make every operation of every class an interface – you simply would not be able to understand such a system! There is also often a performance cost to flexibility, but this is usually a minor consideration compared to the increase in complexity.

Flexibility can
lead to complexity –
so take care.

When you design a system you are trying to capture a very definite set of business semantics in software. Some of these semantics are fluid and change quite rapidly, while others are relatively stable. You need flexibility to help deal with the fluid aspects, but you can simplify systems by dispensing with a certain amount of flexibility for the more stable parts. In a way, this is one of the secrets of good OO analysis and design – identifying the fluid and stable parts of a system and modeling each accordingly.

To be frank, it is more important that a system is correctly modeled than flexibly modeled. Always concentrate on correctly modeling the key business semantics of the system first, and *then* think about flexibility. Remember the KISS rule – keep interfaces sweet and simple!

## 17.8    What we have learned

Interfaces allow software to be designed to a contract rather than to a specific implementation. You have learned the following.

- An interface specifies a set of operations.
  — Interfaces separate specification of functionality from implementation.
  — Interfaces may be attached to classes, subsystems, components and any other classifier and define the services offered by these.
  — If a classifier inside a subsystem realizes a public interface then the subsystem or component also realizes the public interface.
  — Anything that realizes an interface agrees to abide by the contract defined by the set of operations specified in the interface.

- Designing to an implementation:
  — specific classes are connected together;
  — to keep things simple (but rigid), design to an implementation.

- Designing to a contract:
  — a class is connected to an interface that may have many possible realizations;
  — to make things flexible (but possibly more complex), design to a contract.

- Interfaces consist of a set of operations – each operation must have:
  — a complete signature;
  — a specification describing the semantics of the operation;
  — optionally, a stereotype, constraints and tagged values.

- Interfaces can *never* have:
  — attributes;
  — operation implementations (methods);
  — relationships navigable from the interface to anything else.

- Interface syntax:
  — use the "class" style notation when you need to show the operations on the model;
  — use the shorthand "lollipop" style notation when you just want to show the interface without operations.

- Component-based development (CBD) is about constructing software from plug-in parts – you use interfaces to make components "pluggable"; by designing to an interface, you allow the possibility of many different realizations by many different components.

- Finding interfaces:
  — challenge associations;
  — challenge message sends;
  — factor out groups of reusable operations;
  — factor out groups of repeating operations;
  — look for classes that play the same role in the system;
  — look for possibilities for future expansion.

- Subsystems are a type of package.
  — Design subsystems contain design elements:
    - design classes and interfaces;
    - use case realizations;
    - other subsystems.

— Implementation subsystems contain implementation elements:
  - interfaces;
  - components;
  - other subsystems.
— Subsystem icons may optionally have the following compartments:
  - Operations – contains the signatures of the methods that the subsystem makes available (these are realized by public methods of public classes in the subsystem);
  - Specification elements – contains things that specify some aspect of the system, such as use cases or interfaces;
  - Realization elements – contains elements that realize the specifications.
— Subsystems are used to:
  - separate design concerns;
  - represent large-grained components;
  - wrap legacy systems.
— Use interfaces to hide the implementation details of subsystems:
  - the Façade pattern hides a complex implementation behind a simple interface;
  - the layering pattern organizes subsystems into semantically cohesive layers:
    - dependencies between layers should only go one way;
    - all dependencies between layers should be mediated by an interface;
    - example layers include presentation, business logic, and utility layers.

chapter **18**

# Use case realization – design

## 18.1 Chapter roadmap

In this chapter we look at "use case realization – design". This is the process of refining analysis interaction diagrams and class diagrams to show design artefacts. Having already looked in detail at design classes in Chapter 15, we focus here on interaction diagrams. We also discuss the use of interaction diagrams in design to model central mechanisms. These are the strategic design decisions that we make about object persistence, distribution, etc. Finally, we look at using interaction diagrams to capture the high-level interactions within a system by learning how to create subsystem interaction diagrams.

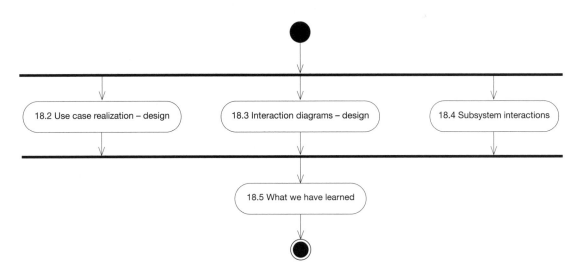

**Figure 18.1**

## 18.2    Use case realization – design

> "Use case realizations – design" are collaborations of design objects and design classes that realize a use case.

A use case realization – design is a collaboration of design objects and classes that realize a use case. There is a «trace» between an analysis use case realization and a design use case realization. The use case realization – design specifies implementation decisions and implements the non-functional requirements. A use case realization – design consists of:

- design interaction diagrams;
- class diagrams containing the participating design classes.

Your focus for use case realizations in analysis was to capture *what* the system needed to do. In design, you are concerned with *how* the system is going to do it. Thus, you now need to specify implementation details that you simply ignored in the analysis stage. Use case realizations – design are therefore much more detailed and complex than the original analysis use case realizations.

It is very important to remember that you only model to help you to understand the system you are trying to build. You should limit the amount of work you do in design to that which is useful – this is what is known as strategic design. There is also tactical design, which you can safely leave to the implementation phase. In fact, the only time you design exhaustively is when you intend to generate most of the code from the model. Even then, use case realizations – design rarely play an active role in automatic code generation, and so you only create these as needed to highlight obscure aspects of system behavior.

## 18.3    Interaction diagrams – design

> In design you may refine key analysis interaction diagrams or create new ones to illustrate central mechanisms such as object persistence.

Interaction diagrams are a key part of your use case realizations – design. Because it can be easier to show large amounts of information on sequence diagrams, you often focus on these in design, rather than on collaboration diagrams.

Interaction diagrams in design may be:

- a refinement of key analysis interaction diagrams with implementation details added;
- entirely new diagrams constructed to illustrate technical issues that have arisen during design.

In design, you introduce a limited number of central mechanisms such as object persistence, object distribution, transactions, etc., and you often construct example interaction diagrams specifically to illustrate these mechanisms. Interaction diagrams that illustrate central mechanisms often cut across use cases.

To understand the role of sequence diagrams in design, we will look at the AddCourse use case we previously discussed in Section 12.8. Here is the AddCourse use case again (Figure 18.2).

| **Use case: AddCourse** |
|---|
| **ID: UC8** |
| **Actors:**<br>Registrar |
| **Preconditions:**<br>The Registrar has logged on to the system. |
| **Flow of events:**<br>1.   The Registrar selects "add course".<br>2.   The system accepts the name of the new course.<br>3.   The system creates the new course. |
| **Postconditions:**<br>A new course has been added to the system. |

**Figure 18.2**

Figure 18.3 shows the analysis interaction diagram that we created in Section 12.8.

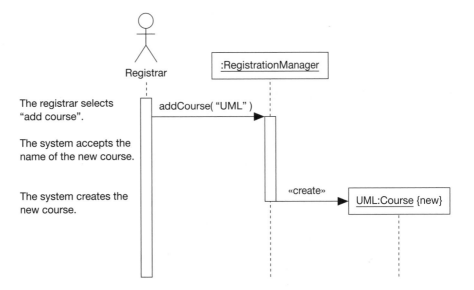

**Figure 18.3**

Figure 18.4 shows a typical sequence diagram for the AddCourse use case in the early stages of design. You can see that we have added the GUI layer, although this hasn't been modeled very deeply. We have also resolved the high-level operations from the analysis sequence diagram into specific methods of classes, complete with parameters. In particular, object construction is now shown by an explicit constructor method invocation.

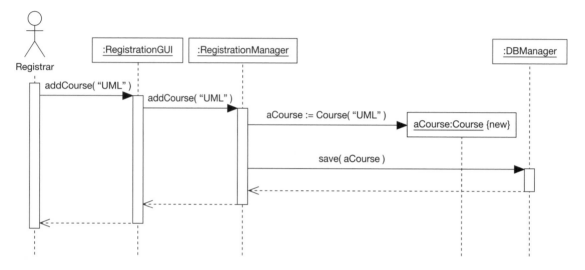

**Figure 18.4**

Figure 18.4 includes a central mechanism – how the Course objects are made persistent. In this case, we have chosen a very simple persistence mechanism – the :RegistrationManager object uses the services of a :DBManager object to store the Course objects in a database. It is essential that this central mechanism, once defined, should be used consistently throughout the rest of the design. We once worked on a large system that had no less than three different persistence mechanisms – clearly, this was two too many!

## 18.4　Subsystem interactions

Subsystem interaction diagrams can show the interactions between parts of the system.

Once you have created a physical architecture of subsystems and interfaces, it is often useful to model use case realizations as interactions between subsystems rather than as interactions between classes. Interactions between subsystems provide a very useful high-level view of how the architecture realizes use cases without going into the low-level details of individual object interactions.

You treat each subsystem as a black box that simply provides services via its operations or, even better, via its published interface or interfaces. You don't have to worry about the object interactions within the subsystem at all. On the whole, it is better to use interfaces rather than subsystem operations, as interfaces are more cohesive and provide a higher degree of encapsulation.

Figure 18.5 shows a subsystem called Customer that has a single interface called CustomerManager.

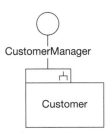

**Figure 18.5**

Figure 18.6 is part of a sequence diagram showing an actor interacting with this subsystem. As the subsystem provides realizations for all of its interfaces (and operations), we show the messages on the interaction diagram going to the subsystem itself. You can qualify the message name with the name of the interface if you want to indicate which specific interface is being used in the interaction.

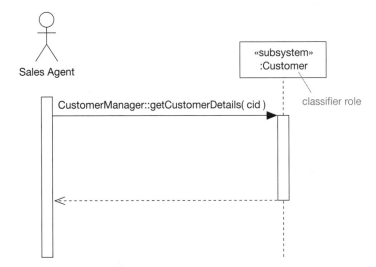

**Figure 18.6**

When you are modeling subsystem interactions, you usually use descriptor form interaction diagrams (see Section 12.5). This is because the instance form interaction diagram would model the interaction with subsystem instances in a particular executing version of the program. You don't usually want, or need, to be that specific!

You can tell that Figure 18.6 is a descriptor form sequence diagram, as the classifier name is not underlined. You treat the Customer subsystem as a black box that services any request for customer details made via its CustomerManager interface. We haven't shown this explicitly on the diagram, but it returns the result as an object of type CustomerDetails. This means that there will be an interaction within the Customer subsystem that gathers information to construct and return this CustomerDetails object. You can show this interaction on another sequence diagram if you need to.

## 18.5    What we have learned

"Use case realization – design" is really just an extension of use case realization in analysis. You have learned the following.

- Use case realizations – design, are collaborations of design objects and classes that realize a use case. They comprise:
    — design interaction diagrams – these are refinements of analysis interaction diagrams;
    — design class diagrams – these are refinements of analysis class diagrams.

- You can use interaction diagrams – design, to model central mechanisms such as object persistence; these mechanisms may cut across many use cases.

- Subsystem interaction diagrams show the interactions between the different parts of the system at a high level:
    — they may contain actors, subsystems, and classes;
    — you normally use descriptor form for subsystem interaction diagrams – instance form is generally too specific.

# chapter 19

# Basic statecharts

## 19.1 Chapter roadmap

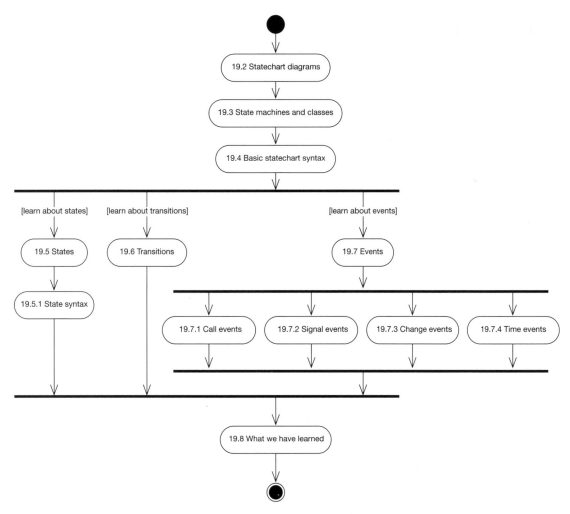

**Figure 19.1**

In this chapter we discuss statecharts. These are an important way of modeling the dynamic behavior of reactive objects. The chapter begins with an introduction to statecharts (Sections 19.2 and 19.3) and then focuses on the basic components of statecharts – states (Section 19.5), transitions (Section 19.6), and events (Section 19.7).

## 19.2    Statechart diagrams

You have already seen some statechart diagrams. Activity diagrams are just a special case of a statechart diagram where the states are action or subactivity states, and the transitions are triggered automatically by the completion of a state's actions and activities. As such, activity diagrams typically use only a small subset of the rich UML statechart syntax.

Although both activity diagrams and statechart diagrams model the dynamic behavior of aspects of the system, they have fundamentally different purposes in modeling. Activity diagrams tend to be used for modeling business processes where several objects participate. Statechart diagrams, on the other hand, tend to be used for modeling the lifecycle history of a single reactive object.

> Activity diagrams are a special case of statechart diagrams.

A reactive object is an object (in the broad sense of the term) that provides the context for the statechart. Reactive objects:

● respond to external events (i.e. events outside of the object context);

● have a clear lifecycle modeled as a progression of states, transitions, and events;

● have current behavior that depends on past behavior.

> A statechart models the state machine for a reactive object.

A statechart contains exactly one state machine for a single reactive object.

The real world is full of reactive objects that can be modeled using state machines. In OO modeling, you can use state machines to model the dynamic behavior of reactive objects such as:

● classes;

● use cases;

● subsystems;

● entire systems.

However, state machines are most commonly used to model the dynamic behavior of classes, and that's what we'll focus on here.

## 19.3 State machines and classes

For each class there may be *one* state machine that models all the transitions between states of all objects of that class in response to events. Events are typically messages sent by other objects, although in some cases the object may internally generate an event in response to time.

Given that objects of a class may participate in many use cases, you can see that the state machine for a class models the behavior of objects of that class across all use cases.

To illustrate state machines we will consider a very simple real-world example. One of the simplest and most obvious real-world objects that constantly cycles though a simple state machine is a light bulb. Figure 19.2 shows how you can send events to a light bulb using a switch. The two events you can send are turnOn (this event models the supply of electric current to the bulb) and turnOff (which cuts off the current).

Events cause transitions between states.

**Figure 19.2**

Every state machine has an initial start state (filled circle) that indicates where the machine begins, and a stop state (bull's eye) that indicates where the machine ends. Typically, you automatically transition from the initial pseudo-state to the first "real" state of the state machine. The initial pseudo-state is thus just used as a convenient marker for the beginning of the series of state transitions.

In Figure 19.2, when the switch is turned to the "On" position, the event turnOn is sent to the bulb. Now, in state machines, events are considered to be instantaneous. In other words, it takes zero time for the event dispatched from the switch to reach the light bulb. Instantaneous events provide an important simplification to state machine theory which makes it much more tractable. Without instantaneous events we might well have race conditions, where two events race from their source to reach the same reactive object. We would have to model this race condition as some sort of state machine!

The bulb receives the event turnOn and changes state to On in response to the event. This is the crux of state machines – objects may change state on receipt of an event. When the event turnOff is sent to the bulb, it changes state to Off.

At some point in time, the event burnOut may occur (when the light bulb burns out) – this terminates the state machine.

## 19.4  Basic statechart syntax

Basic statechart syntax is straightforward and is illustrated in Figure 19.2.

- States are rounded rectangles ("roundtangles"), apart from the initial start state (filled circle) and stop state (bull's eye).
- Transitions indicate possible paths between states, and are modeled by an arrow.
- Events are written over the transitions that they trigger.

The basic semantics are also quite simple. When a reactive object in state A receives the event anEvent, it may transition to state B. Every statechart should have an initial start state (filled circle) that indicates the first state of the sequence. Unless the states cycle endlessly, statecharts should have a stop state (bull's eye) which terminates the sequence of transitions.

We'll look at each element of the statechart in detail in the next few sections.

## 19.5  States

*The UML Reference Manual* [Rumbaugh 1] defines a state as, "a condition or situation during the life of an object during which it satisfies some condition, performs some activity, or waits for some event". The state of an object varies over time, but at any particular point it is determined by:

- the object attribute values;
- the relationships it has to other objects;
- the activities it is performing.

> A state is a semantically significant condition of an object.

Over time, objects send messages to each other, and these messages are events that may cause changes in object state. It is important to think about what we mean by "state" quite carefully. In the case of the light bulb, we could (if we were quantum physicists) decide that every change to any one of the atoms or sub-atomic particles in the light bulb constituted a new state. This is perfectly accurate, but it would give us an infinity of states, most of which would be virtually identical.

However, from the point of view of the user of a light bulb, the only states that make a difference are On and Off. This is the key to successful statechart modeling – you need to identify the states that *make a difference* to your system. Consider the example below.

```
class Color
{
        int red;
        int green;
        int blue;
}
```

If we assume that red, green and blue can each take values 0–255 then, based just on the values of their attributes, objects of this class can have $256*256*256 = 16777216$ possible states! That would be some statechart! However, we must ask ourselves the fundamental question – what is the key semantic difference between each of those states? The answer is none. Each of the 16777216 possible states represent a color, and that's all. In fact, the statechart for this class is very boring, as you can model all of the possibilities by a single state.

In summary, there has to be a semantic "difference that makes a difference" between states for you to bother to model them on a state machine.

### 19.5.1 State syntax

UML state syntax is summarized in Figure 19.3.

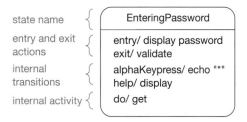

Action syntax: event trigger/ action
Activity syntax: do/ activity

**Figure 19.3**

Actions are instantaneous and uninterruptible.

Each state may contain zero or more actions and activities. Actions are considered to be instantaneous and uninterruptible, whereas activities take a finite amount of time and can be interrupted. Every action in a state is associated with an internal transition that is triggered by an event. There can be any number of actions and internal transitions within a state.

An internal transition allows you to capture the fact that something worth modeling has happened, but that it doesn't cause (or is insufficiently important to warrant modeling as) a transition to a new state. For example, in Figure 19.3, pressing one of the alpha keys on the keyboard is certainly a noteworthy event, but it doesn't cause a transition out of the state EnteringPassword. We model this as an internal event, alphaKeypress, that causes an internal transition that triggers the action echo "*".

There are two special actions – the entry action and the exit action – that are associated with the special events entry and exit. These two events have special semantics. The entry event occurs instantaneously and automatically on entry to the state – it is the first thing that happens when the state is entered, and it causes the associated entry action to execute. The exit event is the very last thing that happens instantaneously and automatically on exit from the state, and it causes the associated exit action to execute.

Activities take finite time and are interruptible.

Activities, on the other hand, take a finite amount of time and may be interrupted by the receipt of an event. The keyword do indicates an activity. Whereas actions always finish because they are atomic, it is possible to interrupt an activity before it has finished processing.

## 19.6 Transitions

UML transition syntax is summarized in Figure 19.4.

Transitions show movement between states.

**Figure 19.4**

Transitions have a simple syntax that may be used for external transitions (shown by an arrow) or internal transitions (nested within a state). Every transition has three optional elements:

- an event – this is an external or internal occurrence that triggers the transition;

- a guard condition – this is a Boolean expression that must evaluate to true before the transition can occur;

- an action – this is a piece of work associated with the transition, and occurs when the transition fires.

You can read Figure 19.4 as follows – "On anEvent if guardCondition is true then perform anAction and immediately enter state B."

## 19.7 Events

Events trigger transitions.

UML defines an event as, "the specification of a noteworthy occurrence that has location in time and space." Events trigger transitions in state machines. Events may be shown externally on transitions, as shown in Figure 19.5, or internally within states.

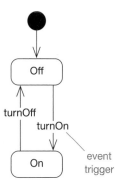

**Figure 19.5**

There are four types of event, each of which has different semantics:

- call event;
- signal event;
- change event;
- time event.

### 19.7.1 Call events

A call event is perhaps the simplest type of event. The receipt of a call event is a request for a set of actions to occur. A call event should have the same signature as a method of the class that provides the context for the state machine. The example in Figure 19.6 shows a fragment from the state machine of a simple BankAccount class. The call events deposit(...) and withdraw(...) correspond to methods of the BankAccount class.

A call event causes a method to be executed.

A sequence of actions may be specified for a call event where each action is separated by a semicolon. These actions may use attributes and operations of the context class. There may be a return value from the call event that must match the return type of the operation.

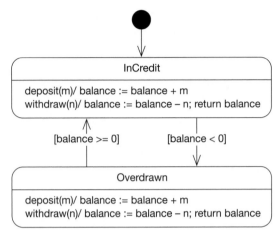

Context: BankAccount class

**Figure 19.6**

In summary, a call event is just a request for a specific method to be invoked on an instance of the context class.

## 19.7.2   Signal events

A signal is a package of information that is sent asynchronously between objects. You model a signal as a stereotyped class that contains all of the communicated information in its attributes. This is illustrated in Figure 19.7.

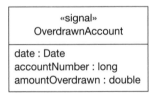

**Figure 19.7**

A signal is a
one-way
asynchronous
communication
between objects.

As a signal only passes information between objects, there is no way that it may have operations apart from the single implicit operation send( targetList ) that allows the sending of the signal to one or more target objects. Signals are not particularly object-oriented as they have no behavior apart from this. We can show sending a signal as follows:

OverdrawnAccount.send( bankManager )

OverdrawnAccount is the signal name, and the implicit send(...) method in this case takes an object called bankManager. This object is the target of the send(...). You can specify a comma-separated list of target objects. If you name one or more *classes* in the parameter list, then the signal is broadcast to all objects of those classes.

You can model the receipt of a signal by a reactive object as a signal event. The event trigger for a signal event is a method that accepts the signal as a parameter, as shown in Figure 19.8.

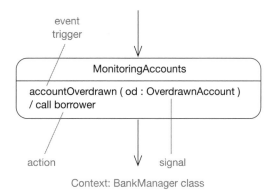

Context: BankManager class

**Figure 19.8**

### 19.7.3 Change events

Change events occur when some Boolean condition changes value from false to true.

A change event has the keyword when, and then a Boolean expression – its use is shown in Figure 19.9. The action associated with the event is performed when the Boolean expression is true. All values in the Boolean expression must be attributes of the context class. From the implementation perspective, a change event implies continually testing the condition while in the state.

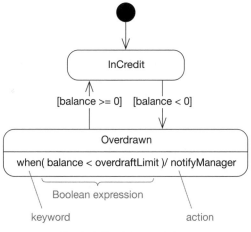

Context: BankAccount class

**Figure 19.9**

Change events are edge triggered. This means that they are triggered by the process of the Boolean condition specified in the when clause *changing* to true. The Boolean condition must go back to false, and then undergo transition to true again, before the change event will be retriggered.

### 19.7.4   Time events

Time events are denoted by the keywords when and after. The keyword when specifies a *particular* moment in time that the event is triggered; after specifies a threshold time *after* which the event is triggered. Examples are after( 3 months ) and when( date = 07/10/2002 ).

> Time events occur in response to time.

It is important to make sure that the time units (hours, days, months, etc.) are carefully specified for each time event. Any symbols in the expression (such as date in the second example above) must correspond to attributes of the reactive object.

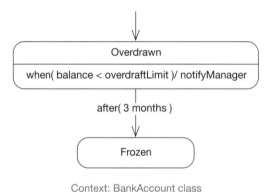

Context: BankAccount class

**Figure 19.10**

The example in Figure 19.10 is a fragment from the statechart of a BankAccount class. You can see that after an Account object has been in the state Overdrawn for three months, it transitions to the state Frozen.

## 19.8   What we have learned

In this chapter you have seen how to construct basic statecharts using states, actions, activities, events, and transitions.

You have learned the following.

- Activity diagrams are a special case of statechart diagrams where:
  — all states are action or subactivity states;
  — transitions are triggered automatically on completion of a state's actions and activities.

- A reactive object provides the context for a statechart.
  — Reactive objects:
    - respond to external events;
    - have a definite lifecycle that can be modeled as a progression of states, transitions, and events;
    - have current behavior that depends on past behavior.
  — State machines model the dynamic behavior of reactive objects – each reactive object has exactly one state machine.
  — Examples of reactive objects:
    - classes (most common);
    - use cases;
    - subsystems;
    - entire systems.

- Actions – pieces of work that are instantaneous and uninterruptible:
  — may occur within a state associated with an internal transition;
  — may occur outside a state associated with an external transition.

- Activities – pieces of work that take a finite time and are interruptible – they may only occur within a state.

- State – a semantically significant condition of an object.
  — Object state is determined by:
    - object attribute values;
    - relationships to other objects;
    - activities the object is performing.
  — State syntax:
    - entry action – performed immediately on entry to the state;
    - exit action – performed immediately on exit from the state;
    - internal transitions – these are caused by events that are not significant enough to warrant a transition to a new state; the event is processed by an internal transition within the state;
    - internal activity – a piece of work that takes a finite amount of time and which may be interrupted.

- Transition – a movement between two states. Transition syntax:
    - event – the event that triggers the transition;
    - guard condition – a Boolean expression that must be true before the transition occurs;
    - action – an action that occurs instantaneously with the transition.

- Event – something of note that occurs to a reactive object. The types of event are:
  — call event:
    - a call for a set of actions to occur;
    - a method invocation on the object;
  — signal event:
    - the receipt of a signal – a signal is an asynchronous one-way communication between objects;
  — change event:
    - occurs when some Boolean condition changes from false to true (i.e. edge is triggered on the false-to-true transition);
  — time event:
    - occurs after a time period;
    - occurs when some time condition becomes true.

# chapter 20

# Advanced statecharts

## 20.1 Chapter roadmap

We begin this chapter with a discussion of composite states. These are states that themselves contain a nested state machine. Section 20.2 gives an introduction to the idea of nested state machines, or submachines. We then discuss two types of composite state – the sequential composite state (20.3) and the concurrent composite state (20.4).

When you have two or more concurrent submachines, you often need to establish some sort of communication between them. We discuss this in Section 20.5 and introduce two communication strategies (using attributes and using sync states) in Sections 20.5.1 and 20.5.2.

In Section 20.6, we introduce the idea of history, which is about giving a superstate "memory" of its final substate before an outgoing transition. In Sections 20.6.1 and 20.6.2 we discuss the two variants of this, shallow and deep history.

Finally, in Section 20.7 we look at how we may summarize nested submachines on statecharts using submachine states.

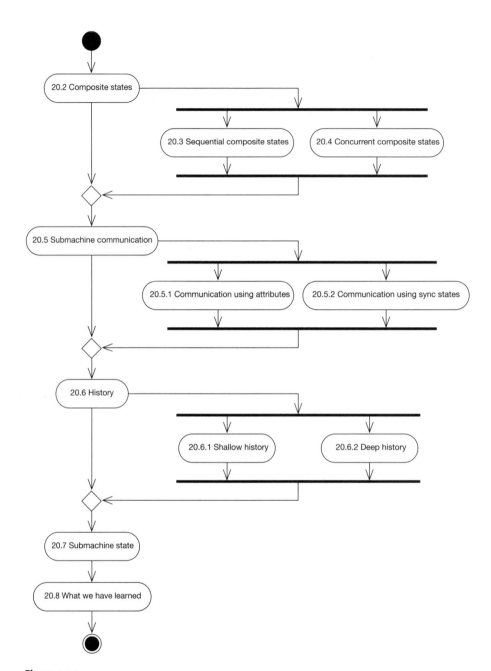

**Figure 20.1**

## 20.2  Composite states

A composite state is a state that contains one or more nested state machines – known as submachines. You can show composite states on a statechart by adding the decomposition indicator to the state icon, as shown in Figure 20.2.

**Figure 20.2**

You can also make decomposition explicit by showing the nested state machines inside a new compartment in the state icon – in this case you don't need the decomposition indicator.

> Composite states contain one or more nested submachines.

Composite states are made up of component states, or substates, to which the composite state is the superstate. Each substate inherits all of the transitions of its superstate(s). We'll see plenty of examples of this in the next few sections.

Each substate may itself be a composite state. Clearly, there is a limit to which this nesting makes sense – for clarity, no more than two or three levels should be used, other than in exceptional circumstances.

If the superstate contains a single nested state machine, then it is known as a sequential composite state. If, however, the superstate contains two or more state machines, these will execute concurrently and it is then known as a concurrent composite state.

## 20.3  Sequential composite states

> Sequential composite states contain a single nested state machine.

A composite state that contains a single nested state machine is known as a sequential composite state. The example in Figure 20.3 shows the state machine for a class called ISPDialer. This class is responsible for dialing in to an internet service provider.

Each substate inherits all of the transitions of its superstate, so both the automatic transition from the DialingISP superstate to the Connected state, and the transition triggered by the cancel event, are inherited by each substate.

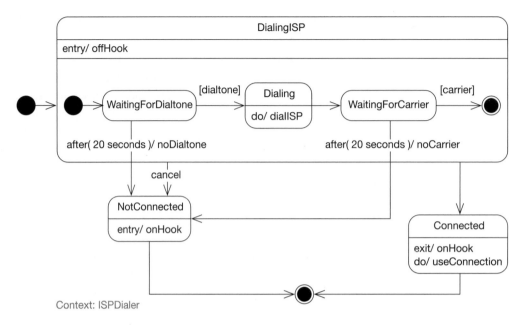

**Figure 20.3**

This is very convenient as it means that on receipt of the cancel event, we will *always* transition from whatever substate we are in to the state NotConnected. Use of superstates and substates can greatly simplify a statechart.

Here is a complete walkthru for the ISPDialer class state machine:

1. We enter the superstate DialingISP and immediately execute the entry action – this puts the modem off-hook.

2. We enter the nested state machine.

3. We enter the state WaitingForDialtone.

   3.1. We wait in the state WaitingForDialtone for a maximum of 20 seconds.

   3.2. If we don't get a dialtone in this time:

      3.2.1. we perform the action noDialtone as we transition to the state NotConnected;

      3.2.2. on entry to NotConnected we put the phone back on the hook;

      3.2.3. we transition to the stop state.

   3.3. If we get a dialtone (i.e. the guard condition [dialtone] evaluates to true) within 20 seconds:

3.3.1. we transition to the state Dialing where we perform the activity diallSP;

3.3.2. as soon as the diallSP activity is finished, we automatically transition to the state WaitingForCarrier;

3.3.3. we wait in the state WaitingForCarrier for a maximum of 20 seconds.

3.3.4. If we don't get a carrier within 20 seconds:

    3.3.4.1. we perform the action noCarrier as we transition to the state NotConnected;

    3.3.4.2 on entry to NotConnected we put the phone back on the hook;

    3.3.4.3 we transition to the stop state.

3.3.5. If we get a carrier within 20 seconds:

    3.3.5.1 we automatically transition from the DialingISP superstate to the Connected state;

    3.3.5.2 we perform the action useConnection until it is finished;

    3.3.5.3 on exit from Connected we put the phone back on the hook;

    3.3.5.4 we transition to the stop state.

4. If at *any point* while we are in the superstate DialingISP we receive the cancel event, we immediately transition to the state NotConnected.

    4.1. On entry to NotConnected we put the phone back on the hook.

    4.2. We transition to the stop state.

## 20.4 Concurrent composite states

Concurrent composite states contain two or more nested submachines that execute concurrently.

Concurrent composite states consist of two or more submachines that execute concurrently. When you enter the superstate, both submachines start executing concurrently – this is a fork. There are two ways you can exit from the superstate:

- both submachines finish – this is a join;
- one of the submachines receives an event or finishes, and makes an explicit transition to a state *outside* the superstate. This does *not* cause a join – there is no synchronization of submachines and the remaining submachine simply terminates.

To investigate concurrent composite states, we need a system that exhibits a degree of concurrency. We will model a simple burglar alarm system that consists of a control box, security and fire sensors, and an alarm box. The state machine for the whole system is shown in Figure 20.4.

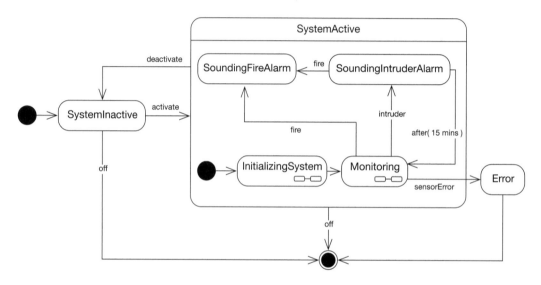

**Figure 20.4**

There are two concurrent composite states in this system, InitializingSystem and Monitoring. The statechart for the InitializingSystem state is shown in Figure 20.5. When we enter this state, there is a fork and two submachines start executing concurrently. In the top submachine, the state InitializingFireSensors runs the initialization process for the fire sensors, and in the bottom submachine the state InitializingSecuritySensors does the same for the security sensors. We can only exit from the InitializingSystem superstate when *both* submachines finish. This is a join, and it synchronizes the submachines such that we can't progress unless both the fire sensors and the security sensors are initialized. This initialization obviously depends on the types of sensors being used but it may, in the simplest case, just be a short "warm up" delay.

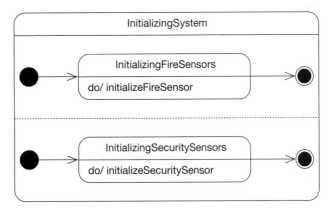

**Figure 20.5**

Sometimes you want to start concurrent threads of control, but do *not* need to synchronize them with a join when they complete. This is the case for the Monitoring concurrent composite state shown in the statechart diagram in Figure 20.6.

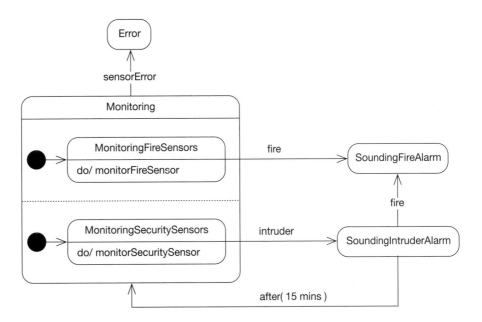

**Figure 20.6**

There are some interesting features in this statechart.

- There is *no* synchronization between the two submachines:
  - — on a fire event we make an explicit transition from MonitoringFireSensors to SoundingFireAlarm that takes us out of the Monitoring superstate – this terminates the other submachine;
  - — similarly, on an intruder event, we make an explicit transition from MonitoringSecuritySensors to SoundingIntruderAlarm that takes us out of the Monitoring superstate – this terminates the other submachine.
- If a fire sensor is triggered, the fire alarm sounds until the system is manually reset.
- If an intruder sensor is triggered, the alarm box sounds the intruder alarm that continues for 15 minutes before the system resets and goes back into the state Monitoring – this is to comply with zoning laws.
- If there is a fire whilst the intruder alarm is sounding, there is an immediate transition from the state SoundingIntruderAlarm to the state SoundingFireAlarm, and the fire alarm sounds. This means that the fire alarm always takes precedence over the intruder alarm.

From this example, you can see how using concurrent composite states, either with or without synchronization, allows you to model concurrency very effectively.

## 20.5    Submachine communication

You have seen in Figure 20.5 how you can use forks and joins to spawn concurrent submachines and then bring them back into synchronization. This is a kind of synchronous communication between the submachines – the concurrent submachines wait for each other until they have *all* finished.

However, very often you need to communicate between submachines but don't want to bring the machines into synchronization to do this. This is called asynchronous communication.

In UML you can achieve asynchronous communication by allowing one submachine to leave "messages" or "flags" as it executes. Other submachines can pick up these flags as and when they are ready. There are two UML mechanisms for achieving this – attributes of the reactive object, and sync states. We'll look at each approach in turn in the next two sections.

### 20.5.1    Communication using attributes

With the attribute mechanism, you assume that the reactive object you are modeling has a set of attributes the values of which may be manipulated by its submachines. The basic strategy for submachine communication using

You can use attribute values to communicate asynchronously between concurrent submachines.

attributes is that one submachine sets attributes, and other submachines use the attribute values in guard conditions on their transitions.

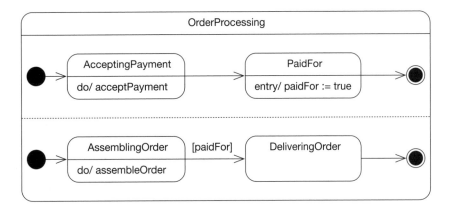

**Figure 20.7**

In the OrderProcessing state shown in Figure 20.7, you can't predict whether a given order will be assembled or paid for first. Some orders may need to wait for new stock to arrive before they can be assembled, and some may be assembled off the shelf. Similarly, some payments might be more or less instantaneous (via credit card for example) and some might take several working days (via check for example). You see that there is a business rule that creates a logical dependency between the two submachines – you can't deliver an order until the order has been assembled *and* the order has been paid for.

In the upper submachine of Figure 20.7, when the AcceptingPayment state is finished, we transition to the state PaidFor where we set the value of the attribute paidFor to true. In the lower state machine, when we have finished AssemblingOrder, we can *only* undergo transition to DeliveringOrder when the attribute paidFor is equal to true. We have achieved asynchronous communication between the two submachines by using an attribute as a flag which one submachine sets, and the other queries – this is a very simple and common mechanism. Finally, both submachines end and synchronize, and we leave the OrderProcessing state.

## 20.5.2 Communication using sync states

A sync state is a special state that has no other purpose than to remember each and every firing of its single input transition. A sync state is like a queue – every time the input transition fires, an entry is stored in the queue. Every time there is a transition *out* of a sync state, an entry is removed from the queue.

You can declare the queue to have a limited number of entries by putting an integer inside the sync state. If you want the sync state to hold an unlimited number of entries, then put an asterisk inside the sync state. The UML syntax for a sync state is shown in Figure 20.8.

sync state holding 2 entries    |    sync state holding unlimited entries

**Figure 20.8**

Sync states provide a very flexible way for concurrent submachines to communicate. One submachine may "leave messages" in a sync state for other submachines to process at their convenience. The two machines *don't* have to synchronize before communication can occur – communication using sync states is asynchronous, just like using attributes. One submachine leaves a message in a sync state and continues about its business. Other submachines pick up this message as and when they are ready.

> Sync states act like a queue in which one submachine can leave a flag to be read by another submachine.

In the example in Figure 20.9, we have taken the example used in Figure 20.7 and achieved exactly the same result using sync states. When we transition from AcceptingPayment to PaidFor, this transition is remembered in the sync state. So when AssemblingOrder finishes, we transition to the join. If a record of the transition from AcceptingPayment to PaidFor is present in the sync state, the join fires and we transition to DeliveringOrder. Otherwise, we wait until an entry appears in the sync state.

One advantage of using sync states rather than attribute values, is that sync states remain silent about *how* the asynchronous communication is actually to be implemented. You can implement this communication using attributes, semaphores, message-oriented middleware (MOM), or some other type of middleware entirely – the sync state only models the seman-

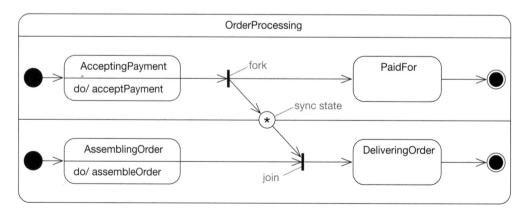

**Figure 20.9**

tics of the communication, *not* its implementation details. Also, sync states allow you to model a queue that can only hold a limited number of entries. It would be more difficult to model this situation with attribute values.

## 20.6 History

You often encounter the following situation when modeling with state machines.

History allows a superstate to "pick up where it left off" when it is returned to after an interruption.

- You are within a substate A of a composite state.
- You transition out of the composite state (and therefore out of substate A).
- You go through one or more external states.
- You transition back into the composite state, *but* would like to continue at the substate A where you left off.

How can you achieve this? Clearly, the composite state needs some way of remembering which substate you were in when you left it. This requirement to pick up where you left off is so common that UML has history state indicators specifically to handle it.

There are two types of history state indicator – the shallow and the deep. We will consider them in the next two sections.

### 20.6.1 Shallow history

Figure 20.10 shows a statechart from the BrowseCatalog use case in an e-commerce system.

In this example you can transition from the BrowseCatalog superstate on three events:

- exit – terminate the state machine and return to whatever you were doing previously (we don't need to consider this in any further detail);
- goToBasket – transition to the composite state DisplayingBasket where the current contents of the shopping basket are displayed;
- goToCheckout – transition to the composite state CheckingOut, where the order summarizing the purchases is presented to the customer.

When you return to BrowseCatalog from DisplayingBasket or CheckingOut, it would be good to return the user to exactly where they were when they left – this is only reasonable.

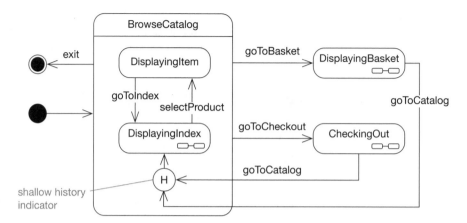

**Figure 20.10**

The history state indicator can have many incoming transitions, but only one outgoing transition. The indicator remembers which substate you were in when you left the superstate. If you then transition from an external state back to the history state, the indicator automatically redirects the transition to the last remembered substate. If this is the first time you have entered the superstate there will be *no* last remembered substate and, in this case, the history state indicator's single outgoing transition fires and you transition to DisplayingIndex.

With history, you give superstates memory of the last active substate before the superstate was exited. With shallow history, you only remember which substate you were in *at the same level* as the history state indicator itself. However, you can see in Figure 20.10 that DisplayingIndex is itself a composite state. Shallow history will not remember the substates within this – for this you need deep history.

## 20.6.2 Deep history

With deep history, you not only remember which substate you were in at the same level as the history state indicator, you remember which sub-substate you were in, to an infinite depth. Thus, in the example in Figure 20.11, you will not only return to either the index or the item display, you will return to the right type of index (alphabetical or by category) *and* to the appropriate page. You could model the same thing without deep history, but it would be much more difficult.

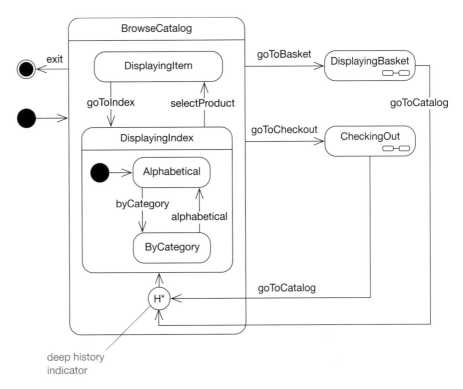

**Figure 20.11**

## 20.7  Submachine state

Statecharts can rapidly become too complex if many states have submachines. Submachine states are a way of simplifying statecharts by allowing you to refer to a submachine that has been fully defined on a different diagram.

The statechart fragment shown in Figure 20.12 models the process of logging on to a website which may or may not recognize the user.

This is a fairly complex diagram. You can simplify it by recording the details of the LoggingOn composite state on a different diagram, and then including a reference to this in a special type of state known as a submachine state. You do this using the keyword include as shown in Figure 20.13.

Submachine states are a very useful notational convenience to simplify statecharts. The semantics are straightforward – wherever you see a submachine state, this is *exactly equivalent* to including the referenced state machine at that point.

Another notational convenience that you may use in conjunction with submachine states is the stubbed state. This is a stub, a vertical or horizontal bar, which indicates a substate within the referenced submachine. Stubbed states are used in Figure 20.13.

A submachine state allows you to summarize a submachine.

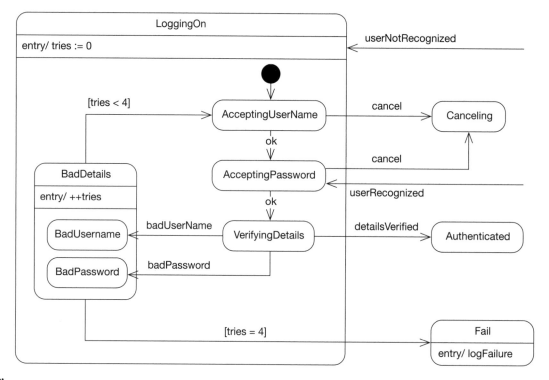

**Figure 20.12**

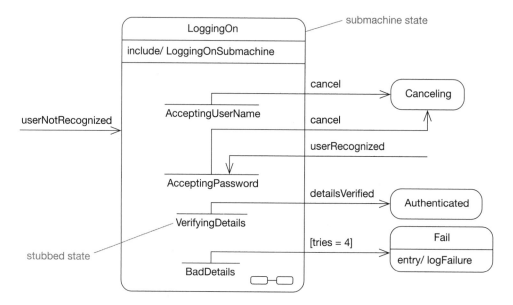

**Figure 20.13**

## 20.8    What we have learned

UML provides a rich statechart syntax that allows you to capture complex behavior in concise statecharts. You have learned the following.

● Composite states can contain one or more nested submachines – substates inherit all of the transitions of their superstate.

● The sequential composite state contains exactly one nested submachine.

● The concurrent composite state contains two or more nested submachines that execute concurrently.
  — There is a fork on entering the state, and the submachines start their concurrent execution.
  — If all the submachines have a stop state, then you can't leave the superstate until all submachines have finished – this is a join.
  — You can leave the superstate without a join if the submachines make explicit transitions to external states.

● Submachine communication:
  — attribute values – one submachine sets the value of an attribute and the other submachines check this value;
  — sync states – act like a queue in which one submachine can leave a flag to be read by another submachine.

● History allows a superstate to remember the last substate before an outgoing transition.
  — Shallow history allows a superstate to remember the last substate at the *same* level as the shallow history indicator before an outgoing transition:
    – on transitioning back into the shallow history indicator, the transition is routed to the last remembered substate;
    – if it is the first entry (no last remembered substate) then the single output transition of the shallow history indicator fires.
  — Deep history allows a superstate to remember the last substate at *any* level before an outgoing transition:
    – on transitioning back into the deep history indicator, the transition is routed to the last remembered substate;
    – if it is the first entry (no last remembered substate) then the single output transition of the deep history indicator fires.

● Submachine states allow you to summarize a submachine:
  — use the keyword include to include a reference to the submachine which occurs on another diagram;
  — summarize the submachine using stubbed states.

part 5

# Implementation

chapter **21**
# The implementation workflow

## 21.1 Chapter roadmap

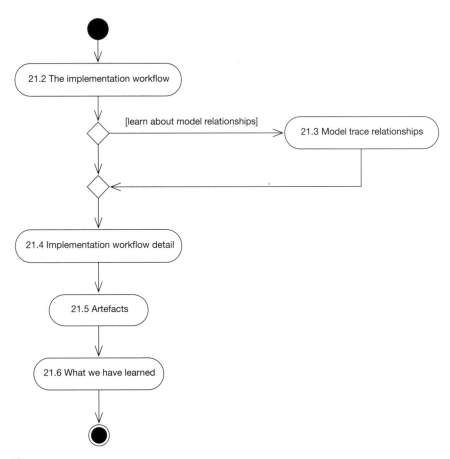

**Figure 21.1**

There is very little work for the OO analyst/designer in the implementation workflow, so this is the most lightweight part of the book. Nevertheless, implementation does bear some scrutiny as, although the primary activity in the implementation workflow is producing code, you will see that there are still some elements of UML modeling involved.

## 21.2   The implementation workflow

> The implementation workflow is the main focus of the Construction phase.

The implementation workflow begins in earnest in the Elaboration phase, and is the main focus of the Construction phase (Figure 21.2).

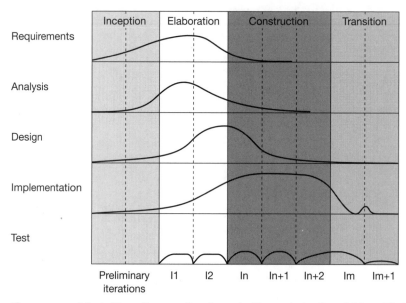

**Figure 21.2**   Adapted from Figure 1.5 [Jacobson 1] with permission from Addison-Wesley

> Implementation is about transforming a design model into executable code.

Implementation is about transforming a design model into executable code. From the point of view of the analyst/designer, the purpose of implementation is to produce an implementation model if that is required. This model involves the (mostly tactical) allocation of design classes to components. How this is done depends, to a great extent, on the target programming language.

The main focus of the implementation workflow is to produce executable code. The production of an implementation model may be a by-product of this, rather than an explicit modeling activity. In fact, many CASE tools allow you to reverse engineer an implementation model from source code. This effectively leaves implementation modeling up to the programmers.

However, there are two cases where an explicit implementation modeling activity, performed by trained OO analyst/designers, might be very important.

- If you intend to generate code directly from the model (forward engineering), you will need to explicitly specify details such as source files and components (unless you take the CASE tool defaults).

- If you are doing CBD to reuse components, the allocation of design classes and interfaces to components becomes a strategic issue. You may want to model this first, rather than leave it to the individual programmer.

In this chapter, we'll look at what's involved in putting together an implementation model.

## 21.3    Model trace relationships

The relationship between the implementation model and the design model is very simple. The implementation model is really just the implementation view of a design model – i.e. it is *part* of the design model. This is shown in Figure 21.3.

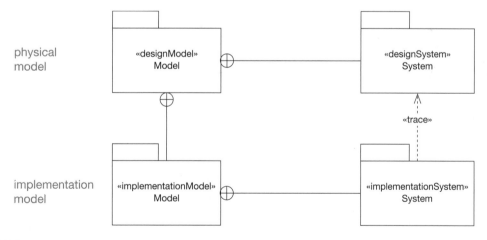

**Figure 21.3**

> The implementation model is part of the design model.

Each design model is for exactly one design system and, not surprisingly, there is a one-to-one «trace» relationship between this design system and the corresponding implementation system. Again, they are just different views of the same thing.

Similarly, there is a one-to-one «trace» relationship between design sub-systems and implementation subsystems. However, whereas design subsystems contain design classes, implementation subsystems contain components that package those classes. The relationship between design subsystems and implementation subsystems is captured in Figure 21.4.

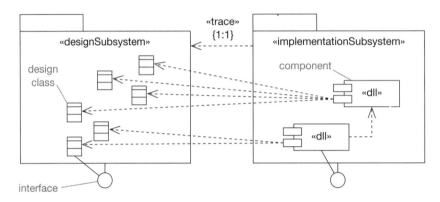

**Figure 21.4**

Because of this one-to-one «trace» relationship, an implementation subsystem realizes exactly the same set of interfaces as its corresponding design subsystem. In implementation subsystems, however, the interfaces are realized by components.

Design subsystems are logical entities that group design elements together, but implementation subsystems should map on to real, physical grouping mechanisms of the target implementation language.

## 21.4    Implementation workflow detail

As you can see from Figure 21.5, the implementation workflow involves the architect, system integrator and component engineer. Individual analyst/designers, or small teams of analyst/designers, may play any of these three roles in the implementation workflow. Their focus will be on producing deployment and implementation models (part of architectural implementation). System integration, class implementation, and unit testing are beyond the scope of this book – these are programming activities rather than analysis and design activities.

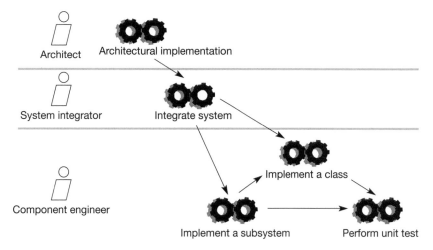

**Figure 21.5**   Reproduced from Figure 10.16 [Jacobson 1] with permission from
Addison-Wesley

## 21.5   Artefacts

The key artefact of the implementation workflow from the point of view of
the OO analyst/designer is the implementation model. This model consists
of two new types of diagram:

- the component diagram – this models the dependencies between the
  software components that constitute the system;
- the deployment diagram – this models the physical computational
  nodes on which the software will be deployed, and the relationships
  between those nodes.

## 21.6   What we have learned

Implementation is primarily about creating code. However, the OO analyst/
designer may be called on to create an implementation model. You have
learned the following.

- The implementation workflow is the main focus of the Construction phase.
- Implementation is about transforming a design model into executable code.

- Implementation modeling is important when:
  - you intend to forward engineer from the model (generate code);
  - you are doing CBD in order to get reuse.

- The implementation model is part of the design model:
  - design subsystems trace to implementation subsystems;
  - design classes are allocated to components;
  - interfaces are realized by components.

- Architectural implementation creates:
  - component diagrams;
  - deployment diagrams.

chapter **22**

# Components

## 22.1 Chapter roadmap

In this chapter we discuss components. We recommend that you read at least Sections 22.2 and 22.3. The example in Section 22.4 is optional, but you may still wish to look at it as it shows the application of a proposed standard UML profile for EJBs. Profiles customize UML with stereotypes, constraints, and tagged values and describe how it should be applied in particular modeling circumstances.

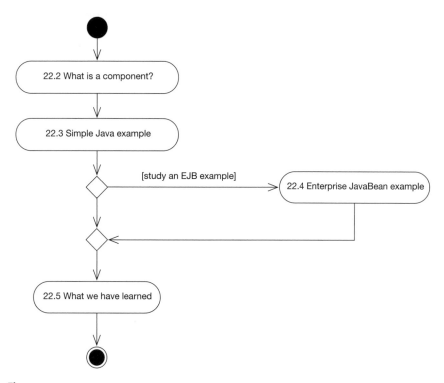

**Figure 22.1**

## 22.2   What is a component?

A component is a physical, replaceable part of a system.

According to *The UML Reference Manual* [Rumbaugh 1], "A component is a physical, replaceable part of a system that packages implementation, and conforms to and provides the realization of a set of interfaces." Components represent tangible, physical things such as an Enterprise JavaBean (EJB) or ActiveX component. A component is a unit of reuse and it has a very broad definition. Any of the artefacts listed below can be considered to be components:

- source files;
- implementation subsystems;
- ActiveX controls;
- JavaBeans;
- Enterprise JavaBeans;
- Java servlets;
- Java Server Pages.

Each component may contain many classes and realize many interfaces.

The component model shows how classes and interfaces are assigned to components. You can show the assignment of a class to a component either as physical containment of the class icon in the component icon, or as a «reside» dependency between the component and the class. These styles are semantically equivalent. Examples of the two notations are shown in Figure 22.2 – class B is assigned to component A using the containment notation, and class D is assigned to component C using the «reside» dependency.

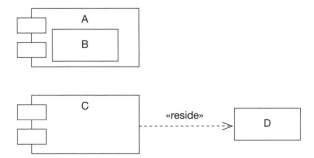

**Figure 22.2**

There is only a descriptor form component diagram. Because components are physical parts of a system, you can only sensibly show
component instances deployed on some physical hardware – they can
never exist in isolation from that hardware. As such, you may show component instances on the deployment diagram as this also shows the
system hardware, but not on the component diagram. You will see how to
use deployment diagrams in Chapter 23.

Components can realize interfaces – this is really shorthand for saying
that a class *inside* the component realizes the interface. Components may
depend on other components. When you want to decouple components
you *always* mediate the dependency with an interface – an example is
shown in Figure 22.3.

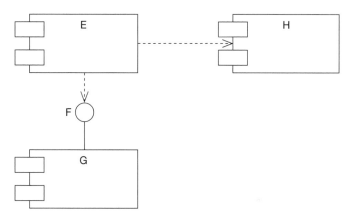

**Figure 22.3**

In this example we have allowed a direct dependency between components
E and H as they are in the same layer of the model and are intimately related.
However, we have used an interface, F, to decouple component E from com-
ponent G as they are in different layers.

## 22.3  Simple Java example

In this section we will illustrate UML component modeling with a very
simple Java example. Figure 22.4 shows the component model for a simple
Java database application. This application uses the Data Access Object
(DAO) pattern described in *Core J2EE™ Patterns* [Alur 1]. The idea behind

this pattern is that a DAO is created that contains code to access a specific database. This DAO is then hidden behind an interface that is used by the clients. Information is passed from the DAO, via the interface to its clients, as a Value Object (VO) that contains a database-neutral representation of the requested information.

One of the many advantages of this pattern is that if you decide to move the data to a different database, you just create a new DAO for that database. The client code, which only uses the interface and is not aware of the DAO, should remain unchanged.

The components are Java class files containing compiled Java bytecode. We have marked these components with the stereotype «JavaClassFile» to indicate this. Stereotyping is used very widely in component modeling as there are so many different types of component.

In Java, a class file *usually* contains the code for a single Java class and this makes the mapping between classes and components simple. In Figure 22.4, the BookReviewApplication component contains a single class also called BookReviewApplication (we have stereotyped this class «JavaApplication» to indicate that it is an executable Java program). This component uses the BookReviewPanel component (that contains a class with the same name), and provides the GUI for the application. We have chosen to use a direct

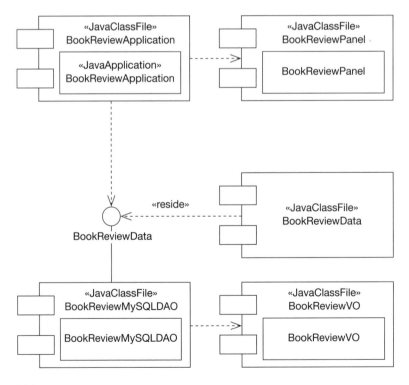

**Figure 22.4**

dependency between the two components, rather than an interface, as the components are intimately related and exist in the same logical layer.

The BookReviewApplication component uses the BookReviewData interface that resides in the BookReviewData component.

The BookReviewData interface is implemented by the BookReviewMySQLDAO component. This component is a DAO that provides access to book review data stored in a MySQL relational database. We could provide other DAOs for other relational databases and, provided they all implemented the BookReviewData interface, they should all be interchangeable as far as the application is concerned.

Looking at Figure 22.4, there are clearly three distinct layers in this model. We can describe these layers using some of the tiers from the five-tier J2EE model described in Alur 1. We have a client tier, a business tier, and an integration tier in this case. There is also an implicit resource tier containing the relational database itself. We can package our components into Java ARchive (JAR) files accordingly, as shown in Figure 22.5.

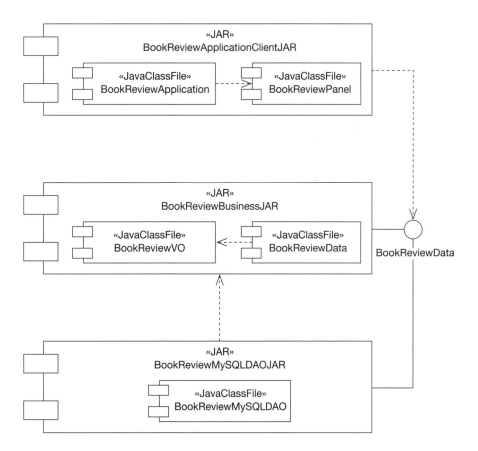

**Figure 22.5**

This example shows that you can have coarse-grained components (the JAR files) that are themselves made up of finer-grained components (the class files). The JAR files provide components suitable for deployment and integration, while the class files provide components suitable for development and testing. It is common to have components at different levels of granularity.

## 22.4 Enterprise JavaBean example

The Enterprise JavaBeans (EJB) architecture provides the distributed component model for Java. An EJB component is deployed into an EJB container running on an application server. This container automatically provides many advanced services to the EJB that would otherwise have to be coded manually. These services include:

- distribution;
- transactions;
- persistence;
- security;
- resource pooling.

Every EJB component has at least four parts – three Java class files (extension .class), and one XML file (extension .xml). The semantics of these parts are summarized in Table 22.1.

**Table 22.1**

| EJB part | Semantics |
|---|---|
| Home interface | Defines the interface for finding or creating EJB instances |
| Remote interface | Defines the interface for the EJB's business methods |
| EJB implementation | Implements the remote and home interfaces |
| Deployment descriptor | An XML file that describes to the EJB container what services the bean requires (e.g. persistence) |

An interesting feature of the EJB architecture is that you *might* expect the EJB implementation to implement the remote and home interfaces, but it does not! These interfaces are, in fact, implemented by an EJB object and a home object that are automatically generated by the EJB container when the EJB is deployed. However, the EJB implementation *must* provide the methods defined in the remote and home interfaces, even though it doesn't physically have an implementation relationship with them.

All the EJB parts are typically packaged into a JAR file, which is a compressed file containing Java class binaries and any other parts. When this JAR file is deployed into an EJB container, the container generates the EJB object and home object and may also generate a client JAR containing stubs for any client programs that wish to use the EJB.

The client JAR provides a client-side implementation for the EJB's home and remote interfaces. This implementation simply forwards message sends via Java Remote Method Invocation (RMI) to the EJB container.

This is clearly quite a complex situation. What are the components here? At a very high level, we can say that we have an EJB component. But when you look closer, you can see that this component has a client-side aspect (the client JAR file) and a server-side aspect (the server JAR file). Looking closer still, you should see that the client JAR realizes two interfaces but is otherwise opaque, as it is the EJB container that generates its implementation. You also see that the server-side JAR contains at least four files – the remote and home interfaces, the EJB implementation, and an XML deployment descriptor.

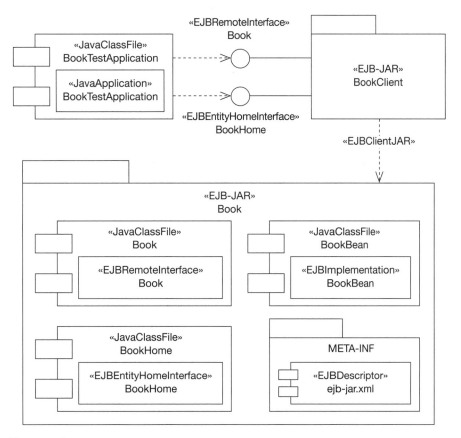

**Figure 22.6**

Let's look at a concrete example – a very simple Java system that uses an EJB to access information about books. We will model a book as an entity EJB. This particular type of EJB is persistent, so we don't have to worry about database access – the container handles that. We will also model an application called BookTestApplication that acts as a test harness for the EJB.

There are several ways to model an EJB, but Rational Corporation has submitted a draft UML profile for EJBs to the Java Community Process [JSR 1] and this is the approach we will use. Please be aware that this draft profile may change. The component diagram for our system is shown in Figure 22.6.

The Rational UML Profile introduces several standard stereotypes for Java and EJBs and these are listed in Table 22.2.

**Table 22.2**

| Stereotype | Stereotyped element | Semantics |
|---|---|---|
| «JavaClassFile» | Component | A file that contains Java bytecode (binaries) – these files have the extension .class |
| «EJBDescriptor» | Component | An XML file that is the deployment descriptor for the EJB |
| «EJBEntityHomeInterface» | Class | A Java interface that is the home interface for the entity EJB |
| «EJBRemoteInterface» | Class | A Java interface that is the remote interface for the EJB |
| «EJBImplementation» | Class | A Java class that provides the implementation for the EJB |
| «EJB-JAR» | Package | A Java Archive that contains one or more EJBs – these files usually have the extension .jar |
| «EJBClientJAR» | Dependency | Indicates that the client is the client JAR for the EJB |

Table 22.2 shows that the Rational UML Profile models JARs as stereotyped packages. We prefer to model JARs as stereotyped components as shown in Figure 22.5. However, provided the semantics of the stereotypes are clear (and they are), either approach is acceptable.

The deployment descriptor component is inside a package called META-INF. Because JAR files are really just a form of zip file (and can be created and viewed with the same tools), directory information for each component is saved when the JAR file is created. The EJB specification states that deployment descriptors should always live in a directory called META-INF, and we can show this very nicely on our component diagram.

## 22.5   What we have learned

Components are the basic units of deployment of a software system. When you create a component diagram, you show how design classes and interfaces are assigned to components.

You have learned the following.

- A component is a physical, replaceable part of a system.
  - Components package design classes. You can show this by:
    - embedding the class icon in the component icon;
    - using a «reside» dependency from the component to the class.
  - Components realize interfaces – this is shorthand for saying that a class inside the component realizes the interface.

- Example components:
  - source files;
  - implementation subsystems;
  - ActiveX controls;
  - JavaBeans;
  - Enterprise JavaBeans;
  - Java servlets;
  - Java Server Pages.

- Components may have dependencies to other components – to reduce coupling, mediate component-to-component dependencies with an interface.

# chapter 23
# Deployment

## 23.1 Chapter roadmap

In this section we look at how to produce a deployment diagram. This is a diagram that shows how the software you are developing will be deployed over physical hardware, and how that hardware is connected. Section 23.4 provides a simple EJB deployment example.

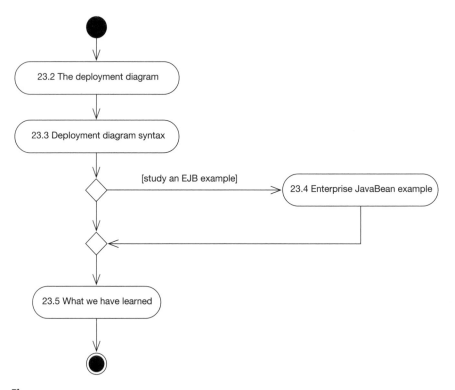

**Figure 23.1**

## 23.2    The deployment diagram

The deployment diagram maps the software architecture on to the hardware architecture.

The deployment diagram shows the physical hardware on which the software system will execute, and how that software is deployed on the hardware.

There are two forms of deployment diagram.

- The descriptor form – contains nodes, relationships between nodes, and components. A node represents a type of hardware (such as a PC). Similarly, a component represents a type of software (such as Microsoft Word).

- The instance form – contains node instances, relationships between node instances, and component instances. A node instance represents a specific, identifiable piece of hardware (such as Jim's PC). A component instance represents a specific instance of a type of software (such as the particular copy of Microsoft Word used to write this). If you don't know (or don't care about) the details of specific instances you can use anonymous instances.

Although we're discussing it as an implementation activity, a first-cut deployment diagram is often created in design as part of the process of deciding the final hardware architecture. You might start by creating a descriptor form deployment diagram limited to nodes and the connections between them. You can then refine this into one or more instance form deployment diagrams, showing possible arrangements of anonymous node instances. When you know the details of the hardware at a deployment site, you can create an instance form deployment diagram showing the actual machines at this site, if so required.

The construction of the deployment diagram is therefore a two-step process.

- In the design workflow – focus mainly on node or node instances and connections.

- In the implementation workflow – focus on assigning physical component instances to node instances (instance form), or components to nodes (descriptor form).

## 23.3 Deployment diagram syntax

The descriptor form deployment diagram shows types of components deployed on types of hardware.

The syntax for descriptor form deployment diagrams is very simple, as shown in Figure 23.2.

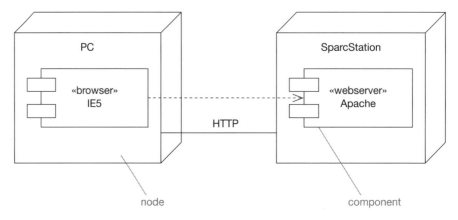

**Figure 23.2**

Nodes are shown as cubes labeled with the name of the *type* of physical hardware that they represent. In this case we have PCs and Sparc Stations. The relationship between the nodes shows that there is a connection between PCs and Sparc Stations, and that the HTTP protocol runs over this connection.

You can deploy components on each node. In this simple example, PCs can run Internet Explorer 5, and the Sparc Stations can run the Apache web server. The dependency between the two components *must* involve the HTTP protocol, as this is the only way that the nodes are connected.

The instance form deployment diagram is very similar. Figure 23.3 shows an instance form of Figure 23.2. You have to remember that instance form deployment diagrams model *specific* pieces of hardware (node instances) on which are deployed *specific* pieces of software (component instances).

In this instance form deployment diagram, there are two specific PCs, Jim's machine and Ila's machine. Both PCs are running their own copy of IE5 and are communicating with the server, homer, via HTTP. The server is running an anonymous instance of the Apache web server.

The instance form deployment diagram shows component instances deployed on specific pieces of hardware.

The instance form deployment diagram tends to be the most widely used, as you very often need to model the specific hardware at a particular client site.

According to *The UML User Guide* [Booch 2], deployment diagrams are the most stereotyped part of UML. You can assign your own icons to stereotypes, and this allows you to use symbols in the deployment diagram that

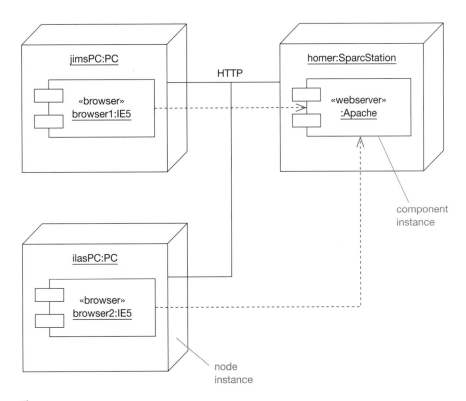

**Figure 23.3**

look as much like the actual hardware as possible. This makes it easy to read the deployment diagram at a glance. Having an extensive collection of clip-art can help with this! An example of a fully stereotyped descriptor form deployment diagram is shown in Figure 23.4.

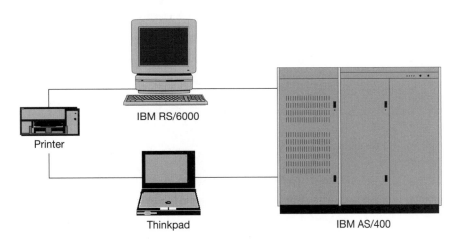

**Figure 23.4**

## 23.4    Enterprise JavaBean example

We'll take the EJB example from Section 22.4 and deploy it on some hardware. If you haven't already read Section 22.4, then you may like to look at it now.

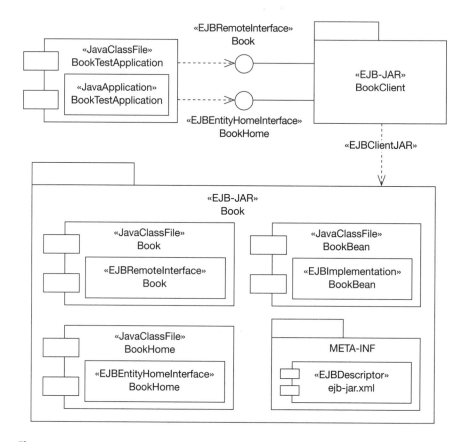

**Figure 23.5**

Figure 23.5 shows the component diagram we created for the Book entity EJB. In order to deploy this, we need to make the following implementation decisions.

● What hardware will we use for the client?

● What hardware will we use for the server?

● What software will we use for the EJB container?

We will use Windows 2000 PCs for both the client and the server. We will use JBoss for the EJB container – JBoss is an open source EJB container available from www.jboss.org.

An instance form deployment model for this system is shown in Figure 23.6.

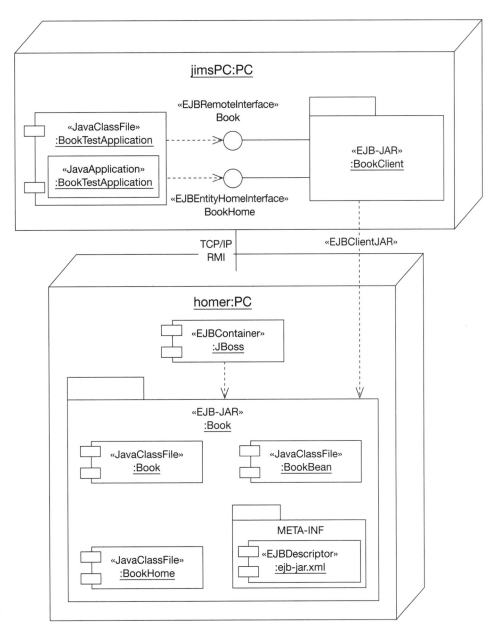

**Figure 23.6**

In this model we have two node instances, jimsPC and homer. These nodes are connected by the Java RMI (Remote Method Invocation) protocol running over a TCP/IP network. The machine jimsPC runs the client application, which uses the client JAR (:BookClient) to access the EJB. The server JAR (:Book) contains the EJB, and this is deployed into a JBoss EJB container on homer.

## 23.5 What we have learned

Deployment diagrams allow you to model the distribution of your software system over physical hardware.

You have learned the following.

- The deployment diagram maps the software architecture on to the hardware architecture.

- The descriptor form deployment diagram may be used to model what types of hardware, software, and connections there will be in the final deployed system.

  — It describes a whole set of possible deployments.
  — It shows:
    - nodes – what types of hardware run the system;
    - relationships – the types of connections between the nodes;
    - components – the types of component deployed on particular nodes.

- The instance form deployment diagram shows a particular deployment of the system over specific, identifiable pieces of hardware.

  — It describes one specific deployment of the system, perhaps at a specific user site.
  — It shows:

- node instances – specific pieces of hardware;
- relationship instances – specific relationships between node instances;
- component instances – specific, identifiable pieces of software deployed on a node instance; for example, a particular copy of Microsoft Office with a unique serial number.

● In the design workflow you can create a "first-cut" deployment diagram by identifying nodes or node instances, and relationships – you refine this as part of the implementation workflow by adding components or component instances.

● You can use stereotypes with associated icons to make the deployment diagram look like the hardware it is modeling.

# Appendix 1

# Example use case model

## A1.1 Introduction

Our experience is that UML models are antagonistic to paper. If you've ever printed out a large UML model, including specifications, then you'll know precisely what we mean! UML models are best viewed in a flexible, hypertext medium. At this time, this means either a CASE tool or a website.

We have therefore decided to provide a complete UML worked example on our website (www.umlandtheunifiedprocess.com) rather than include it in this book. In the example we walk through the OO analysis and design activities required to create a small web-based e-commerce application. We present a few simplified highlights of the model in this appendix to give you a taste for what is available on the site!

## A1.2 Use case model

The use case model is for a simple e-commerce system that sells books and CDs. Figure A1.1 shows the final result of use case modeling.

The use case model will give you a fair idea of what this system does, but please refer to the website for more details and background.

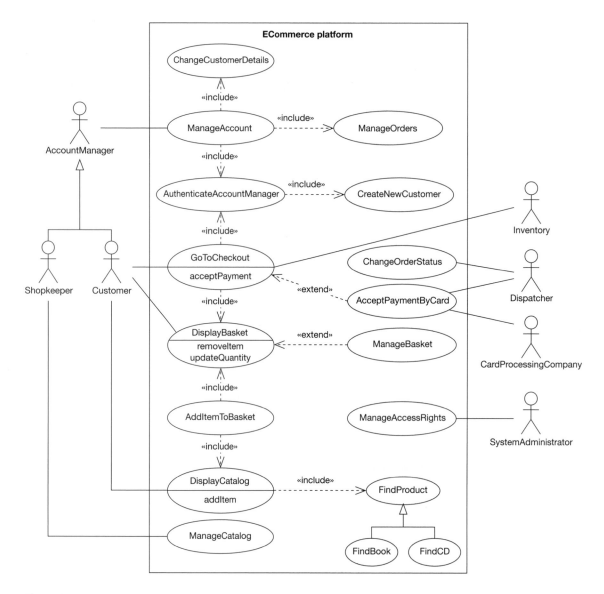

**Figure A1.1**

## A1.3   Example use cases

We will look at a subset of the use case model – see Figure A1.2.

In the use case specifications we have included all of the important use case detail, but have omitted general document information (such as company branding, author information, version information, and other

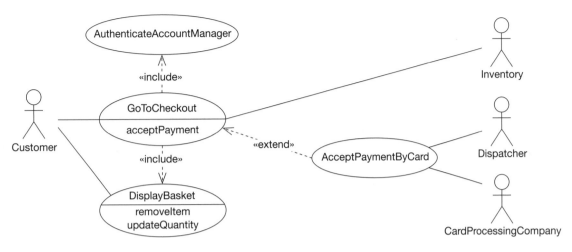

**Figure A1.2**

| Use case: GoToCheckout |
|---|
| **ID: UC12** |
| **Actors:**<br>A2 Customer |
| **Includes:**<br>UC3 AuthenticateAccountManager<br>UC7 DisplayBasket |
| **Extension points:**<br><acceptPayment> |
| **Preconditions:** |
| **Flow of events:**<br>1.   The Customer selects "checkout".<br>2.   include( AuthenticateAccountManager )<br>3.   include( DisplayBasket )<br>4.   If the Customer selects "proceed to checkout"<br>    4.1  The system communicates with the Inventory actor to determine which parts of the order can be fulfilled immediately.<br>    4.2  If there are any items in the order that can't be dispatched immediately<br>        4.2.1  The system informs the Customer that some items are unavailable and that these items have been removed from the order.<br>    4.3  The system presents the final order to the Customer and asks for confirmation to debit the card.<br>    4.4  If the Customer accepts the final order<br>        <acceptPayment> |
| **Postconditions:** |

**Figure A1.3**

attributes). These things tend to be company-specific, and many companies have standard headers that are applied to all documents.

Although the use case specification may be stored directly in a UML CASE tool, support for it is often quite weak, being limited to plain text. For this reason, many modelers save the use case specification in a richer document format, such as Word or XML, and link to these external documents from the use case model in the CASE tool. See Appendix 2 for some ideas about using XML to record use case specifications.

| Extension use case: AcceptPaymentByCard |
|---|
| **ID: UC1** |
| **Extends:**<br>UC12 GoToCheckout at \<acceptPayment\> |
| **Insertion segment:**<br>1.  The system retrieves the Customer's credit card details.<br>2.  The system sends a message to the CardProcessingCompany that includes the merchant ID, merchant authentication, the Customer credit card details, and the amount of the order.<br>3.  The CardProcessingCompany validates the transaction.<br>4.  If the transaction succeeds<br>    4.1  The Customer is notified that they have been billed.<br>    4.2  The Customer is given an order reference number for tracking the order.<br>    4.3  The Dispatcher is sent the order.<br>5.  If there is not enough credit<br>    5.1  The system informs the Customer that there was not enough credit on the card to process the order.<br>    5.2  The Customer is given the option to change to another credit card.<br>6.  If there is some other error.<br>    6.1  The Customer is notified that the order can't be processed at this time and to try again later. |

**Figure A1.4**

| Use case: AuthenticateAccountManager |
|---|
| **ID: UC3** |
| **Actors:**<br>A3 AccountManager |
| **Includes:**<br>UC6 CreateNewCustomer |
| **Extension points:** |
| **Preconditions:**<br>1.  The AccountManager has not yet been logged on by the system. |
| **Flow of events:**<br>1.  If the system automatically identifies the AccountManager<br>    1.1. The system logs the AccountManager on as a Customer or a Shopkeeper.<br>2.  If the system can't identify the AccountManager automatically<br>    2.1. The system presents the options "existing customer" or "new customer".<br>    2.2. If the AccountManager selects "existing customer"<br>        2.2.1. While the AccountManager is not authenticated and the number of logon<br>               attempts by the AccountManager is less than or equal to 3<br>            2.2.1.1.  The system asks the AccountManager for their customer name<br>                      and password.<br>            2.2.1.2.  The system logs the AccountManager on as a Customer.<br>    2.3. If the AccountManager selects "new customer"<br>        2.3.1.  include( CreateNewCustomer )<br>        2.3.2.  The system logs on the new Customer. |
| **Alternate flow:**<br>At any time the AccountManager may cancel the process and go to another part of the<br>system, or leave the system entirely. |
| **Postconditions:** |

**Figure A1.5**

| Use case: DisplayBasket |
|---|
| **ID: UC7** |
| **Actors:**<br>A2 Customer |
| **Extension points:**<br><removeItem><br><updateQuantity> |
| **Preconditions:** |
| **Flow of events:**<br>1.  If there are no items in the basket<br>    1.1. The system displays the message "No items in basket yet".<br>    1.2. The use case terminates.<br>2.  The system displays a list of all of the items in the Customer's shopping basket. This list is a series of lines that include product ID, item name, quantity, item price, and total price.<br>    <removeItem><br>    <updateQuantity> |
| **Alternate flow:**<br>At any point the Customer may leave the shopping basket screen. |
| **Postconditions:** |

**Figure A1.6**

# Appendix 2
# XML and use cases

## 2.1   Using XML for use case templates

As you have seen, UML 1.4 does not define a formal standard for documenting use cases. Modelers either have to use the often rather limited facilities offered by UML CASE tools, or define their own approach. The most common approach at the moment seems to be to create the use case model in a CASE tool, and then link the use cases and actors to external documents that contain their detailed specifications. These documents are usually created on a word processor. However, a word processor isn't the best tool for this, as although it allows you to format and structure the use case and actor specifications, it does not allow you to capture the semantics of that structure.

We believe that structured XML documents are the natural format for use case specifications. XML is a semantic markup language, so it separates the semantic structure of the document from its formatting. Once you have a use case or actor specification captured as an XML document, you can transform it in many different ways using XSL [Kay 1]. You can render specifications as HTML, PDF, or word processor documents, and you can also query the specifications to extract specific information.

The structure of XML documents may be described using Document Type Definitions (DTDs) or the XML Schema Definition Language. We present some simple XML schema for actors and use cases on our website. They are available to download and use under the GNU General Public License (see www.gnu.org for details). We are improving these XML schema over time, as we use them and receive feedback on them.

Detailed descriptions of XML and XSL are beyond the scope of both this book and our website. However, on the site we provide useful links to XML and XSL learning resources.

# Bibliography

Our main bibliography is online at www.umlandtheunifiedprocess.com. Here is a short bibliography for those texts specifically referred to in the book.

[Alur 1], *Core J2EE™ Patterns*, Deepak Alur, John Crupi, Dan Malks, Sun Microsystems Press, 2001, 0130648841

[Ambler 1], *The Unified Process Inception Phase*, Scott W. Ambler, Larry L. Constantine, CMP Books, 2000, 1929629109

[Ambler 2], *The Unified Process Elaboration Phase*, Scott W. Ambler, Larry L. Constantine, Roger Smith, CMP Books, 2000, 1929629052

[Ambler 3], *The Unified Process Construction Phase*, Scott W. Ambler, Larry L. Constantine, CMP Books, 2000, 192962901X

[Booch 1], *Object Solutions*, Grady Booch, Addison-Wesley, 1995, 0805305947

[Booch 2], *The Unified Modeling Language User Guide*, Grady Booch, Ivar Jacobson, James Rumbaugh, Addison-Wesley, 1998, 0201571684

[Chomsky 1], *Syntactic Structures*, Noam Chomsky, Peter Lang Publishing, 1975, 3110154129

[Gamma 1], *Design Patterns*, Erich Gamma, Richard Helm, Ralph Johnson, John Vlissides, Addison-Wesley, 1995, 0201633612

[Jacobson 1], *Unified Software Development Process*, Ivar Jacobson, Grady Booch, James Rumbaugh, Addison-Wesley, 1999, 0201571692

[JSR 1], *JSR-000026*, UML Profile for EJB, available to download at www.jcp.org, Rational Software Corporation

[Kay 1], *XSLT Programmer's Reference* 2nd Edition, Michael Kay, Wrox Press Inc, 2001, 1861005067

[Kruchten 1], *The Rational Unified Process, An Introduction*, Philippe Kruchten, Addison-Wesley, 2000, 0201707101

[Meyer 1], *Object Oriented Software Construction*, Bertrand Meyer, Prentice Hall, 1997, 0136291554

[Pitts 1], *XML Black Book* 2nd Edition, Natalie Pitts, Coriolis Group, 2000, 1576107833

[Rumbaugh 1], *The Unified Modeling Language Reference Manual*, James Rumbaugh, Ivar Jacobson, Grady Booch, Addison-Wesley, 1998, 020130998X

# Index